What people are saying about *Writing to Win Federal Gr*

Kester and Cassidy have provided a comprehensive tool that will equip grant writers—both seasoned and novice—with knowledge that will enable them to be proactive at every level of the proposal process. From standard checklists to finely detailed MOUs to annotated sample proposals, **Writing to Win Federal Grants—The Workbook** *will prove an integral instrument for anyone tackling the federal proposal process.*

Danell Hetrick
Director of Grant Writing and Communications
Batesville Area Chamber of Commerce

As a senior grant professional, I wish that I'd had this book before I wrote my first federal application! Karen and Cheryl's experience and expertise shine brightly as reflected in the content, tips, and checklists. This book is a much-needed, user-friendly, and valuable resource for all grant professionals!

Linda G. Butler, MSW, ACSW, LISW-S
President, Butler Consulting
Past GPA National Board Member

I hold both Karen and Cheryl in the highest regard for their experience, success, and contributions to the grants profession. I am so grateful to them for sharing their expertise—and will be the first in line to buy this book!

Micki Vandeloo, GPC
President, Lakeview Consulting

As the Rosetta Stone helped reveal ancient hieroglyphs and languages, so too will **Writing to Win Federal Grants** *and* **Writing to Win Federal Grants—The Workbook** *lead, guide, and help you interpret your way through what can be the difficult-to-decipher language of federal grant requests. This is your number-one go-to book for writing federal grant proposals from a duo of experts. Buy it today!*

Kay C. Tabscott
Co-Principal, Development Research Partners

My hat's off to Cheryl and Karen for doing such a wonderful job of summarizing the proposal process into a very detailed and concise, easy-to-understand workbook. Anybody can pick this workbook up—from the beginner employee assigned to put a grant proposal together to the more seasoned grants manager looking to get a refresher on topics such as logic models, partnership agreements, or letters of support. I really enjoyed how the workbook got straight to business and flowed more as an informative conversation than a boring lecture.

Joey Estrada, PMP
Business Development and Grants Program Manager
Texas Military Forces, Texas Army National Guard

I've read many books on grant writing and applied for many grants. This book stands out. The authors do a great job of demystifying federal grants so you can go into the process informed, including how to interpret grant guidelines, how to create a strong logic model and budget (with several examples), and what to expect postaward. There are also samples of successful federal proposals. I haven't seen this content offered in any other resource.

Genevieve Richardson, GPC
Nonprofit and Grants Information Center
Dayton Metro Library

The authors share skill, advice, and many templates as they generously coach you in techniques, offer resources, and reveal tricks of the trade gathered from years of experience and success. They tell us "you can do this too" as you craft quality proposals like the ones they are known for. Who wouldn't want such consummate grant professionals on their own Grants Dream Team?

Dale E. Bruce, JD
Grants Consultant

I have been working in the grants field for almost thirty years now and wish that this book had been around when I first started with grants! The hints and suggestions in this book as well as the templates are excellent references and guides to anyone who will be working with grants.

Kathy P. Brunot, CGMS, GPC
Vice President, Administration and Compliance
Boys & Girls Club of Valdosta

Writing to Win Federal Grants—The Workbook *is the book I wish I'd had when we first began preparing our grant proposal. The workbook offers clear descriptions, step-by-step explanations, and varied examples to help demystify a complex and frequently overwhelming process. If you are not fortunate enough to have one of the authors as your grant writer, this is the book for you!*

Pat Stansfield
TRiO/SSS Project Director
Kaskaskia College

After nineteen years of writing and managing grants, I have read many books on grants, but this book stands apart. The authors do an outstanding job of taking the mystery out of federal grants, and these tools can be used for state/local and private grants too. I intend to use this book as a staff guide for grants management as well as for grant writing.

Kenneth R. Holton, Certified Grants Management Specialist
Manager, Capital Programming and Grants Management
Jacksonville Transportation Authority

Writing to Win Federal Grants

The Workbook

Cheryl L. Kester, CFRE
Karen L. Cassidy, GPC

*Charity*Channel

PRESS

Writing to Win Federal Grants—The Workbook

One of the **In the Trenches**™ series

Published by
CharityChannel Press, an imprint of CharityChannel LLC
424 Church Street, Suite 2000
Nashville, TN 37219 USA

CharityChannel.com

ISBN Print Book: 978-1-938077-72-2 | ISBN eBook: 978-1-938077-73-9

Library of Congress Control Number: 2015949538

13 12 11 10 9 8 7 6 5 4 3 2 1

Printed in the United States of America

This and most CharityChannel Press books are available at special quantity discounts for bulk purchases for sales promotions, premiums, fundraising, or educational use. For information, contact CharityChannel Press, 424 Church Street, Suite 2000, Nashville, TN 37219 USA, +1 949-589-5938.

Publisher's Acknowledgments

This book was produced by a team dedicated to excellence; please send your feedback to editors@charitychannel.com.

We first wish to acknowledge the tens of thousands of peers who call charitychannel.com their online professional home. Your enthusiastic support for the **In the Trenches™** series is the wind in our sails.

Members of the team who produced this book include:

Editors

Acquisitions Editor: Linda Lysakowski

Comprehensive Editor: Melanie Palmer

Copy Editor: Jill McLain

Production

In the Trenches Series Design: Deborah Perdue

Layout Editor: Jill McLain

Administrative

CharityChannel LLC: Stephen Nill, CEO

Marketing and Public Relations: John Millen

About the Authors

Cheryl Kester

Cheryl L. Kester is a Certified Fundraising Executive (CFRE). As owner of The Kester Group, she provides grant seeking and grant evaluation services for a range of clients nationwide. With almost thirty years of experience in the nonprofit sector, Cheryl has extensive expertise serving academic, faith-based, public safety, health care, and social service organizations. She has helped secure more than $96 million in state, federal, and foundation grants and contracts. An engaging speaker, Cheryl teaches grants classes, presents at conferences, and conducts board workshops. She also serves as a grant reviewer for private and federal funders. She is a member of the Association of Fundraising Professionals (AFP), the Council for the Advancement and Support of Education (CASE), and the Grant Professionals Association (GPA). In 2012, Cheryl received the GPA president's award for service to the grants profession and the association.

Cheryl's proposals have secured funds from several state and federal departments and agencies:

- Arkansas Biomedical Research Infrastructure Network (NIH sub-awards)

- Arkansas Department of Health

- Arkansas Workforce Investment Board

- Colorado Department of Public Health and Environment

- Department of Agriculture (USDA)

- Department of Education (National Professional Development, TRIO programs [Student Support Services, Upward Bound], Title III, Title V, Title VI [International Studies and Foreign Language])

- Department of Health and Human Services (ACF, CDC, and HRSA)

- Department of Homeland Security (FEMA)

- Department of Labor

- Department of State

- Environmental Protection Agency

- National Endowment for the Arts

- National Science Foundation

- West Virginia Department of Education

Karen Cassidy

Karen L. Cassidy, GPC and Principal of Governmental Grants Professionals LLC, began her career in the US House of Representatives working for Congressmen Bob Wise and Dick Gephardt. Transitioning into the nonprofit field, Karen applied her knowledge to help educational institutions and nonprofit organizations obtain and manage more than $250 million in grant awards. With nearly twenty-five years of experience, Karen helps organizations design programs and evaluation strategies, develop grant proposals, and report outcomes. She is presently serving as an evaluator on several foundation and federal grants.

A knowledgeable and energetic trainer, Karen leads workshops and teaches seminars on many topics, including federal grant proposal development at conferences, universities, and community nonprofits. Her experience developing successful proposals led her to become a reviewer for federal and private funders, providing her with unique insight.

Karen is one of the founding members of the St. Louis Regional Chapter, Grant Professionals Association (GPA). In October 2011, she was elected to serve on the national GPA board of directors. She earned her GPC (Grant Professional Certification) credential from the Grant Professionals Certification Institute in 2011.

Karen's proposals have secured grants from several departments and agencies:

- ◆ Corporation for National and Community Service

- ◆ Department of Commerce

- ◆ Department of Education (Office of Innovation and Improvement, FIPSE, Title V, Upward Bound, Veterans Upward Bound, and Title III)

- ◆ Department of Health and Human Services (ACF, ACYF, CDC, HRSA, NIH, and SAMHSA)

- ◆ Department of Homeland Security

- ◆ Department of Housing and Urban Development

- ◆ Department of Labor

- ◆ Department of State

- ◆ Department of Treasury

- ◆ Department of Veterans Affairs

- ◆ Environmental Protection Agency

- ◆ National Endowment for the Humanities

- ◆ National Science Foundation

- ◆ Small Business Administration

- ◆ USAID

Authors' Acknowledgments

We wish to thank all of our clients and colleagues who were willing to share copies of their grant proposals or excerpts, such as logic models. We have learned so much from you and are grateful for your support.

- ◆ Pima County Community College, Tucson, Arizona

- ◆ John Brown University, Siloam Springs, Arkansas

- ◆ Sabine Volunteer Fire Department, Liberty City, Texas

- ◆ Ozarks Medical Center, West Plains, Missouri

- ◆ Stapleton Foundation for Sustainable Urban Communities, Stapleton, Colorado

Contents

Foreword...xvii

Introduction..xix

Part One—Resources for Federal Grant Writing..1

    Chapter One...3
    Getting Ready for Federal Grants

    Chapter Two..13
    Finding the Right Grant Opportunity

    Chapter Three..25
    Federal Forms

    Chapter Four...49
    Logic Models

    Chapter Five...67
    Budgets and Budget Narratives

    Chapter Six..85
    Partnerships and the ABCs of MOUs

    Chapter Seven...101
    Organizational Charts and Letters of Support

    Chapter Eight...117
    Postaward Policies and Tools

Part Two—Annotated Sample Proposals 133

Annotated Application 1 137
Using Diagrams, Maps, and Tables Effectively

Annotated Application 2 177
Faith-Based Applicant Delivering Community Services

Annotated Application 3 223
Working With Tight Space Restrictions

Annotated Application 4 239
Writing for Online Applications

Index 247

Summary of Chapters

Part One—Resources for Federal Grant Writing 1

Chapter One 3
Getting Ready for Federal Grants. In this chapter, we provide you an
overview of the federal funding process to get us all started. Resources in
this chapter include multiple checklists, an organizational readiness self-
assessment, documents you need for applications, and a one-page summary
of key organizational information.

Chapter Two 13
Finding the Right Grant Opportunity. This chapter digs more deeply
into listings of grant opportunities in the Catalog of Federal Domestic
Assistance, walking you step by step through interpreting a program listing.
Resources for you include an RFA feasibility checklist (deciding go or no-go
on a specific grant opportunity), a program summary form, and forms for
organizing your research.

Chapter Three 25
Federal Forms. This chapter is all about the standard federal forms. After a
brief introduction describing the most commonly used forms, you get copies
of each form, with notes from us about how to fill them out and "gotchas."

Chapter Four 49
Logic Models. In this chapter, you receive a variety of completed logic
models that you can use in your own program planning. We also provide
blank templates of simple, traditional logic model styles.

Chapter Five 67
Budgets and Budget Narratives. This chapter offers a quick reminder of
the federal budget categories and how they work. Resources in this chapter
include an extensive everything-but-the-kitchen sink budget item checklist,
budget templates for grants that have matching funds and grants that do not,
plus models of documenting in-kind contributions.

Chapter Six. 85
Partnerships and the ABCs of MOUs . In this chapter, we focus on the varying levels of partnerships and collaborations and how best to document those relationships. Resources include partnership rosters suitable for internal use or inserting into grant proposals, three actual MOUs for different types of agreements, and a build-your-own MOU template.

Chapter Seven. 101
Organizational Charts and Letters of Support. This chapter focuses on samples of common proposal attachments that are not provided in the annotated proposals in **Part Two**. Resources include organizational charts from small and large organizations, a letter of support, and a letter of commitment.

Chapter Eight. 117
Postaward Policies and Tools. This chapter focuses mainly on how preaward personnel (grant writers and program personnel) interact with postaward management. Starting with a checklist for whom to notify when a grant is received, other resources include a summary of awarded programs form, several sample trip report/travel expense forms, and sample time and effort reports.

Part Two—Annotated Sample Proposals. 133

Annotated Application 1. 137
Using Diagrams, Maps, and Tables Effectively. The first annotated proposal uses diagrams, maps, and tables in its thirty-five-page narrative to communicate information clearly and avoid reader fatigue. This example also contains a fully developed work plan. The abstract and most of the application's attachments are included.

Annotated Application 2. 177
Faith-Based Applicant Delivering Community Services. The second annotated proposal is of a similar length. It contains the proposal's abstract and budget narrative. Faith-based organizations should look to this application as a model for how to present themselves in grant applications. However, all readers can garner good strategies for writing strong federal proposals from this example, since the applicant's faith orientation was not a deciding factor in winning the grant.

Annotated Application 3. 223
Working With Tight Space Restrictions. The third annotated application is included because it is an excellent example of how to present a well-thought-out project plan in fewer pages than would have been preferred. It was only nine pages long, including what would normally be considered the abstract. The page limits forced the author to be as brief as possible in her language and to summarize important content in diagrams and tables, without sacrificing specificity.

Annotated Application 4 239
Writing for Online Applications. The fourth and final application is provided as an example of a narrative that was prepared in a word processor for submission online via the funding agency's proprietary system (not Grants. gov). This meant that all formatting that could have been used to set off or emphasize text was stripped out once the text was pasted into the application screen. Such applications are becoming more common, even among federal agencies, so we wanted to include an example for you. Don't let the short narrative fool you into thinking this application was simple. The application also required substantial data and other information to be entered directly into a series of online forms.

Foreword

Throughout my twenty-five-plus years of preparing grant proposals, I have had to deal with many requirements and formats. The application that is burned in my memory requested information on our history, current activities, recent accomplishments, future plans, population served, partners, rationale, proposed solution, implementation plan, anticipated results, and evidence proving our success.

All in nine pages. Double-spaced.

I knew federal proposals had a reputation for being challenging. I had heard my colleagues shriek in horror as deadlines approached. But, I thought, federal proposals come with detailed instructions. How much harder are they *really* than foundation and corporate proposals? Everything you need to know is written down, either in the solicitation or those helpful circulars that OMB publishes. Right?

I was wrong. Even with those instructions, it was incredibly confusing.

I made it through my first federal proposal and went on to successfully write several more. But I wish I'd had this book way back then. *Writing to Win Federal Grants—The Workbook* takes the mystery out of federal grants. And I can think of no two better guides through the federal maze than Cheryl Kester and Karen Cassidy.

I met Cheryl ten years ago at my first Grant Professionals Association conference when I attended one of her workshops. I was awed by her clear, engaging way of presenting information and the useful tools she shared. A few years later, I met Karen when we served together on the Grant Professionals Association board of directors. I was impressed with her quick grasp of complex topics and the straightforward way she presented practical solutions. Combined, they represent decades of experience with winning millions of dollars in federal grants from various agencies and for many different types of organizations. They are both first-rate teachers.

With this book, it is like having Cheryl and Karen sitting next to you—answering questions, offering tactical advice, providing encouragement.

Part One provides all those tools you wish you had and several you didn't know you needed, such as a memorandum of understanding. As I read through the chapters, I found improved ways of accomplishing tasks, such as the "Checklist of Standard Documents," which reminds you where the document is located and the last time it was updated. I also greatly appreciated how they walk you through a Catalog of Federal Domestic Assistance entry to explain what each section means.

Logic models have left more than one grant professional quaking with fear. This book not only provides examples of different formats, but it also explains how to lead a group in brainstorming development of the logic model elements. I've seen logic models explained in other books, but this is the first time I've received training in how to help the program staff create the model.

That's what makes this book stand out: It not only gives you the tools, but it also tells you why you need them and how to use them.

My first foray into federal proposals came about two months into a new job. The project director handed me a draft of the proposal and asked me to critique it. The first thing I did was read a successful proposal that my nonprofit had submitted to the same agency so I could get a sense of what a "good" proposal contained. While reading the winning proposal did give me a sense of what the agency was looking for, what I was missing was insight into *why* the proposal was written the way it was. The annotated sample proposals in **Part Two** of this book would have taught me exactly what I needed to know.

Beyond the very practical benefits of *Writing to Win Federal Grants—The Workbook*, it is remarkable that it was written at all. In these days of fierce competition for decreasing funding, it would be understandable if these two seasoned grant consultants wanted to keep their trade secrets to themselves.

Instead, they have written a book that raises the competency of the entire grants profession.

Teri S. Blandon, CFRE, GPC
Vice President for Institutional Advancement, Global Communities
Contributing Author, *You and Your Nonprofit*

Introduction

We are excited that *Writing To Win Federal Grants* is one of CharityChannel's first book/workbook duos to be written and released simultaneously. As we were composing *Writing to Win Federal Grants: A Must-Have for your Fundraising Toolbox*, we found we had many tools that we wanted to share with our readers. But the book was already bursting at the seams, and we didn't want it to overwhelm beginners.

Checklists, forms, and templates that we knew you could use make up the first half of this workbook. These are all tools we created or borrowed and continue to adapt when needed. Now we share them with you. Whenever possible, tools such as checklists and forms fit on one or two pages so that you can photocopy them right out of this book to use.

But also consider them springboards. Feel free to adapt and modify the tools for your own purposes. (And we'd love it if you sent us a note telling us how you used these tools and sharing your new versions.) But it's usually easier to start with existing content than a blank page.

We also thought it was critical to include complete federal grant applications to share with you. We sure would have liked to have had some models to follow when we were learning to write federal applications. All of the proposals included in this workbook were funded. The proposals are annotated to point out parts to which reviewers responded positively and parts that we think helped push the application over to the winning side.

We would love it if you purchased both of our books. But each does stand alone, independent from the other. A sidebar that looks like the one to the right will let you know when the *Writing to Win Federal Grants* book provides more information about a particular subject. However, you can use the resources in this workbook without having to read the other text.

> The companion book, *Writing to Win Federal Grants: A Must-Have for Your Fundraising Toolbox*, shows and tells you how to complete important sections of your grant narrative, budget, and other attachments.
>
> **Dig Deeper**

If you are new to seeking government grants, this workbook will help you become comfortable with putting together a winning proposal. If you are more experienced, the tools and resources in this workbook will help make your job easier and more efficient. Regardless of who you are and where you are in your career, you can take away practical tools to use for the proposal you are working on today.

Part One

Resources for Federal Grant Writing

In the first part of this workbook, we focus on providing for you an array of resources to make your job of researching, pursuing, and managing federal grants easier. It is chock-full of checklists and forms that come from real grant professionals in the trenches who use these documents every day. These are internal documents that you can use at your organization to manage your workflow and keep things organized.

In addition, we spend one chapter walking you through the most common federal forms. These are forms provided to you by the funding agency. We highlight aspects about these documents that can be confusing or that can trip you up if you don't pay attention to each agency's own quirky way of doing things. We remind you that if an agency's instructions vary from what we have provided, absolutely follow the agency's directions. After all, we can't possibly cover every quirk out there.

Finally, this section concludes with models of documents that you often have to attach to or include in your federal proposals. In each case, it is our intent to share several different types of organizational charts and logic models so that you can select and adapt the model that works best for you.

If there is something you were hoping to find in Part One, such as sample timelines, check Part Two. Part Two contains four complete federal proposals, some with attachments. In the case of items such as timelines, there are multiple examples, shown in context, within the sample proposals that provide excellent models you can use.

Chapter One

Getting Ready for Federal Grants

IN THIS CHAPTER

···→ Basic terminology and key concepts

···→ Assessing your readiness for federal grants

···→ Preparing to apply

We pretty much assume that you are familiar with grants in general and that you are now expanding your expertise into winning state and federal grants. But we will cover some basic concepts and give a very brief overview of how federal grants usually work as an introduction.

Throughout both *Writing to Win Federal Grants* books, we use the term "organization" to refer to whoever it is that will be applying for the federal grant. And sometimes we will just say "you." Often the organization will be a nonprofit, but not always. Several other types of applicants may compete for federal funds as well, including government entities, such as tribes, states, territories, counties, and municipalities. Publicly owned utilities and hospitals along with state colleges and universities are frequently eligible. Even for-profit corporations may sometimes apply. So we just call all prospective applicants "organizations."

To keep things straight, we refer to the federal agency to whom you are applying as the agency, funding agency, or funder.

The companion book, *Writing to Win Federal Grants*, introduces the most common federal funding vehicles and describes the difference among grants, cooperative agreements, contracts, and grant/loan agreements.

Dig Deeper

So organization equals the one asking for money, and agency equals the one investing the money. In addition, although we talk about grants in this workbook, for simplicity, that term also includes cooperative agreements and contracts.

You'll also notice right away that we talk about competing for a grant and about grant competitions. That's because there are (usually) hundreds of applicants vying for a small pool of federal dollars. The funding agency invites any qualified organization to send in an application that explains why it is the best investment of government funds—why giving that organization a grant will achieve the greatest public good. Here's how that works.

> The companion *Writing to Win Federal Grants* book provides more in-depth information about the grant-seeking process, if you want to learn more.
> If you read that book, this section is a great quick review, or you can skip on ahead to the self-assessment and preparation tools.
>
> **Dig Deeper**

Quick Overview of Federal Grant Process

Keeping in mind that you will be able to find an exception to almost any generality we make about how to apply for and win federal grants, here is our summary of how federal grants usually work:

◆ Funding opportunity gets announced. This may happen once a year in one big announcement or one at a time as competitions come open. Regardless, the public almost always gets some notice that a funding opportunity will be open for competition.

◆ Prospective applicants review grant guidelines. Out of the thousands of grant competitions held every year, there may be only one or two that are a good fit for your organization. So review the information about particular grants you are interested in to see if you should apply.

◆ Organizations obtain application materials. If you decide you are going to apply, then you usually download complete application materials and instructions from either the agency's website or the federal government's one-stop grants center, Grants.gov.

◆ You submit a completed application. Be sure to follow the submission instructions from the agency to which you are applying. While many applications will be submitted through Grants.gov, your funding agency may require a different submission method.

◆ Grant reviewers read and score applications. Real people, usually three to five, read your application. These are called

> The companion *Writing to Win Federal Grants* book gives you firsthand advice on preparing and compiling all of the sections of a typical federal grant application.
>
> **Dig Deeper**

grant reviewers. Reviewers use a score sheet provided by the funding agency to grade each application and award points to each section.

◆ Funding agencies work their magic. The agency staff prioritize grant applications by their numeric score and any other criteria they are using and reach a decision about who gets funded and who does not.

◆ Grant recipients receive funding notification. A Notice of Grant Award or similar document will be sent to successful applicants to let them know they will receive a grant if they agree to the funding agency's terms.

Getting the highest score possible on your grant application must be your goal in life. You need every single point. Sometimes competition is so fierce that only applications scoring ninety-nine or one hundred points (out of one hundred) will be awarded. If too many grants earn one hundred points, the funding agency may not have a large enough budget to give everyone a grant and then has to use other methods to select who gets a grant and who doesn't.

important

◆ Grant recipients implement the grant program and submit reports. This may sound like the easy part, but ensuring that federal funds get spent properly and that your project achieves its promised objectives can take a lot of oversight. You usually have to submit annual reports in order to receive the next year's funding for multiyear grants and a final report to remain in good standing with the government for future grants.

Assessing Your Readiness for Federal Grants

We know you are interested in winning federal grants. We know you want to strengthen your proposal-writing skills. But before you jump into your first federal proposal, pause for a bit. Take a careful look at your organization to determine whether you are ready to handle federal funds. Use the checklist on the next page to perform a self-assessment of your organization's readiness to compete for and properly manage federal grants.

The companion *Writing to Win Federal Grants* book discusses each item in the checklist on the next page in more detail.

Dig
Deeper

The Organizational Self-Assessment table provided on the next page gives you a clear checklist to help you assess your organization's readiness to successfully pursue federal grants.

Organizational Self-Assessment: Readiness for Federal Grants

Category	Assessment Question	Yes	No
Clear mission	Is your mission statement clear and precise?		
Strategic plan	Do you have a current strategic plan with clear organizational goals?		
Fundable programs	Do you have programs already designed or programs you wish to launch that are eligible for federal funding?		
	Do you have a general budget for these programs?		
Financial stability/cash flow	Do you have enough cash on hand to wait (perhaps months) to be reimbursed for grant expenses?		
Accounting practices	Can you track grant funds separately from the organization's general budget?		
Financial records	Do you have at least three years of financial statements?		
	Do you have audited financial statements?		
Track record	Do you have evidence of success/expertise serving your target community/population?		
Personnel	Can existing personnel be freed up from their current responsibilities to take on grant duties, or can you attract qualified new personnel?		
	Do your bookkeeping, human resources/payroll, and data personnel have time to add grant-related duties?		
	Does your executive director have time to supervise the grant, monitor the funds, and oversee grant personnel?		
Space	Do you have adequate space in which to deliver your grant activities?		
Data tracking	Do you have a reliable method to track grant activities and people served?		
Evaluation expertise	Do you have the ability to evaluate grant activities and prepare regular reports?		
Nonprofit status (possibly optional)	If you intend to apply for grants as a nonprofit, do you have nonprofit status recognized by your state?		
	If you intend to apply for grants as a nonprofit, have you received your 501(c)(3) ruling from the IRS?		

A "no" answer to any single item in the self-assessment checklist may not necessarily be an indication that you have insufficient capacity or resources to manage a federal grant. However, you should examine any "no" answer thoughtfully and consider a grant's possible impact on your organization.

Several "yes" answers are a good sign. Before you even find the right grant opportunity to apply to, do as much as you can to prepare in advance. Why is this important? Because many times, you learn of a grant opportunity when the deadline is only a few weeks away. Doing as much work as you can ahead of time positions you to be more competitive. Sometimes you have to be able to move very quickly when the right grant opportunity for your organization comes along.

Collecting Existing Resources for Future Proposal Content

We recommend that you collect existing materials that will be useful sources of proposal content. You will frequently use content from these sources in several proposal sections, including the case for need, evidence of your organization's previous successes, or evidence of your ability to conduct project evaluations.

Even if you eventually rewrite most or all of the preexisting content that you pull from other documents, we find that starting with content that has already been created can help us get over "blank-page syndrome." The bonus for you is that usually text from existing brochures or websites has already been approved and vetted through your organization's leadership.

It's a good idea to create a folder into which you can toss paper copies of newsletters, annual reports, and brochures that you can use as source material for upcoming proposals. Or create an electronic folder on a shared drive into which you can save electronic copies of press releases, email announcements, resumes, and other potential attachments.

 practical tip

The table on the next page provides for you a checklist of documents it will be useful to gather. It also explains how you will most often use those documents in support of your grant proposal.

Checklist of Internal Documents to Gather for Proposal Content

Internal Documents	Common Uses	Obtained
Strategic plan (should be no more than three to five years old, with evidence it is updated regularly)	◆ To develop program goals and objectives ◆ To demonstrate that proposed project is an organizational priority	
Annual report	◆ May contain data to support case for need ◆ Evidence of previous successes can be used to support program plans or evaluation design ◆ Can also demonstrate capacity of the organization to design and deliver projects similar in scope or complexity to the proposed project	
Evaluation reports	◆ Can demonstrate capacity to measure outcomes and achieve results ◆ May contain data that support the case for need ◆ Also demonstrates organization is successful at delivering projects similar in scope or complexity to the proposed project	
Newsletters, program brochures, and other informational publications	◆ Describe the organization, its mission, the people it serves ◆ Typically include good summaries of major programs ◆ May have some history of the organization, such as when it was founded or by whom	
Previous grant proposals	◆ Useful for describing the population you serve ◆ Can provide content for any section of the proposal	

Documents to Include in Federal Proposals

The materials we just discussed are useful for helping you tell your organization's story, but rarely would you include any of them in an application package. We also recommend that you collect copies of the documents in the next checklist, because you will often need to include these in grant applications.

Standard Documents Needed for Federal Grants

Organization's Documents	Digital Copy Available	Location/File Owner	Last Updated
Sample entry			
IRS 501(c)(3) letter	✓	Saved to "grants/fed docs" folder on F: drive	
IRS 501(c)(3) letter			
Organization's mission statement			
Board roster			
Current annual budget			
Most recent audited financials			
Most recent IRS Form 990			
Organizational chart			
Articles of incorporation			
Bylaws			
Resumes of key personnel			
◆ Executive director			
◆ Program director or principal investigator			
◆ Other: _____			
Job descriptions for positions to be filled with grant funds			
Signed certifications and assurances (SF-424B or SF-424D)			

You will need electronic versions of all of these documents. You may have to scan in some of the older documents (such as your Articles of Incorporation). Your auditors should be able to send you a PDF version of your audit and financial statements. In addition, items like job descriptions, the organizational chart, or the budget will probably all need editing or reformatting before you can submit them. Eventually, you'll want to convert all of these items into PDFs so that they can be uploaded to online application systems.

It's a good idea to have a backup plan. If one person at your organization submits all grant proposals, do you have a way to access that person's files in an emergency? Commonly needed documents can be saved to a shared directory on your network or an Internet file-sharing site. Make sure at least two people can access everything, and make sure that at least two people are signed up to use Grants.gov or whatever submission system your funding agency requires applicants to use.

 practical tip

Standard Grant Information List

We've had you running all over your organization gathering together documents. Some, such as the Articles of Incorporation, may not have seen the light of day since 1957. At first, you may have a difficult time convincing the owners of documents like the board roster or your annual budget to let you have copies. If you run into any brick walls, that's fine. You can always wait until you have an application that actually requires those documents. We're just trying to save you a bit of time by helping you collect them in advance.

In addition to those documents, there are some basic organizational facts that you should collect and put on one sheet for quick reference at application time. We know—you can recite the mailing address by heart, and you will be the contact person on every grant proposal.

Still, there might be times when you are swamped and need help from the new intern or administrative assistant completing some forms. Or maybe you have emergency surgery and someone else has to finish your grant proposal. If you've left your copy of the Standard Grant Information Form that we've provided on the next page on top of your desk, then you will be a hero from your hospital bed. That is, if you've filled it out.

The information on this form stays pretty static. Aside from financial information, including fringe benefit rates that need to be updated, most of the other content you have to collect only once.

Standard Grant Information Form

Organizational Information	
Applicant's legal name:	
Payee name (if different):	
Mailing address:	
Physical address (if different):	
Telephone:	
Fax:	
Date organization was founded:	
EIN (federal tax ID):	
DUNS number:	
Mission statement:	
Congressional district:	
Grants.gov user ID and password:	
Contact Information	
First name:	
Last name:	
Contact title:	
Address:	
Telephone:	
Email address:	
Executive director (if different from contact person):	
Executive director email:	
Executive director phone:	
Financial Information	
Amount of annual operating budget: (total budgeted expenses for the current fiscal year)	
Fringe benefits rate for full-time employees:	
Fringe benefits rate for part-time employees (including payroll taxes):	

Forms You Can Sign ahead of Time

We are almost done helping you get ready to apply, and we're going to talk about actually working on a proposal soon. We promise. But there is one more preparatory step you can take now.

Chapter Three discusses the most common application forms. It tells you how to get copies and how to complete them properly. We're pausing here to talk about forms that require only a signature instead of filling in several fields.

Certifications and assurances are typically longer documents. By signing them, your organization promises it is complying with certain laws and regulations. The first time you apply for a federal grant, your executive director/CEO/president will need to read these very carefully. Sometimes the board of directors, your organization's attorney, or your human resources department will need to review them as well.

This takes time, and you don't want to be rushed. The documents must be signed by a person, such as the executive director, chief operating officer, or board president, who has the legal authority to make assurances to the federal government. This is usually not the grant professional or a development officer.

The small table below lists the most common forms that don't change from application to application. Get them signed once, and keep a copy in your files.

Federal Forms Requiring Advance Approval and/or Signature(s)

Form Number	Form Title	Reviewed/ Approved By	Date Approved/ Signed	Signed Copy on File
SF-424B (or SF-424D)	Assurances for non-construction/construction programs			
SF-LLL	Disclosure of lobbying activities			
Grants.gov lobbying form	Certification regarding lobbying			

Now that you have done all of this groundwork, you are ready to begin searching for the right grant opportunity.

To Recap

◆ First assess whether your organization has the capacity to implement a federal grant if you win one.

◆ Once you have determined that you are ready for federal grant seeking, gather together the standard information that can help you complete proposals.

◆ Give yourself time to get legal requirements reviewed by an attorney, board member, or your executive director so that your organization can sign various certifications and assurances in good faith.

Chapter Two

Finding the Right Grant Opportunity

IN THIS CHAPTER

···→ Searching federal resources

···→ Deciding whether to apply

···→ Organizing your research

Sometimes information about the right grant opportunity for your organization just drops in your lap. Someone forwards a grant announcement to you. Or you signed up to receive notifications from Grants.gov or the Federal Register (federalregister.gov) when grant competitions open.

That's great when it happens. The downside to receiving information this way is that you suddenly have to rearrange your schedule and scramble to meet an unexpected deadline that may be only a few weeks away. We've all been there, and you can be successful responding to grant opportunities you learn about this way.

Even better is when you can carve out some time to do some proactive research and try to identify grant opportunities early, before the guidelines are posted and the clock starts ticking. One way to do this is to search the Catalog of Federal Domestic Assistance (CFDA) at cfda.gov for grant programs that are relevant to your organization.

The CFDA is a free government resource that is an index of all grant programs. All grant programs remain on the list whether there is a current competition open or not. Even grant competitions that are open only every few years are listed in the CFDA. Some people find it easier to identify potential grant programs through searching the CFDA. Then they can contact

There's an entire chapter on multiple methods of finding grant opportunities for your organization in the companion *Writing to Win Federal Grants* book.

Dig Deeper

the funding agency to ask about the next competition or to try to obtain a copy of the RFA for the most recent closed competition. Any tactic like this that helps you get a jump-start on planning your project and meeting the proposal's requirements can put you ahead of the competition and save you much stress from scrambling at the last minute.

The most effective way to use the CFDA is to search by keywords relevant to your organization and your mission. For example, we conducted a search on the keywords "housing" *and* "seniors." We also asked the search to limit results to grants only.

A list of potential funding programs was returned. We selected one called the "Housing Counseling Assistance Program" to research further. When we click on that funding name, a complete summary is displayed.

In the excerpt below, we have copied the entire text of the entry for the Housing Counseling Assistance Program. We've annotated it to point out key elements to watch for. Don't get concerned when you see all of this text. We are going to walk through it together, and our notes are there to point out for you what we think is important. Notice that a website address and contact information appear at the end of the entry.

EXCERPT...

Program Information

Program Number/Title (010):
14.169 Housing Counseling Assistance Program

Federal Agency (030):
Office of Housing-Federal Housing Commissioner, Department of Housing and Urban Development

Authorization (040):
Housing and Urban Development Act of 1968, as amended.

Objectives (050):
To counsel homeowners, homebuyers, prospective renters and tenants under HUD, conventional and other government programs in improving their housing conditions and in meeting the responsibilities of tenancy and homeownership.

> This tells you the program's purpose—an overview of what funds should be used for.

EXCERPT...

Program Information

Types of Assistance (060):

PROJECT GRANTS

Uses and Use Restrictions (070):
To provide housing counseling grants to HUD-approved local housing counseling agencies; to HUD-approved national and regional intermediaries; Multi-state Organizations; and to State housing finance agencies. Grants provide a variety of housing counseling services, including single family home buying, homeownership, mortgage default, HECM, rental, and rental delinquency under HUD and other programs.

This gets more specific, with actual allowed activities.

Eligibility Requirements (080)

Applicant Eligibility (081):
Qualified public or private nonprofit organizations. There are four categories of eligible applicants: (1) HUD-approved local housing counseling agency; (2) HUD-approved national or regional intermediary; (3) State housing finance agency; and (4) multi-state organizations.

This section tells you what type of applicants are eligible to apply.

Beneficiary Eligibility (082):
Individuals, groups of individuals, and families who are renters, tenants, homeowners, and home buyers under HUD, conventional and other government programs.

Beneficiary eligibility describes who is eligible to receive services from grant recipients.

Credentials/Documentation (083):
To be eligible to apply for a housing counseling grant through the SuperNOFA, agencies, except state housing finance agencies, must be HUD approved. To become a HUD-approved housing counseling agency, applicants must (1) meet the requirements of the Housing Counseling Handbook 7610.1 as revised; (2) consult the HUD website to learn about the eligibility requirements for becoming HUD-approved and obtain application (available on the HUD website at www.hud.gov/offices/hsg/sfh/hcc/hcc_homes.cfm); and (3) return application to the HUD Homeownership Center (HOC) with jurisdiction, or, if appropriate, HUD Headquarters. This program is excluded from coverage under OMB Circular No. A-87.

This section explains that potential applicants must be prequalified as being eligible by the funding agency by a certain date. Not all programs require this.

Application and Award Process (090)

Preapplication Coordination (091):
The availability of funds is announced on HUD's website at www.hud.gov. There is no application kit. For a copy of the NOFA, applicants can visit the HUD website (www.hud.gov). Environmental impact information is not required for this program. This program is excluded from coverage under E.O. 12372.

This section explains that this program doesn't have a traditional application. The NOFA contains the guidelines for completing an application.

EXCERPT...

Program Information

Application Procedures (092):
OMB Circular No. A-102 applies to this program. OMB Circular No. A-110 applies to this program. Applicants must submit by the required date the items and forms requested in the NOFA, such as a description of the housing counseling services to be provided, and indicators by which benefits / impact will be measured.

> OMB Circulars used to contain the rules for how to manage and spend grant funds. In 2014, these were superseded by what is called the "Super Circular." Do an online search for COFAR to find the new rules.

Award Procedure (093):
Applicants will be evaluated competitively and ranked against all other applicants that applied in the same funding category. National and regional intermediaries are rated and ranked by HUD Headquarters. Local agencies, multi-state organizations and State housing finance agencies are rated and ranked by the Homeownership Center (HOC) with jurisdiction. A funding formula outlined in the NOFA is used to calculate awards. This program is subject to the administrative requirements established in OMB Circular A-102, Grants and Cooperative Agreements with State and Local Governments, which was implemented by 24 CFR part 85; OMB Circular A-110, Uniform Administrative Requirements for Grants and Other Agreements with Institutions of Higher Education, Hospitals and Other Nonprofit Organizations, which was implemented by 24 CFR part 84; and OMB Circular A-133, Audits of States, Local Governments and Nonprofit Organizations, which was implemented by 24 CFR Parts 84 and 85. Grants awarded under this program are also subject to the cost principles in OMB Circular A-87 for State and local governments and Indian tribal governments and OMB Circular A-122 for nonprofit organizations.

> Lots of detail here, but this text basically explains how applicants of different sizes will be evaluated.
>
> The references to OMB Circulars and Code of Federal Regulations (CFR) have now been replaced by the "Super Circular." (See previous note.)
>
> It's a good idea to give the revised spending and accounting rules to your accounting staff and ask if you are in compliance.

Deadlines (094):
Not Applicable.

Range of Approval/Disapproval Time (095):
Award announcements typically occur 5-7 months after applications are received.

Appeals (096):
Applicants for housing counseling grants may appeal their denial of a grant award or the insufficiency of the grant amount to HUD.

Renewals (097):
Grantees must submit a new application and compete through the NOFA each year.

EXCERPT...

Program Information

Assistance Consideration (100)

Formula and Matching Requirements (101):
This program has no statutory formula.
Matching requirements are not applicable to this program.
MOE requirements are not applicable to this program.

Some grants require applicants to match grant funds with other money. That is a "matching requirement."

Length and Time Phasing of Assistance (102):
Funding assistance is for a discrete period of time, generally 1 year. Grantees invoice HUD on a periodic basis for housing counseling services delivered. Payments of grant funds are subsequently made to grantees via direct deposit/electronic funds transfer (DD/EFT). Method of awarding/releasing assistance: quarterly.

This section and the Renewals section (097) on the previous page tell you that these grants are for one year only and that you have to reapply every year.

Post Assistance Requirements (110)

Reports (111):
Not Applicable.

Audits (112):
Not Applicable.

Records (113):
As required in grant document and Housing Counseling Handbook, HUD 7610.1.

These are the rules about record keeping you will have to follow if you receive a grant.

Financial Information (120)

Account Identification (121):
86-0156-0-1-604.

Obligations (122):
(Project Grants (Cooperative Agreements)) FY 11 $79,036,966; FY 12 est $40,050,000; and FY 13 est $45,500,000

This is the total amount of grant funding expected to be available.

Range and Average of Financial Assistance (123):
Range and average of financial assistance: For Fiscal Year 2012, the minimum request from a local agency was $15,000 and the maximum request from an intermediary was $3,000,000. The average local agency counseling grant was approximately $20,500. The average intermediary award was approximately $990,000.

This is the amount of individual grants. It indicates how much you should and could apply for.

Program Accomplishments (130):
Not Applicable.

Regulations, Guidelines, and Literature (140):
Not Applicable.

EXCERPT...

Program Information

Information Contacts (150)

Regional or Local Office (151) :

None. Persons are encouraged to contact the Homeownership Center serving their State (see http://www.hud.gov/offices/hsg/sfh/hoc/hsghocs.cfm), or the nearest local HUD Office. See Catalog address Appendix IV for a list of offices.

> Always do anything that is "encouraged."

Headquarters Office (152):
Wanda L. Sampedro, 451 7th Street, SW, Washington, District of Columbia 20410 Email: info@fhaoutreach.com Phone: (800) 225-5342.

Website Address (153):
http://portal.hud.gov/hudportal/HUD?src=/program_offices/housing/sfh/hcc/hcc_home

If you noticed, this particular entry included the amount of money Congress is expected to authorize for grants in this program for the next three years. Unanticipated circumstances like sequestration or government shutdowns may affect these future plans. Nothing is certain. But you could use a listing like this to begin planning your application one, two, or three years into the future.

Considering the steps applicants have to take to prequalify and the regulations you would have to get to know ahead of time, you may need three years to get ready!

We selected this housing assistance funding opportunity pretty much at random. Not all will be as overwhelming as this one, and not all will require steps like prequalifying. We just wanted to walk you through a more complicated example to help you break it into workable chunks to review.

What we've just shown you from the CFDA is not the same thing as the actual grant guidelines. A CFDA listing can help you identify programs to which you may want to apply, but you need to do more research before you can decide. Read everything possible on the agency's website. Then try to obtain last year's grant guidelines—or this year's if the announcement is already open. These will tell you what actually has to go into an application.

important

Reviewing Guidelines to Find the Best Fit

Guidelines are completely separate from any descriptions of a funding program you will find in the CFDA or on the agency's website. Remember, the CFDA is a catalog. It lists only grant programs, and the descriptions don't change that much. Guidelines, the rules for how you complete an application, can change each time there is a new competition.

What grant professionals are used to calling "the guidelines" go by many names and acronyms in the government grants world. Here are some:

◆ Request for applications (RFA)

◆ Request for proposals (RFP)

◆ Program solicitation

◆ Notice of funding availability (NOFA) or notice of funding opportunity (NOFO)

◆ Solicitation for grant applications (SGA)

◆ Broad agency announcement (BAA)

◆ Annual program statement (APS)

◆ Federal funding announcement

◆ Program guidance, or the guidance

All of these refer to the same thing: the instructions that tell you that there is funding available and how you can win it.

Whether you have just found out about a grant that is due in thirty days or you are reading last year's guidelines, we have provided a feasibility checklist to help you zero in on the most important parts of the guidelines first. Skipping straight to decision points, such as the deadline, matching requirements, or eligibility, can save you a lot of time and a lot of reading.

Notice that we call this document a "prioritized" checklist. Items are in rough priority order, with the most important decision points at the top. Often a single "no" answer to an item close to the top of the list is a deal breaker, and you need go no further in assessing that particular opportunity.

> All of the items in the checklist that follows are explained in detail in **Chapter Five** of the *Writing to Win Federal Grants* book.
>
> **Dig Deeper**

The form ends with a place to record your decision to apply or not apply and a place for the signature of your boss or other appropriate leader who is approving of the decision to apply or not apply. We can tell you from long experience that it's worth your time to complete such a checklist and keep it on file. It's Murphy's Law that if you don't keep a record of a decision not to apply, that's when an influential board member or your boss wants you to explain how you let a perfectly wonderful grant opportunity slip through your fingers. It's nice having that backup that documents the decision not to apply when you need it.

Federal/State Funding Opportunity Feasibility Analysis

Funding Opportunity Name: _____ Today's Date: _____

Deadline: _____ Size of Awards: _____ per year for _____ years

Match Required? Y / N   If yes, at what ratio? _____

Total Number of Pages to be Submitted: _____

Prioritized Checklist for Reviewing an RFA

Category	Assessment Question	Yes	No
Purpose	Is there a close match between our organization's mission and experience and the funding agency's purpose for providing this grant?		
Eligibility	Is our type of organization eligible to apply for this opportunity?		
Deadline	Is the time between now and the deadline sufficient for us to prepare this proposal?		
Funding amount	Can we fit the budget for our proposed program between the funding floor (minimum grant allowed) and the funding ceiling (maximum award)?		
Matching requirements	Can we meet any matching funds requirement?		
Type of match required	May in-kind contributions count toward the match?		
Number of awards	Is the number of anticipated awards high enough that our organization is likely to be competitive?		
Partnering requirements	Do we have time to establish relationships, or do we have existing relationships with required partners, or are we members of an eligible coalition?		
Level of evaluation	Do we have the resources and expertise (and are there sufficient funds allowed in the grant budget) to hire an external evaluator or for us to complete the level of evaluation expected by this agency?		
Regularity of competition	Will we have another opportunity to apply for this program in the future if we decide not to pursue it now?		
Technical assistance	Will there be a workshop or webinar offered by the funding agency to help applicants know how to apply?		
Prior experience	Will new applicants receive as many points as applicants with previous grants or prior experience?		
Priority/ bonus points	Can we meet any required or optional competitive preference priorities or otherwise earn bonus points?		
Decision to Write This Proposal: Y / N Approved by: _____			

We have also found it useful to attach an executive summary of a grant opportunity to the feasibility checklist. You can then forward both to the executive director or other decision maker with a note explaining why you recommend pursuing or not pursuing that particular opportunity. If the decision is made to apply, the executive summary is a great way to help launch program and budget planning.

On the next page, we share an example of just such a summary form that was used to communicate the details about the funding opportunity to which Annotated Application 2 in **Part Two** of this workbook was written. It communicates the information about a specific funding opportunity that our bosses and clients usually find most useful. Of course, we often adapted our form to reflect some unique quality of the particular grant opportunity under consideration. In this situation, we emphasized that the applicant had to choose to apply within one of two budget ranges and the opportunity to earn bonus points.

Feel free to take this summary form and adapt it for the needs of your organization and to reflect the particular funding opportunities you are assessing. Other information that we commonly include on such summary forms includes the following when applicable:

◆ An award floor (minimum grant request)

◆ Partnership requirements

◆ Allowable activities

◆ Budget restrictions or requirements (such as a cost that is disallowed or a requirement to set aside a certain portion of the budget for something like evaluation)

◆ Any special evaluation requirements (such as being required to participate in the funder's national evaluation effort or to use random control groups when delivering services)

Sample Program Summary Form

Community-Centered Healthy Marriage and Relationship Grants

Funding Number: HHS-2011-ACF-OFA-FM-0193

Application Due Date: 4:30 pm Eastern/3:30 pm Central   07/28/2011

Award Period: Three Years

Project Period: October 1, 2011 – September 30, 2012 (Y1)

Award Amounts: Must select from (see p. 3 for description of project sizes)
- Range A: $800,000 to $2,500,000 or
- Range B: $300,000 to $799,999

Matching Funds: No match required

Annual Award Amounts: NOTE Award Amounts do NOT increase annually, so if staff receive raises, must cut funds in other budget lines in Years 2 and 3.

Bonus Points:
- Five points awarded to previous recipients whose federal reports show good progress in meeting project objectives
- Four points to applicants that include: comprehensive services to foster Job and Career Advancement including, but not limited to: job development, job training, soft- and hard-skills training, subsidized employment, and work experience.
- Two points to applicants that include partnerships with child support agencies (signed MOU or third-party agreement required)

Required Activities:
Projects MUST choose from among the following:
   (I) Public advertising campaigns on the value of marriage and the skills needed to increase marital stability and health.
  (II) Education in high schools on the value of marriage, relationship skills, and budgeting.
 (III) Marriage education, marriage skills, and relationship skills programs that may include parenting skills, financial management, conflict resolution, and job and career advancement.
 (IV) Pre-marital education and marriage skills training for engaged couples and for couples or individuals interested in marriage.
  (V) Marriage enhancement and marriage skills training programs for married couples.
 (VI) Divorce reduction programs that teach relationship skills.
(VII) Marriage mentoring programs which use married couples as role models and mentors in at-risk communities.

Also of Note:
- Strong emphasis on serving economically challenged individuals, especially TANF recipients or former TANF recipients.
- Consider ways to partner with state/community agencies to incorporate job skills into the project.
- Evidence of case management and linkage to other community services strongly advised.
- Clear relationship with and plan to use services of Domestic Violence resources/agencies in the community as part of required services.

Organizing Your Research

Considering that you may need to track several grant opportunities every year, gather your grant summary forms and feasibility checklists into a binder or folder on your computer. A summary sheet similar to the one below can help you keep your research organized.

This research tracker first lists the program the organization wishes to get funded. Then summaries of likely prospects are attached to the original research request.

Sample Completed Research Tracker

Program for Which Funding Is Sought	
Program area:	Higher Education Exchange Programs
Organizational needs:	Students are interested in learning about other cultures, developing language skills, learning new approaches to their study area of interest. The University is seeking scholarship funding to enable the exchange participation for students with demonstrated academic merit who need financial assistance. Similarly faculty members are interested in learning about curriculum and teaching their subject area in other cultures. Funds for short or long-term faculty exchange are needed.
Likely funding source(s):	U.S. Department of Education, U.S. Department of State
Existing or new program:	New
Funding needed by:	Ongoing
Other information:	Faculty members have contacts with other institutions located in a variety of countries. Additionally, the University has executed study-abroad agreements with other institutions across the globe. A complete list is available in the University's International Office, and with the Dean of International Programs for this school.
Potential Funding Prospect #1	
Agency name:	U.S. Department of Education, Office of Postsecondary Education (OPE), Fund for the Improvement of Post-Secondary Education (FIPSE)
Program:	U.S. – Brazil Higher Education Consortia Program
CFDA Number:	84.116M
Federal agency contact name:	Ms. Program Officer
Historic or projected deadline(s):	March, annually
Federal agency contact phone and email:	(000) 555-1212 msprogramofficer@ed.gov
Stated program description:	The program, jointly administered by the U.S. Department of Education and the Brazilian Ministry of Education, provides grants for up to four years to consortia of at least two academic institutions each from Brazil and the United States. The program fosters the exchange of students and faculty within the context of bilateral curricular development.

To Recap

◆ Set aside regular time to conduct prospect research and to get to know the programs for which you are most likely eligible so that you can plan ahead.

◆ You have access to free resources, such as the Catalog for Federal Domestic Assistance and Grants.gov.

◆ Once you find a potential funding opportunity, obtain the most current copy of the guidelines (RFA) and use our RFA feasibility checklist to determine if it is a good fit for your organization at this time.

◆ Program summaries can be helpful to your organization's leaders when making decisions about whether or not to apply. They can also help you keep track of the results of your research.

Chapter Three

Federal Forms

IN THIS CHAPTER

- ···→ An introduction to standard federal forms

- ···→ Annotated sample forms with tips on completing them

- ···→ Official instructions with the forms

Ah, forms. At least we no longer have to fill them out with a typewriter, trying to position the paper so our text will go in the right box—and missing it most of the time.

You will get to know several federal forms. Most federal proposals have a "cover page" that identifies the applicant and provides basic information about the proposed project. Your applications will usually have a budget form and the certifications and assurances we talked about in **Chapter One**. There may be a few additional forms required as well.

Every funding agency is a bit different. Some may have their own versions of "standard" forms. For example, the Department of Education sometimes requires applicants to complete and submit a "Department of Education Budget Information for Non-Construction Programs (ED-524)" instead of the usual SF-424A "Budget Information—Non-Construction Programs."

Another agency may instruct you to fill out a form somewhat differently than you usually do. Always read the RFA carefully for the exact forms to be included in your application. Your first choice is always to use forms included in your Grants.gov application package, but if there is a form missing, you can obtain it online from Grants.gov or the funding agency's website.

On the pages that follow, we introduce the most commonly used forms. We then provide you with a copy of each form and our notes with tips for completing them. When you open forms

Chapter Fifteen of the companion *Writing to Win Federal Grants* book discusses thoroughly attachments other than forms you may be required to submit with your application. These may include staff resumes, works cited, or proof of nonprofit status.

Dig Deeper

from within your Grants.gov package, certain fields may be highlighted in yellow, but be sure to follow the instructions in your particular application package, since you should not assume that you have to complete only the highlighted fields.

SF-424 "Application for Federal Assistance"

Titled the "Application for Federal Assistance," the SF-424 is also sometimes called the "cover sheet." This form summarizes data about the applicant, the project, and the budget. You enter your organization's contact information, tax identification number, DUNS number, the project start and end dates, and the congressional districts served.

When you press the "submit" button, the form will automatically fill in the name of the person authorized to sign your grant proposal. This person is known as the authorized organizational representative, or AOR.

But before you launch into reviewing the form, a note about Executive Order 12372. The SF-424 will ask you if the grant for which you are applying is subject to Executive Order 12372. Your RFA will tell you the answer to this question.

Basically, this order from the president allows each state to maintain a single point of contact (SPOC) for all federal grants submitted by applicants from that state. If your program is required to follow EO 12372, all you do is notify your state's SPOC office of your application.

If you do need to follow this executive order for your application, the White House has an easy-to-follow web page that provides the contact information for the SPOC office for each state that participates in the program: whitehouse.gov/omb/grants_spoc.

If you are applying through Grants.gov, there is a section titled "Mandatory Documents" on the "Grant Application Page." Don't assume that this contains every "mandatory document." Always compare the mandatory documents listed in the guidelines with those in the list. Also do not assume that documents in the "Optional Documents" list are actually optional. Something required may be there instead. Then again, you may have to go searching for a form that was omitted from the package.

practical tip

OMB Number: 4040-0004
Expiration Date: 03/31/2012

Application for Federal Assistance SF-424

* 1. Type of Submission:	* 2. Type of Application:	* If Revision, select appropriate letter(s):
☐ Preapplication	☐ New	
☐ Application	☐ Continuation	* Other (Specify):
☐ Changed/Corrected Application	☐ Revision	

* 3. Date Received:	4. Applicant Identifier:
Completed by Grants.gov upon submission.	

5a. Federal Entity Identifier:	* 5b. Federal Award Identifier:

State Use Only:

6. Date Received by State:	7. State Application Identifier:

8. APPLICANT INFORMATION:

* a. Legal Name:

* b. Employer/Taxpayer Identification Number (EIN/TIN):	* c. Organizational DUNS:

d. Address:

* Street1:

Street2:

* City:

County/Parish:

* State:

Province:

* Country: USA: UNITED STATES

* Zip / Postal Code:

e. Organizational Unit:

Department Name:	Division Name:

f. Name and contact information of person to be contacted on matters involving this application:

Prefix: * First Name:

Middle Name:

* Last Name:

Suffix:

Title:

Organizational Affiliation:

* Telephone Number:	Fax Number:

* Email:

> If some fields are highlighted, the ones that are not highlighted are usually auto-filled by Grants.gov or by the agency upon receipt. The applicant does not complete them. The instructions for the SF-424 that appear after this form provide more information about completing each field.

> Most of the rest of the information on page 1 of this form can be drawn from your organization's Standard Grant Information Form. (See **Chapter One**.)

Application for Federal Assistance SF-424

9. Type of Applicant 1: Select Applicant Type:

Type of Applicant 2: Select Applicant Type:

Type of Applicant 3: Select Applicant Type:

* Other (specify):

> The type of applicant option will be a drop-down menu from which to select.

* **10. Name of Federal Agency:**

11. Catalog of Federal Domestic Assistance Number:

CFDA Title:

> Sometimes fields such as the name of the federal agency and the funding opportunity number will be prefilled by Grants.gov. If not, obtain the information from the RFA.

* **12. Funding Opportunity Number:**

* Title:

13. Competition Identification Number:

Title:

14. Areas Affected by Project (Cities, Counties, States, etc.):

[Add Attachment] [Delete Attachment] [View Attachment]

* **15. Descriptive Title of Applicant's Project:**

Attach supporting documents as specified in agency instructions.

[Add Attachments] [Delete Attachments] [View Attachments]

> Sometimes, this "Add Attachments" button is the place you are told to upload your abstract. Other agencies insist you upload nothing in the SF-424. Follow the directions for each package every time.

Application for Federal Assistance SF-424

16. Congressional Districts Of:

* a. Applicant [   ]   * b. Program/Project [   ]

Attach an additional list of Program/Project Congressional Districts if needed.

[   ]   Add Attachment   [Attachment]   [View Atta]

17. Proposed Project:

* a. Start Date: [   ]   * b. End Date: [   ]

> The RFA may set the project start and end dates for you. If not, you will have to estimate.

18. Estimated Funding ($):

* a. Federal [   ]
* b. Applicant [   ]
* c. State [   ]
* d. Local [   ]
* e. Other [   ]
* f. Program Income [   ]
* g. TOTAL [   ]

> For the estimated funding, sometimes you enter only the amounts for Year One. Other times you enter the total amount for the entire funding period. Be sure to read your RFA for each competition.

* 19. Is Application Subject to Review By State Under Executive Order 12372 Process?

[ ] a. This application was made available to the State under the Executive Order 12372 Process for review on [   ]

[ ] b. Program is subject to E.O. 12372 but has not been selected by the State for review.

[ ] c. Program is not covered by E.O. 12372.

> You find the answer to the question about Executive Order 12372 on a case-by-case basis from the RFA itself.

* 20. Is the Applicant Delinquent On Any Federal Debt? (If "Yes," provide explanation in attachment.)

[ ] Yes   [ ] No

If "Yes", provide explanation and attach

[   ]   Add Attachment   Delete Attachment   View Attachment

21. *By signing this application, I certify (1) to the statements contained in the list of certifications** and (2) that the statements herein are true, complete and accurate to the best of my knowledge. I also provide the required assurances** and agree to comply with any resulting terms if I accept an award. I am aware that any false, fictitious, or fraudulent statements or claims may subject me to criminal, civil, or administrative penalties. (U.S. Code, Title 218, Section 1001)

[ ] ** I AGREE

** The list of certifications and assurances, or an internet site where you may obtain this list, is contained in the announcement or agency specific instructions.

Authorized Representative:

Prefix: [   ]   * First Name: [   ]

Middle Name: [   ]

* Last Name: [   ]

Suffix: [   ]

* Title: [   ]

* Telephone Number: [   ]   Fax Number: [   ]

* Email: [   ]

* Signature of Authorized Representative: [Completed by Grants.gov upon submission.]   * Date Signed: [Completed by Grants.gov upon submission.]

> The information you enter here should match the name and contact information for the authorized organizational representative on file for your organization with Grants.gov. It may or may not be the same person listed as the contact person on page 1 of this form.

INSTRUCTIONS FOR THE SF-424

This is a standard form required for use as a cover sheet for submission of pre-applications and applications and related information under discretionary programs. Some of the items are required and some are optional at the discretion of the applicant or the federal agency (agency). Required fields on the form are identified with an asterisk (*) and are also specified as "Required" in the instructions below. In addition to these instructions, applicants must consult agency instructions to determine other specific requirements.

Item	Entry:	Item	Entry:
1.	**Type of Submission:** (Required) Select one type of submission in accordance with agency instructions. • Pre-application • Application • Changed/Corrected Application – Check if this submission is to change or correct a previously submitted application. Unless requested by the agency, applicants may not use this form to submit changes after the closing date.	10.	**Name Of Federal Agency:** (Required) Enter the name of the federal agency from which assistance is being requested with this application.
		11.	**Catalog Of Federal Domestic Assistance Number/Title:** Enter the Catalog of Federal Domestic Assistance number and title of the program under which assistance is requested, as found in the program announcement, if applicable.
2.	**Type of Application:** (Required) Select one type of application in accordance with agency instructions. • New – An application that is being submitted to an agency for the first time. • Continuation - An extension for an additional funding/budget period for a project with a projected completion date. This can include renewals. • Revision - Any change in the federal government's financial obligation or contingent liability from an existing obligation. If a revision, enter the appropriate letter(s). More than one may be selected. If "Other" is selected, please specify in text box provided. A. Increase Award D. Decrease Duration B. Decrease Award E. Other (specify) C. Increase Duration	12.	**Funding Opportunity Number/Title:** (Required) Enter the Funding Opportunity Number and title of the opportunity under which assistance is requested, as found in the program announcement.
		13.	**Competition Identification Number/Title:** Enter the competition identification number and title of the competition under which assistance is requested, if applicable.
		14.	**Areas Affected By Project:** This data element is intended for use only by programs for which the area(s) affected are likely to be different than the place(s) of performance reported on the SF-424 Project/Performance Site Location(s) Form. Add attachment to enter additional areas, if needed.
3.	**Date Received:** Leave this field blank. This date will be assigned by the Federal agency.	15.	**Descriptive Title of Applicant's Project:** (Required) Enter a brief descriptive title of the project. If appropriate, attach a map showing project location (e.g., construction or ~~real~~ projects). For pre-applications, attach a su~~mmary~~ the project.
4.	**Applicant Identifier:** Enter the entity identifier assigned buy the Federal agency, if any, or the applicant's control number if applicable.		
5a.	**Federal Entity Identifier:** Enter the number assigned to your organization by the federal agency, if any.	16.	**Congressional Districts Of:** 15a. ~~Re~~qui~~re~~ applicant's congressional district. 15b. Ente~~r~~ by the program or project. Enter in the format: 2 characters state abbreviation – 3 characters district number, e.g., CA-005 for California 5th district, CA-012 for California 12 district, NC-103 for North Carolina's 103 district. If all congressional districts in a state are affected, enter "all" for the district number, e.g., MD-all for all congressional districts in Maryland. If nationwide, i.e. all districts within all states are affected, enter US-all. If the program/project is outside the US, enter 00-000. This optional data element is intended for use only by programs for which the area(s) affected are likely to be different than place(s) of performance reported on the SF-424 Project/Performance Site Location(s) Form. Attach an additional list of program/project congressional districts, if needed.
5b.	**Federal Award Identifier:** For new applications leave blank. For a continuation or revision to an existing award, enter the previously assigned federal award identifier number. If a changed/corrected application, enter the federal identifier in accordance with agency instructions.		
6.	**Date Received by State:** Leave this field blank. This date will be assigned by the state, if applicable.		
7.	**State Application Identifier:** Leave this field blank. This identifier will be assigned by the state, if applicable.		
8.	**Applicant Information:** Enter the following in accordance with agency instructions:		
	a. Legal Name: (Required) Enter the legal name of applicant that will undertake the assistance activity. This is the organization that has registered with the Central Contractor Registry (CCR). Information on registering with CCR may be obtained by visiting www.Grants.gov.	17.	**Proposed Project Start and End Dates:** (Required) Enter the proposed start date and end date of the project.
	b. Employer/Taxpayer Number (EIN/TIN): (Required) Enter the employer or taxpayer identification number (EIN or TIN) as assigned by the Internal Revenue Service. If your organization is not in the US, enter 44-4444444.	18.	**Estimated Funding:** (Required) Enter the amount requested, or to be contributed during the first funding/budget period by each contributor. Value of in-kind contributions should be included on appropriate lines, as applicable. If the action will result in a dollar change to an existing award, indicate only the amount of the change. For decreases, enclose the amounts in parentheses.
	c. Organizational DUNS: (Required) Enter the organization's DUNS or DUNS+4 number received from Dun and Bradstreet. Information on obtaining a DUNS number may be obtained by visiting www.Grants.gov.	19.	**Is Application Subject to Review by State Under Executive Order 12372 Process?** (Required) Applicants should contact the State Single Point of Contact (SPOC) for Federal Executive Order 12372 to determine whether the application is subject to the State intergovernmental review process. Select the appropriate box. If "a." is selected, enter the date the application was submitted to the State.
	d. Address: Enter address: Street 1 (Required); city (Required); County/Parish, State (Required if country is US), Province, Country (Required), 9-digit zip/postal code (Required if country US).	20.	**Is the Applicant Delinquent on any Federal Debt?** (Required) Select the appropriate box. This question applies to the applicant organization, not the person who signs as the authorized representative. Categories of federal debt include; but, may not be limited to: delinquent audit disallowances, loans and taxes. If yes, include an explanation in an attachment.

Follow carefully the rules for entering your congressional district number(s).

	e. Organizational Unit: Enter the name of the primary organizational unit, department or division that will undertake the assistance activity. **f. Name and contact information of person to be contacted on matters involving this application:** Enter the first and last name (Required); prefix, middle name, suffix, title. Enter organizational affiliation if affiliated with an organization other than that in 7.a. Telephone number and email (Required); fax number.	21.	**Authorized Representative:** To be signed and dated by the authorized representative of the applicant organization. Enter the first and last name (Required); prefix, middle name, suffix. Enter title, telephone number, email (Required); and fax number. A copy of the governing body's authorization for you to sign this application as the official representative must be on file in the applicant's office. (Certain federal agencies may require that this authorization be submitted as part of the application.)
9.	Type of Applicant: (Required) Select up to three applicant type(s) in accordance with agency instructions.		
	A. State Government B. County Government C. City or Township Government D. Special District Government E. Regional Organization F. U.S. Territory or Possession G. Independent School District H. Public/State Controlled Institution of Higher Education I. Indian/Native American Tribal Government (Federally Recognized) J. Indian/Native American Tribal Government (Other than Federally Recognized) K. Indian/Native American Tribally Designated Organization L. Public/Indian Housing Authority	M. Nonprofit N. Private Institution of Higher Education O. Individual P. For-Profit Organization (Other than Small Business) Q. Small Business R. Hispanic-serving Institution S. Historically Black Colleges and Universities (HBCUs) T. Tribally Controlled Colleges and Universities (TCCUs) U. Alaska Native and Native Hawaiian Serving Institutions V. Non-US Entity W. Other (specify)		

SF-424A "Budget Information"

You usually enter your proposed budget on the form titled "Budget Information—Non-Construction Programs," the SF-424A, or one similar to it. An agency may ask you to use a modified version of the SF-424A or its own agency-specific budget form. As always, use the versions of forms that are included in your funding package, and follow directions in the RFA.

On most budget forms, you will be entering subtotals for each budget category, not detail. These subtotals go on page 2 of the form. If you are applying for a multiyear program, some agencies have you enter the annual budget for each subsequent year in Section E on page 3. Notice that Section E asks you for future funding needs. The first "future funding period" is the second year of your grant. Don't make the mistake of repeating your year-one budget in Section E.

On the other hand, some funding agencies want you to enter the budget for only the first year, even if it is a multiyear project. The guidelines for the program to which you are applying will state this clearly if this is the funder's preference.

The numbers entered on this form need to match the budget numbers in box 18 on page 3 of the cover sheet (SF-424), "Estimated Funding." They also must match the numbers as presented in your budget narrative.

It sounds simple, but mistakes can happen when working across documents. One of the most common errors is when a spreadsheet formula accidentally omits a cell or row. Usually any discrepancies of one dollar or two are caused by slight differences in how numbers were rounded up or down by your spreadsheet.

Using your calculator to manually double-check addition in your budget usually catches any small glitches like this.

OMB Number: 4040-0006
Expiration Date: 06/30/2014

BUDGET INFORMATION - Non-Construction Programs

SECTION A - BUDGET SUMMARY

Grant Program Function or Activity (a)	Catalog of Federal Domestic Assistance Number (b)	Estimated Unobligated Funds		New or Revised Budget		
		Federal (c)	Non-Federal (d)	Federal (e)	Non-Federal (f)	Total (g)
1.		$	$	$	$	$
2.						
3.						
4.						
5. Totals		$	$	$	$	$

> Most of the time, you will use Row 1 only. Sometimes, Box 1a and Box 1b will autofill. Other times, enter the name and funding number yourself carefully from the RFA. These two boxes will then populate boxes on other pages of this form.

> For most applications, you will enter your total grant amount into column (e). Only enter something into column (f) if matching funds are required.

Standard Form 424A (Rev. 7- 97)
Prescribed by OMB (Circular A -102) Page 1

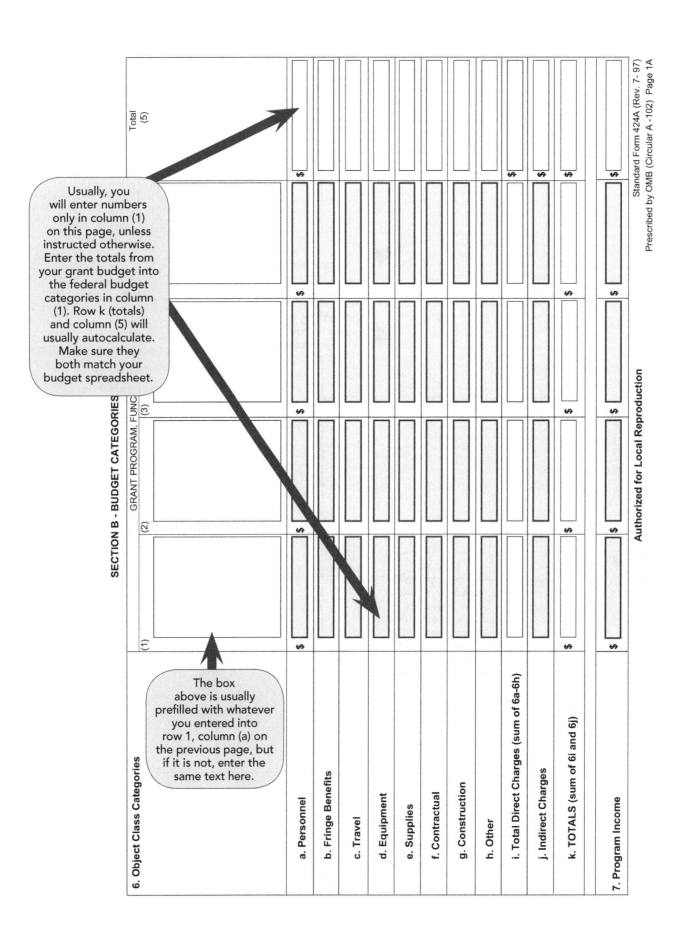

SECTION B - BUDGET CATEGORIES

GRANT PROGRAM, FUNC

6. Object Class Categories

a. Personnel
b. Fringe Benefits
c. Travel
d. Equipment
e. Supplies
f. Contractual
g. Construction
h. Other
i. Total Direct Charges (sum of 6a-6h)
j. Indirect Charges
k. TOTALS (sum of 6i and 6j)

7. Program Income

Usually, you will enter numbers only in column (1) on this page, unless instructed otherwise. Enter the totals from your grant budget into the federal budget categories in column (1). Row k (totals) and column (5) will usually autocalculate. Make sure they both match your budget spreadsheet.

The box above is usually prefilled with whatever you entered into row 1, column (a) on the previous page, but if it is not, enter the same text here.

Total
(5)

Authorized for Local Reproduction

Standard Form 424A (Rev. 7- 97)
Prescribed by OMB (Circular A -102)   Page 1A

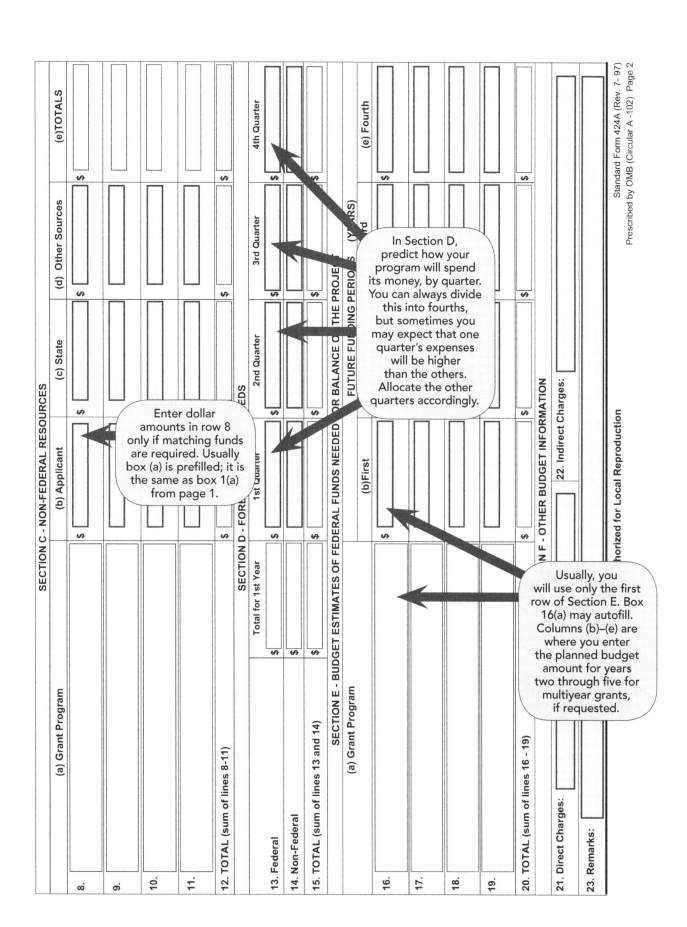

Enter dollar amounts in row 8 only if matching funds are required. Usually box (a) is prefilled; it is the same as box 1(a) from page 1.

In Section D, predict how your program will spend its money, by quarter. You can always divide this into fourths, but sometimes you may expect that one quarter's expenses will be higher than the others. Allocate the other quarters accordingly.

Usually, you will use only the first row of Section E. Box 16(a) may autofill. Columns (b)–(e) are where you enter the planned budget amount for years two through five for multiyear grants, if requested.

SECTION C - NON-FEDERAL RESOURCES

(a) Grant Program   (b) Applicant   (c) State   (d) Other Sources   (e)TOTALS

8.
9.
10.
11.
12. TOTAL (sum of lines 8-11)

SECTION D - FORECASTED CASH NEEDS

Total for 1st Year   1st Quarter   2nd Quarter   3rd Quarter   4th Quarter

13. Federal
14. Non-Federal
15. TOTAL (sum of lines 13 and 14)

SECTION E - BUDGET ESTIMATES OF FEDERAL FUNDS NEEDED FOR BALANCE OF THE PROJECT

FUTURE FUNDING PERIODS (YEARS)

(a) Grant Program   (b)First   (c)   (d)   (e) Fourth

16.
17.
18.
19.
20. TOTAL (sum of lines 16 - 19)

SECTION F - OTHER BUDGET INFORMATION

21. Direct Charges: 22. Indirect Charges:

23. Remarks:

Authorized for Local Reproduction

Standard Form 424A (Rev. 7- 97)   Page 2
Prescribed by OMB (Circular A -102)

Instructions For Completing SF-424A Budget Information for Non-Construction Programs

General Instructions

This form is designed so that application can be made for funds from one or more grant programs. In preparing the budget, adhere to any existing Federal grantor agency guidelines which prescribe how and whether budgeted amounts should be separately shown for different functions or activities within the program. For some programs, grantor agencies may require budgets to be separately shown by function or activity. For other programs, grantor agencies may require a breakdown by function or activity. Sections A, B, C, and D should include budget estimates for the whole project except when applying for assistance which requires Federal authorization in annual or other funding period increments. In the latter case, Sections A, B, C, and D should provide the budget for the first budget period (usually a year) and Section E should present the need for Federal assistance in the subsequent budget periods. All applications should contain a breakdown by the object class categories shown in Lines a-k of Section B.

Section A. Budget Summary Lines 1-4 Columns (a) and (b)

For applications pertaining to a single Federal grant program (Federal Domestic Assistance Catalog number) and not requiring a functional or activity breakdown, enter on Line 1 under Column (a) the Catalog program title and the Catalog number in Column (b).

For applications pertaining to a single program requiring budget amounts by multiple functions or activities, enter the name of each activity or function on each line in Column (a), and enter the Catalog number in Column (b). For applications pertaining to multiple programs where none of the programs require a breakdown by function or activity, enter the Catalog program title on each line in Column (a) and the respective Catalog number on each line in Column (b).

For applications pertaining to multiple programs where one or more programs require a breakdown by function or activity, prepare a separate sheet for each program requiring the breakdown. Additional sheets should be used when one form does not provide adequate space for all breakdown of data required. However, when more than one sheet is used, the first page should provide the summary totals by programs.

Lines 1-4, Columns (c) through (g)

For new applications, leave Column (c) and (d) blank. For each line entry in Columns (a) and (b), enter in Columns (e), (f), and (g) the appropriate amounts of funds needed to support the project for the first funding period (usually a year).

For continuing grant program applications, submit these forms before the end of each funding period as required by the grantor agency. Enter in Columns (c) and (d) the estimated amounts of funds which will remain unobligated at the end of the grant funding period only if the Federal grantor agency instructions provide for this. Otherwise, leave these columns blank. Enter in columns (e) and (f) the amounts of funds needed for the upcoming period. The amount(s) in Column (g) should be the sum of amounts in Columns (e) and (f).

For supplemental grants and changes to existing grants, do not use Columns (c) and (d). Enter in Column (e) the amount of the increase or decrease of Federal funds and enter in Column (f) the amount of the increase or decrease of non-Federal funds. In Column (g) enter the new total budgeted amount (Federal and non-Federal) which includes the total previous authorized budgeted amounts plus or minus, as appropriate, the amounts shown in Columns (e) and (f). The amount(s) in Column (g) should not equal the sum of amounts in Columns (e) and (f).

Line 5 - Show the totals for all columns used.

Section B Budget Categories

In the column headings (1) through (4), enter the titles of the same programs, functions, and activities shown on Lines 1-4, Column (a), Section A. When additional sheets are prepared for Section A, provide similar column headings on each sheet. For each program, function or activity, fill in the total requirements for funds (both Federal and non-Federal) by object class categories.

Line 6a-i - Show the totals of Lines 6a to 6h in each column.

Line 6j - Show the amount of indirect cost.

Line 6k -Enter the total of amounts on Lines 6i and 6j. For all applications for new grants and continuation grants the total amount in column (5), Line 6k, should be the same as the total amount shown in Section A, Column (g), Line 5. For supplemental grants and changes to grants, the total amount of the increase or decrease as shown in Columns (1)-(4), Line 6k should be the same as the sum of the amounts in Section A, Columns (e) and (f) on Line 5.

Line 7 -Enter the estimated amount of income, if any, expected to be generated from this project. Do not add or subtract this amount from the total project amount. Show under the program narrative statement the nature and source of income. The estimated amount of program income may be considered by the Federal grantor agency in determining the total amount of the grant.

Section C. Non-Federal Resources

Lines 8-11 Enter amounts of non-Federal resources that will be used on the grant. If in-kind contributions are included, provide a brief explanation on a separate sheet.

> **Column (a)** -Enter the program titles identical to Column (a), Section A. A breakdown by function or activity is not necessary.
>
> **Column (b)** -Enter the contribution to be made by the applicant.
>
> **Column (c)** -Enter the amount of the State's cash and in-kind contribution if the applicant is not a State or State agency. Applicants which are a State or State agencies should leave this column blank.
>
> **Column (d)** -Enter the amount of cash and in-kind contributions to be made from all other sources.
>
> **Column (e)** - Enter totals of Columns (b), (c), and (d).

Line 12 -Enter the total for each of Columns (b)-(e). The amount in Column (e) should be equal to the amount on Line 5, Column (f), Section A.

Section D. Forecasted Cash Needs

Line 13 -Enter the amount of cash needed by quarter from the grantor agency during the first year.

Line 14 -Enter the amount of cash from all other sources needed by quarter during the first year.

Line 15 - Enter the totals of amounts on Lines 13 and 14.

Section E. Budget Estimates of Federal Funds Needed for Balance of the Project

Lines 16-19 -Enter in Column (a) the same grant program titles shown in Column (a), Section A. A breakdown by function or activity is not necessary. For new applications and continuation grant applications, enter in the proper columns amounts of Federal funds which will be needed to complete the program or project over the succeeding funding periods (usually in years). This section need not be completed for revisions (amendments, changes, or supplements) to funds for the current year of existing grants.

If more than four lines are needed to list the program titles, submit additional schedules as necessary.

Line 20 -Enter the total for each of the Columns (b)-(e). When additional schedules are prepared for this Section, annotate accordingly and show the overall totals on this line.

Section F. Other Budget Information

Line 21 -Use this space to explain amounts for individual direct object class cost categories that may appear to be out of the ordinary or to explain the details as required by the Federal grantor agency.

Line 22 -Enter the type of indirect rate (provisional, predetermined, final or fixed) that will be in effect during the funding period, the estimated amount of the base to which the rate is applied, and the total indirect expense.

Line 23 -Provide any other explanations or comments deemed necessary.

SF-424B "Assurances—Non-Construction Programs" or SF-424D "Assurances—Construction Programs"

The assurances documents are not really forms. Instead, they are long lists of statements that are signed at the end. Each statement "certifies" or "assures" the federal government that your organization will follow certain laws or regulations. This is why we recommend that you have legal counsel review these forms for you the first time you submit a federal application (and if the assurances documents ever change) so you can be absolutely certain that you are in compliance.

Insist that someone in senior leadership sign this document. Even though the name of your authorized organizational representative (AOR) will likely go on the version that is submitted through Grants.gov, you want proof that your executive director, board chair, or some other person with the authority to enter into contractual agreements on behalf of the organization reviewed and signed it. If you are a grant professional or a program person, that's not you.

> This is important enough to repeat. Print out the Assurances (the SF-424B) and have your executive director (or whomever signs contracts) sign a hard copy. Keep a copy in your files. This way you are off the hook if the person who signed the Assurances failed to read and understand them!
>
>

Keep a hard copy of the signed document in your file, even if you submit all grants electronically.

Here's the good news: The assurances document rarely changes. If you know you are going to be applying for a federal grant, go get one of these now and get it approved when it's not urgent.

As the title of each version makes clear, you select whether you complete and submit version B or version D based on whether your program includes construction. If you are applying through Grants.gov, the application package usually automatically includes the correct version for you. We have included version B, for non-construction programs, as the following sample.

ASSURANCES - NON-CONSTRUCTION PROGRAMS

> This document is not a form per se. As early as possible in the application process, have your organization's legal counsel (and possibly HR) review this document and state that you are in full compliance. Keep a signed paper copy on file.

Public reporting burden for this collection of information is estimated to average 15 minutes per response, incl[...] instructions, searching existing data sources, gathering and maintaining the data needed, and completing and [...] information. Send comments regarding the burden estimate or any other aspect of this collection of information [...] reducing this burden, to the Office of Management and Budget, Paperwork Reduction Project (0348-0040), W[...]

PLEASE DO NOT RETURN YOUR COMPLETED FORM TO THE OFFICE OF MANAGEMENT A[...] IT TO THE ADDRESS PROVIDED BY THE SPONSORING AGENCY.

NOTE: Certain of these assurances may not be applicable to your project or program. If you have questi[...] awarding agency. Further, certain Federal awarding agencies may require applicants to certify to a[...] If such is the case, you will be notified.

As the duly authorized representative of the applicant, I certify that the applicant:

1. Has the legal authority to apply for Federal assistance and the institutional, managerial and financial capability (including funds sufficient to pay the non-Federal share of project cost) to ensure proper planning, management and completion of the project described in this application.

2. Will give the awarding agency, the Comptroller General of the United States and, if appropriate, the State, through any authorized representative, access to and the right to examine all records, books, papers, or documents related to the award; and will establish a proper accounting system in accordance with generally accepted accounting standards or agency directives.

3. Will establish safeguards to prohibit employees from using their positions for a purpose that constitutes or presents the appearance of personal or organizational conflict of interest, or personal gain.

4. Will initiate and complete the work within the applicable time frame after receipt of approval of the awarding agency.

5. Will comply with the Intergovernmental Personnel Act of 1970 (42 U.S.C. §§4728-4763) relating to prescribed standards for merit systems for programs funded under one of the 19 statutes or regulations specified in Appendix A of OPM's Standards for a Merit System of Personnel Administration (5 C.F.R. 900, Subpart F).

6. Will comply with all Federal statutes relating to nondiscrimination. These include but are not limited to: (a) Title VI of the Civil Rights Act of 1964 (P.L. 88-352) which prohibits discrimination on the basis of race, color or national origin; (b) Title IX of the Education Amendments of 1972, as amended (20 U.S.C.§§1681-1683, and 1685-1686), which prohibits discrimination on the basis of sex; (c) Section 504 of the Rehabilitation

Act of 1973, as amended (29 U.S.C. §794), which prohibits discrimination on the basis of handicaps; (d) the Age Discrimination Act of 1975, as amended (42 U.S.C. §§6101-6107), which prohibits discrimination on the basis of age; (e) the Drug Abuse Office and Treatment Act of 1972 (P.L. 92-255), as amended, relating to nondiscrimination on the basis of drug abuse; (f) the Comprehensive Alcohol Abuse and Alcoholism Prevention, Treatment and Rehabilitation Act of 1970 (P.L. 91-616), as amended, relating to nondiscrimination on the basis of alcohol abuse or alcoholism; (g) §§523 and 527 of the Public Health Service Act of 1912 (42 U.S.C. §§290 dd-3 and 290 ee- 3), as amended, relating to confidentiality of alcohol and drug abuse patient records; (h) Title VIII of the Civil Rights Act of 1968 (42 U.S.C. §§3601 et seq.), as amended, relating to nondiscrimination in the sale, rental or financing of housing; (i) any other nondiscrimination provisions in the specific statute(s) under which application for Federal assistance is being made; and, (j) the requirements of any other nondiscrimination statute(s) which may apply to the application.

7. Will comply, or has already complied, with the requirements of Titles II and III of the Uniform Relocation Assistance and Real Property Acquisition Policies Act of 1970 (P.L. 91-646) which provide for fair and equitable treatment of persons displaced or whose property is acquired as a result of Federal or federally-assisted programs. These requirements apply to all interests in real property acquired for project purposes regardless of Federal participation in purchases.

8. Will comply, as applicable, with provisions of the Hatch Act (5 U.S.C. §§1501-1508 and 7324-7328) which limit the political activities of employees whose principal employment activities are funded in whole or in part with Federal funds.

9. Will comply, as applicable, with the provisions of the Davis-Bacon Act (40 U.S.C. §§276a to 276a-7), the Copeland Act (40 U.S.C. §276c and 18 U.S.C. §874), and the Contract Work Hours and Safety Standards Act (40 U.S.C. §§327-333), regarding labor standards for federally-assisted construction subagreements.

10. Will comply, if applicable, with flood insurance purchase requirements of Section 102(a) of the Flood Disaster Protection Act of 1973 (P.L. 93-234) which requires recipients in a special flood hazard area to participate in the program and to purchase flood insurance if the total cost of insurable construction and acquisition is $10,000 or more.

11. Will comply with environmental standards which may be prescribed pursuant to the following: (a) institution of environmental quality control measures under the National Environmental Policy Act of 1969 (P.L. 91-190) and Executive Order (EO) 11514; (b) notification of violating facilities pursuant to EO 11738; (c) protection of wetlands pursuant to EO 11990; (d) evaluation of flood hazards in floodplains in accordance with EO 11988; (e) assurance of project consistency with the approved State management program developed under the Coastal Zone Management Act of 1972 (16 U.S.C. §§1451 et seq.); (f) conformity of Federal actions to State (Clean Air) Implementation Plans under Section 176(c) of the Clean Air Act of 1955, as amended (42 U.S.C. §§7401 et seq.); (g) protection of underground sources of drinking water under the Safe Drinking Water Act of 1974, as amended (P.L. 93-523); and, (h) protection of endangered species under the Endangered Species Act of 1973, as amended (P.L. 93-205).

12. Will comply with the Wild and Scenic Rivers Act of 1968 (16 U.S.C. §§1271 et seq.) related to protecting components or potential components of the national wild and scenic rivers system.

13. Will assist the awarding agency in assuring compliance with Section 106 of the National Historic Preservation Act of 1966, as amended (16 U.S.C. §470), EO 11593 (identification and protection of historic properties), and the Archaeological and Historic Preservation Act of 1974 (16 U.S.C. §§469a-1 et seq.).

14. Will comply with P.L. 93-348 regarding the protection of human subjects involved in research, development, and related activities supported by this award of assistance.

15. Will comply with the Laboratory Animal Welfare Act of 1966 (P.L. 89-544, as amended, 7 U.S.C. §§2131 et seq.) pertaining to the care, handling, and treatment of warm blooded animals held for research, teaching, or other activities supported by this award of assistance.

16. Will comply with the Lead-Based Paint Poisoning Prevention Act (42 U.S.C. §§4801 et seq.) which prohibits the use of lead-based paint in construction or rehabilitation of residence structures.

17. Will cause to be performed the required financial and compliance audits in accordance with the Single Audit Act Amendments of 1996 and OMB Circular No. A-133, "Audits of States, Local Governments, and Non-Profit Organizations."

18. Will comply with all applicable requirements of all other Federal laws, executive orders, regulations, and policies governing this program.

19. Will comply with the requirements of Section 106(g) of the Trafficking Victims Protection Act (TVPA) of 2000, as amended (22 U.S.C. 7104) which prohibits grant award recipients or a sub-recipient from (1) Engaging in severe forms of trafficking in persons during the period of time that the award is in effect (2) Procuring a commercial sex act during the period of time that the award is in effect or (3) Using forced labor in the performance of the award or subawards under the award.

* SIGNATURE OF AUTHORIZED CERTIFYING OFFICIAL	* TITLE
Completed on submission to Grants.gov	
* APPLICANT ORGANIZATION	* DATE SUBMITTED
	Completed on submission to Grants.gov

Standard Form 424B (Rev. 7-97) Back

When you submit through Grants.gov, this form is automatically "signed" with the name of the AOR, and the applicant is then committed to full compliance. This is why you must ensure that it has been thoroughly reviewed before submission.

Certification Regarding Lobbying and SF-LLL

It is a common misconception that nonprofits are not allowed to engage in advocacy work, or lobbying. For some nonprofits, advocacy is their primary mission. However, engaging in advocacy may not mean that you pay a lobbyist. If you are applying for federal funds and you engage in advocacy, you must disclose that fact and provide some information if you pay a lobbyist or lobbying firm.

The "Certification Regarding Lobbying" has that title on it, but in application packages, it is commonly referred to as the Grants.gov lobbying form. So file that tip away. While most 501(c)(3) organizations do not engage in outright lobbying, some do. Some even hire lobbyists, and this is allowed, as long as it is disclosed.

In the Certification Regarding Lobbying, you are promising two things: (1) that you never have used—and never, ever will use—federal funds to pay for lobbying, and (2) that if your organization does engage in allowable lobbying activities, you are also submitting an SF-LLL. While you may employ a lobbyist with the organization's other funds, it is never allowable to use federal funds for this purpose.

Again, we're not lawyers. (Thank goodness!) We're sharing our opinion of how lobbying and advocacy work and how that might impact your federal grant seeking. Our best advice for you is to give both of the following forms to an attorney. Fork over the few hundred bucks to make sure you are doing everything right. It will be a wise investment.

 practical tip

If your organization has hired a lobbyist, then you complete the SF-LLL with the name and address of your lobbyist. But if you do not have a lobbyist, you should still submit an SF-LLL. Just enter your organization's name and then indicate "not applicable" in the first and last name boxes.

CERTIFICATION REGARDING LOBBYING

Certification for Contracts, Grants, Loans, and Cooperative Agreements

The undersigned certifies, to the best of his or her knowledge and belief, that:

(1) No Federal appropriated funds have been paid or will be paid, by or on behalf of the person for influencing or attempting to influence an officer or employee of an agency, a Congress, an officer or employee of Congress, or an employee of a Member of Congress the awarding of any Federal contract, the making of any Federal grant, the making of ar entering into of any cooperative agreement, and the extension, continuation, renewal, ar modification of any Federal contract, grant, loan, or cooperative agreement.

> This document is most commonly called "the Grants.gov lobbying form." This is another document that should be reviewed by your executive director or legal counsel. Keep a paper copy signed by that person on file. Upon submission, the form will be "autosigned."

(2) If any funds other than Federal appropriated funds have been paid or will be paid to any person for influencing or attempting to influence an officer or employee of any agency, a Member of Congress, an officer or employee of Congress, or an employee of a Member of Congress in connection with this Federal contract, grant, loan, or cooperative agreement, the undersigned shall complete and submit Standard Form-LLL, "Disclosure of Lobbying Activities," in accordance with its instructions.

(3) The undersigned shall require that the language of this certification be included in the award documents for all subawards at all tiers (including subcontracts, subgrants, and contracts under grants, loans, and cooperative agreements) and that all subrecipients shall certify and disclose accordingly. is a material representation of fact upon which reliance was placed when this transactio entered into. Submission of this certification is a prerequisite for making or entering into imposed by section 1352, title 31, U.S. Code. Any person who fails to file the required c subject to a civil penalty of not less than $10,00 0 and not more than $100,000 for each

> Notice that if your organization does engage in lobbying, you must also complete an SF-LLL, which is the next form provided in this section.

Statement for Loan Guarantees and Loan Insurance

The undersigned states, to the best of his or her knowledge and belief, that:

If any funds have been paid or will be paid to any person for influencing or attempting to influence an officer or employee of any agency, a Member of Congress, an officer or employee of Congress, or an employee of a Member of Congress in connection with this commitment providing for the United States to insure or guarantee a loan, the undersigned shall complete and submit Standard Form-LLL, "Disclosure of Lobbying Activities," in accordance with its instructions. Submission of this statement is a prerequisite for making or entering into this transaction imposed by section 1352, title 31, U.S. Code. Any person who fails to file the required statement shall be subjec t to a civil penalty of not less than $10,000 and not more than $100,000 for each such failure.

* APPLICANT'S ORGANIZATION

* PRINTED NAME AND TITLE OF AUTHORIZED REPRESENTATIVE

Prefix:	* First Name:	Middle Name:
* Last Name:	Suffix:	* Title:

* SIGNATURE: `Completed on submission to Grants.gov`   * DATE: `Completed on submission to Grants.gov`

DISCLOSURE OF LOBBYING ACTIVITIES

Complete this form to disclose lobbying activities pursuant to 31 U.S.C.1352

> If this form is not applicable to your organization, it's usually better to submit a copy of this form and to put n/a into all required form fields than to omit the form from your application package.

1. * Type of Federal Action:
- [ ] a. contract
- [X] b. grant
- [ ] c. cooperative agreement
- [ ] d. loan
- [ ] e. loan guarantee
- [ ] f. loan insurance

2. * Status of Federal Action:
- [ ] a. bid/offer/application
- [X] b. initial award
- [ ] c. post-award

3. * Report Type:
- [X] a. initial filing
- [ ] b. material chang

4. Name and Address of Reporting Entity:

[X] Prime   [ ] SubAwardee

* Name

* Street 1   Street 2

* City   State   Zip

Congressional District, if known:

5. If Reporting Entity in No.4 is Subawardee, Enter Name and Address of Prime:

6. * Federal Department/Agency:

7. * Federal Program Name/Description:

CFDA Number, *if applicable:*

8. Federal Action Number, *if known:*

9. Award Amount, *if known:*

$

10. a. Name and Address of Lobbying Registrant:

Prefix   * First Name   Middle Name

* Last Name   Suffix

* Street 1   Street 2

* City   State   Zip

b. Individual Performing Services (including address if different from No. 10a)

Prefix   * First Name   Middle Name

* Last Name   Suffix

* Street 1   Street 2

* City   State   Zip

11. Information requested through this form is authorized by title 31 U.S.C. section 1352. This disclosure of lobbying activities is a material representation of fact upon which reliance was placed by the tier above when the transaction was made or entered into. This disclosure is required pursuant to 31 U.S.C. 1352. This information will be reported to the Congress semi-annually and will be available for public inspection. Any person who fails to file the required disclosure shall be subject to a civil penalty of not less than $10,000 and not more than $100,000 for each such failure.

* Signature: Completed on submission to Grants.gov

*Name: Prefix   * First Name   Middle Name

* Last Name   Suffix

Title: Telephone No.:   Date: Completed on submission to Grants.gov

Federal Use Only:

Authorized for Local Reproduction
Standard Form - LLL (Rev. 7-97)

Faith-Based EEO Survey

The Survey Ensuring Equal Opportunity for Applicants is also often just called the "faith-based EEO survey." It collects basic data about organizations applying for federal grants. It's usually optional, but it helps the government keep track of how many faith-based organizations receive grants and how small or large they are.

This is an easy one. Since the form asks for information about the size of your staff and budget, we recommend updating those pieces of information once a year.

While the Faith-Based EEO Survey form is optional, it's not hard or time consuming to fill out. We recommend providing it if you can, if it's relevant to your organization. If applicants do not return this survey, the Congress and administration have no way to measure how many faith-based organizations receive federal funding.

practical tip

OMB Number: 1894-0010
Expiration Date: 05/31/2012

Survey on Ensuring Equal Opportunity For Applicants

Purpose:

The Federal government is committed to ensuring that all qualified applicants, small or large, non-religious or faith-based, have an equal opportunity to compete for Federal funding. In order for us to better understand the population of applicants for Federal funds, we are asking nonprofit private organizations (not including private universities) to fill out this survey.

Upon receipt, the survey will be separated from the application. Information provided on the survey will not be considered in any way in making funding decisions and will not be included in the Federal grants database. While your help in this data collection process is greatly appreciated, completion of this survey is voluntary.

Instructions for Submitting the Survey

If you are applying using a hard copy application, please place the completed survey in an envelope labeled "Applicant Survey." Seal the envelope and include it along with your application package. If you are applying electronically, please submit this survey along with your application.

Applicant's (Organization) Name:	
Applicant's DUNS Name:	
Federal Program:	
CFDA Number:	

1. Has the applicant ever received a grant or contract from the Federal government?

   ☐ Yes   ☐ No

2. Is the applicant a faith-based organization?

   ☐ Yes   ☐ No

3. Is the applicant a secular organization?

   ☐ Yes   ☐ No

4. Does the applicant have 501(c)(3) status?

   ☐ Yes   ☐ No

5. Is the applicant a local affiliate of a national organization?

   ☐ Yes   ☐ No

6. How many full-time equivalent employees does the applicant have? (Check only one box).

   ☐ 3 or fewer   ☐ 15-50

   ☐ 4-5   ☐ 51-100

   ☐ 6-14   ☐ over 100

7. What is the size of the applicant's annual budget? (Check only one box.)

   ☐ **Less Than $150,000**

   ☐ **$150,000 - $299,999**

   ☐ **$300,000 - $499,999**

   ☐ **$500,000 - $999,999**

   ☐ **$1,000,000 - $4,999,999**

   ☐ **$5,000,000 or more**

Survey Instructions on Ensuring Equal Opportunity for Applicants

Provide the applicant's (organization) name and DUNS number and the grant name and CFDA number.

1. Self-explanatory.

2. Self-identify.

3. Self-identify.

4. 501(c)(3) status is a legal designation provided on application to the Internal Revenue Service by eligible organizations. Some grant programs may require nonprofit applicants to have 501(c)(3) status. Other grant programs do not.

5. Self-explanatory.

6. For example, two part-time employees who each work half-time equal one full-time equivalent employee. If the applicant is a local affiliate of a national organization, the responses to survey questions 2 and 3 should reflect the staff and budget size of the local affiliate.

7. Annual budget means the amount of money your organization spends each year on all of its activities.

Paperwork Burden Statement

According to the Paperwork Reduction Act of 1995, no persons are required to respond to a collection of information unless such collection displays a valid OMB control number. Public reporting burden for this collection of information is estimated to average 5 minutes per response, including time for reviewing instructions, searching existing data sources, gathering and maintaining the data needed, and completing and reviewing the collection of information. The obligation to respond to this collection is voluntary (EO 13198 and 13199).

If you have comments concerning the accuracy of the time estimate(s) or suggestions for improving the form, please write to: The Agency Contact listed in this grant application package.

Project/Performance Site Location(s)

The next form after the survey is the Project/Performance Site Locations form. This form is pretty clear. The funding agency wants you to say where your project or program will take place. If you will deliver grant-funded activities at multiple locations, provide the address of each site.

OMB Number: 4040-0010

Project/Performance Site Location(s)

Project/Performance Site Primary Location

☐ I am submitting an application as an individual, and not on beh[alf of a] local or tribal government, academia, or other type of organiza[tion.]

Organization Name:

DUNS Number:

* Street1:

Street2:

* City: County:

* State:

Province:

* Country: USA: UNITED STATES

* ZIP / Postal Code: * Project/ Performance Site Congressional District:

> If you have a grant project taking place at multiple locations, list each location on this form. From within the Grants.gov package, you usually have the option to keep selecting an "add location" button until all of your locations have been entered.

Project/Performance Site Location 1

☐ I am submitting an application as an individual, and not on behalf of a company, state, local or tribal government, academia, or other type of organization.

Organization Name:

DUNS Number:

* Street1:

Street2:

* City: County:

* State:

Province:

* Country: USA: UNITED STATES

* ZIP / Postal Code: * Project/ Performance Site Congressional District:

Additional Location(s)   [Add Attachment] [Delete Attachment] [View Attachment]

Other Miscellaneous Forms

Funding agencies have an array of other forms from which to choose that they may ask you to complete. Larger agencies, such as the National Science Foundation (NSF) and Department of Education (ED), often have created supplemental forms for their applicants, and they sometimes create their own versions of the standard forms, such as the budget form (SF-424A).

Other agencies will have forms that you may need to complete. For example, the Department of Education may require a form called "Certification Regarding Debarment, Suspension, Ineligibility and Voluntary Exclusion." The Department of Health and Human Services requires you to submit a form that you are a drug-free workplace.

Finding Forms

The forms you need for your proposal are not always inside the application package you downloaded. If they are not, use the RFA to make a list of every form you need to complete. If a required form is missing from your application package, you can obtain one online. Start with your funding agency to see if it provides links to forms. Grants.gov also maintains a collection of most of the forms a federal agency would require you to submit. At the Grants.gov website, search for "forms repository" if it's not easy to find the forms by following the menus.

To Recap

◆ You can get some forms work out of the way early by getting any certifications and assurances reviewed by the organization's leadership or legal counsel, getting them signed, and then filing them away for future use.

◆ Most application packages use some or all of the standard forms, but always be on the lookout for agency-specific forms or instructions for completing a form differently.

◆ If there are forms required for your application that are not included in your application package, search first on the funding agency's website for versions of the forms they want you to use. You can always obtain generic versions of forms from the Grants.gov forms repository as a last resort. The repository is currently available at www.grants.gov/web/grants/forms.html or under the "Forms" tab on the Grants.gov website.

Chapter Four

Logic Models

IN THIS CHAPTER

- ···→ Purpose of a logic model

- ···→ A logic model by any other name . . .

- ···→ Some logic model examples

- ···→ Logic model tips

Logic models. Merely mentioning them is enough to make some people want to run from the room screaming. But before you jump out of your chair, relax. Logic models are nothing more than a summary of your grant proposal in table or illustration form. In fact, a completed logic model gives you a great point from which to start drafting your project narrative.

Now here's the good news: You don't have to create logic models on your own. In fact, you will probably need the input of program staff. The companion *Writing to Win Federal Grants* book offers tips and even an exercise for working with program staff to complete a logic model for your project.

In this chapter, we offer you several different styles of logic models so you can find one that fits your own style best. You can take materials from this chapter into the program planning meeting to help others overcome any fears they may have.

Purpose of a Logic Model

A well-constructed logic model is evident to reviewers. It offers convincing evidence that your organization can pull off the project as proposed. It shows your organization has thought through its program and is prepared to implement and collect data to prove its effectiveness.

Think of your logic model as a brief outline of your program. Focus on brevity. Logic models tend to be only one or two pages long. More than that may mean one of three things:

◆ you are measuring far too many things;

◆ your project lacks focus; or

◆ you have included too many details that likely belong in your project narrative.

Remember, the logic model is just supposed to be an overview of the program. Many times reviewers will look at your logic model first to help orient them to the project before they begin reviewing the narrative. Essentially, it's the PowerPoint introduction to your project.

The companion *Writing to Win Federal Grants* book gives a detailed explanation of each of these elements, along with examples. It also provides additional completed logic models that are simpler than the ones in this chapter.

Dig Deeper

The following are the main elements of most logic models:

◆ A short definition of the problem you are addressing

◆ What resources you need to solve the problem

◆ How you will use these resources (activities)

◆ What services will be delivered (outputs)

◆ How participants will benefit (outcomes)

◆ If benefits are achieved, how they solve the defined problem (impact)

The basic logic model elements are laid out in the diagram on the facing page. The diagram is based on a combined W.K. Kellogg and United Way of America model. It focuses on what a logic model should communicate to its readers.

When we are creating a logic model, we typically begin with the need in the community we wish to address. Then we determine what we want the outcomes of our efforts to be. This is the goal or impact. With the ultimate goal in mind, many program people and grant professionals find it easier to build the logic model backward from the goal rather than forward from the inputs.

A Basic Logic Model Template

If you have to create a logic model and your funding agency has not given you any guidance as to its content, you may want to start small. It's hard to get much simpler than the five-column logic model template provided below. You could use the same columns, but some people prefer to put "Impact" on the far left, instead of the far right, to indicate that everything is driven by the ultimate outcome.

Logic Model Template 1

Inputs	Activities	Outputs	Outcomes	Impact

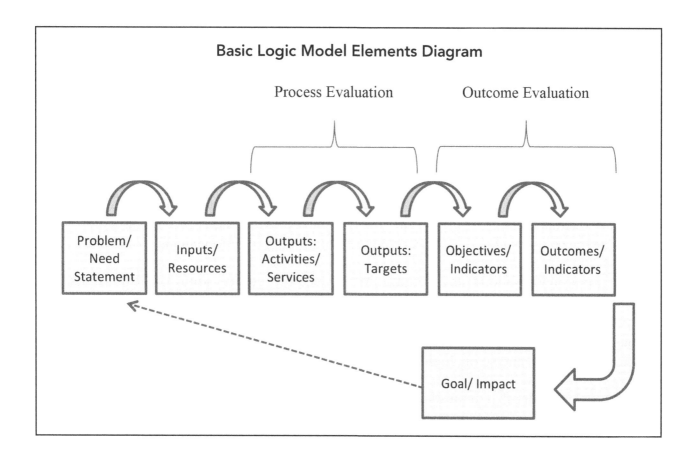

Once you've got some experience with logic models, or if you need to provide more detail, you can use a version of the second template below. It does start with the goal. It also includes a problem or community need that the project wishes to address. It also adds a column for targets, or performance measures. This is something commonly requested by funders.

Logic Model Template 2

Goal/ Impact	Problem/ Need Statement	Inputs/ Resources	Outputs/ Activities & Services	Outputs/ Targets	Objectives/ Indicators	Outcomes/ Indicators

Additional Logic Model Examples

If you're like us, a blank page can be uninspiring. So we are providing several completed logic models pulled from actual funded proposals. Sometimes the style of the logic model was determined by the funder who provided the template. Other times the style came from the project's evaluator or was created by program staff.

The models on the following pages are presented roughly in order from simpler to more complex. The simplest logic model we have to offer is included in Sample Annotated Proposal 3 in **Part Two** of this workbook.

Sample Logic Model 1—Expanded Traditional Format

The first logic model sample came from Sample Annotated Proposal 1 in **Part Two**. You might find it useful to come back to this chapter to compare the logic model against the proposal content.

Sample Logic Model 2—Theory of Change Format

What we are calling a logic model in this chapter can go by many names in many circles. Some funding agencies, evaluators, and program experts prefer to call such program diagrams "theory of change models." Whatever the title is at the top of the page, you will immediately recognize the column titles since they are very similar to the traditional logic model titles.

The Corporation for National and Community Service now requires some applicants to use a theory of change model like Sample Logic Model 2. See how similar it is to the logic model templates. It's organized somewhat differently. It is also able to communicate the contributions of many partners serving several different populations in the community. These are listed as Agency 1, Agency 2, and so on, in the sample.

This particular model also requests applicants to break their outcomes down into three categories: short term, medium term, and long term. Some funding agencies will give you definitions of these terms. In this particular case, the funder has determined that "short-term outcomes" are those realized within three to six months, "mid-term outcomes" are realized within six months to one year, and "long-term outcomes" take longer than one year to accomplish.

If the funder gives no definition, then you determine for yourself what constitutes short term as opposed to mid term. We recommend that you communicate your definitions clearly in your project narrative and in your model if there is room.

Sample Logic Model 3—Connections Model

As you may have discovered, you can spend a lot of time formatting a logic model, trying to squeeze everything in just so. Trying to make clear the relationships among items from one column to the next can be a real challenge, especially if you need readers to follow an individual item from left to right, across all columns.

One solution is to put each item in its own box. You can then draw arrows showing how boxes connect, affect one another, and interrelate. The sample logic model labeled "Connections Model" took just this approach.

Basically, the major column boundaries are "imagined." All column content is communicated in a series of text boxes that are then connected by arrows. The main column headings were required by the funding agency and include short-, medium-, and long-term outcomes. This type of design is relatively common in public health settings.

Sample Logic Model 4—Additions to Traditional Model

The fourth and final completed logic model we share with you came from a template provided by the funding agency. In other words, we had to fill in preexisting boxes and columns. Even though the applicant completing the model was a community college, the funding agency is the US Department of Agriculture (USDA). USDA asks applicants to discuss different types of outcomes (knowledge, actions, and conditions) rather than define outcomes by a time frame.

Also added to the USDA model are (1) a place to describe the problem or community need to be addressed ("Situation"), (2) assumptions upon which the proposed project plan is based, and (3) any external factors that may negatively impact the success of the project.

Logic models can go by many other names, such as:

◆ Theory of change model

◆ Logframe

◆ Logical framework

◆ Program matrix

important

These boxes summarize and support content that you also provide in more detail in the project narrative such as need, the evidence basis for your planned activities, and identifying possible barriers or challenges to the project's success.

Sample Logic Model 1 – Expanded Traditional Format

Goal/Impact	Problem/Need Statement	Inputs/Resources	Outputs/Activities & Services	Outputs/Targets	Objectives/Indicators	Outcomes/Indicators
Reduce hospital readmissions for cardiac patients (defined as readmitted for any cause within 30 days of original discharge). Improve patient satisfaction with regard to care. Improve patient and/or caregiver health literacy with regard to cardiac diagnoses. Improve OMC staff knowledge with regard to implementing evidenced-based practices	Socio-economic factors, negatively impact health outcomes including readmission rates, patient satisfaction and health literacy. OMC intends to implement an evidenced-based Quality Improvement model called the Model for Improvement. The model will be overlaid with specific re-designs in the hospital's discharge process for cardiac patients that supports a reduction in readmissions.	1. Patients 2. Hospital Medical Staff 3. Hospital Social Services Staff 4. Hospital Pharmacy staff 5. Councils with Physicians and Other Providers 6. Patients 7. Caregivers/ family 8. Electronic Health Records 9. Information Technology Staff 10. Evaluation Team	1. OMC team will be trained in implementing evidenced-based practices. 2. Using Model for Improvement the existing discharge process will be evaluated 3. Changes to existing discharge process will be established and staff will be trained. 4. A Discharge Advocate will be named. 5. Patients will be assigned to a Discharge Advocate. 6. Discharge Advocate will monitor patient's progress while in the hospital and will work across departments to support the patient's transition to home or other care.	A quality improvement model known as the Model for Improvement will be implemented. A new discharge process will be developed and implemented.	Trainings conducted. A cardiac care team will be developed with team members including a Discharge Advocate, physician, patient care nurse, pharmacy and other support service members (i.e., nutrition, rehab, etc.). This care team will refine the planned re-designed discharge process and begin its implementation. Discharge process developed and implemented. Discharge process reviewed and evaluated to determine if results appear promising in terms of readmission rates. Discharge process reviewed and evaluated in terms of patient/family/ caregiver satisfaction.	100% of evaluation team will be trained on the implementation of the Model for Improvement. 100% of cardiac care team members will be trained on the use of the LACES evaluation tool for assessing patients at high-risk for readmission. New team member trainings will be offered at least quarterly. Hospital readmission rates (defined as readmitted within 30 days of discharge) will decrease by 10% over baseline in year one, 20% over baseline in year 2 and 30% over baseline in year 3 for patients originally admitted with a cardiac diagnosis.

Sample Logic Model 1 – Expanded Traditional Format, continued

Goal/Impact	Problem/Need Statement	Inputs/Resources	Outputs/Activities & Services	Outputs/Targets	Objectives/Indicators	Outcomes/Indicators
			7. If transitioned home, Discharge Advocate will administer LACES tool to determine risk value for readmission. 8. Team will review care and discharge orders with patient/family/caregivers to build health literacy. 9. Follow-up services end 31 days after discharge unless readmitted. If readmitted, follow-up services end 31 days following final discharge to home.		Health literacy of patient/family/caregiver improves. Follow-up services end 31 days after discharge unless readmitted. If readmitted, follow-up services end 31 days following final discharge to home.	25% of patients in year one, 30% in year two, and 50% in year three will make and complete follow-up care visits with their physician or clinic as indicated on discharge orders. 100% of patients will receive follow-up phone calls (if low to moderate risk) or home visits (if high-risk) within 2 days of discharge. Risk for readmission will be measured using LACES measurement tool. 70% of patients/family members/caregivers will report feeling more confident and informed about the patient's condition and care.

Sample Logic Model 2 – Theory of Change Model

Project Resources	Core Project Components	Evidence of Project Implementation and Participation	Evidence of Change		
			Outcomes		
Inputs	Activities	Outputs	Short-Term	Medium-Term	Long-Term
What we invest (# and type of AmeriCorps members)	What we do	Direct products from program activities	Changes in knowledge, skills, attitudes, opinions	Changes in behavior or action that result from participants' new knowledge	Meaningful changes, often in their condition or status in life
<u>General</u> • Evidenced-based programming addressing identified community needs <u>Agency 1</u> • Supervision • Orientation and Training • Match through food pantry <u>Agency 2</u> • Educational Advocates supervising AmeriCorps members • Training • Match through __.	<u>AmeriCorps Members</u> Provide training, orientation and support to AmeriCorps members, preparing them to deliver high quality services to the community and personally grow <u>Educational Advocates</u> Using the evidenced-based Check and Connect model, educational advocates will work with youth 6 through 10th grade to ensure the youth is making adequate academic progress, advocate for education and family supports as needed.	<u>AmeriCorps Members</u> • X AmeriCorps members will participate in training and orientation • X AmeriCorps members will participate in AmeriCorps activities (National Day of Service, AmeriCorps Days) • X AmeriCorps members will complete their term of service.	<u>AmeriCorps Members</u> • AmeriCorps members will establish personal goals • AmeriCorps members will complete X of Y professional growth opportunities gaining skills such as CPR, first aid, etc. <u>Youth</u> • Absenteeism will decrease • Truancy will decrease • Youth will report feeling better about themselves • Youth will present a better attitude at school	<u>AmeriCorps Members</u> • AmeriCorps members will establish a plan for using their educational award and will begin completing identified action steps. <u>Youth</u> • Youth will meet the educational requirements to advance to the next grade level. • Schools will report improved scores on the annual achievement tests	<u>AmeriCorps Members</u> • AmeriCorps member will utilize education award to obtain post-secondary degree <u>Youth</u> • Education levels increase in the community • Fewer children live in poverty <u>Family</u> • Family stability improves • Poverty rates decrease

Sample Logic Model 2 – Theory of Change Model, continued

What we invest (# and type of AmeriCorps members)	What we do	Direct products from program activities	Changes in knowledge, skills, attitudes, opinions	Changes in behavior or action that result from participants' new knowledge	Meaningful changes, often in their condition or status in life
Agency 3 • Student and volunteer recruitment through the Leadership and Volunteerism Center • Program support Agency 4 • Support for AmeriCorps members to work in schools Agency 5 • Support for AmeriCorps members to work in schools Agency 6 • Advisory capacity to ensure coordination across programs on youth violence prevention initiatives. Agency 7 • Outreach and coordination CNCS & IL Commission • Funding for X FTE AmeriCorps Members including Y full-time and Z minimum time members • Technical assistance	Economic Opportunity Families identified as food insecure will receive assistance from the food pantry that stabilizes the household along with referrals to other stabilizing supports. Families will receive computer training that supports job searches and improves employability. Families will also receive support with budgeting. Youth Violence Prevention Using an evidenced-based curriculum, youth participating in summer programming will engage in organized activities designed to promote self-confidence, self-awareness and goal-setting behavior that encourages them to envision a positive future.	Youth • X Youth will make appropriate progress in school • X youth will improve their reading level by at least one-full grade • X youth will achieve at least 90% attendance in school Family • X families will receive food pantry support and referrals to other stabilizing services • Y computers will be distributed to families enabling them to search for jobs, practice computer skills and allow their children to have access to computers for school work. Community • X Youth will make appropriate progress in school • X youth will improve their reading level by at least one-full grade • X youth will achieve at least 90% attendance in school	Family • Families will report increased stability • Families will report increased food security Community • Youth report an increase in community awareness and engagement Family • Families report improved engagement with the schools • Families report improved engagement with their children • Families report improvements in household income and stability Community • Youth participation in community activities increases.	Family • Families report improved engagement with the schools • Families report improved engagement with their children • Families report improvements in household income and stability Community • Youth participation in community activities increases.	Community • Education levels increase in the community • Graduation rates improve in the school district • Youth violence decreases in the community • Poverty decreases in the community • Youth violence rates decrease

Sample Logic Model 3 – Connections Model

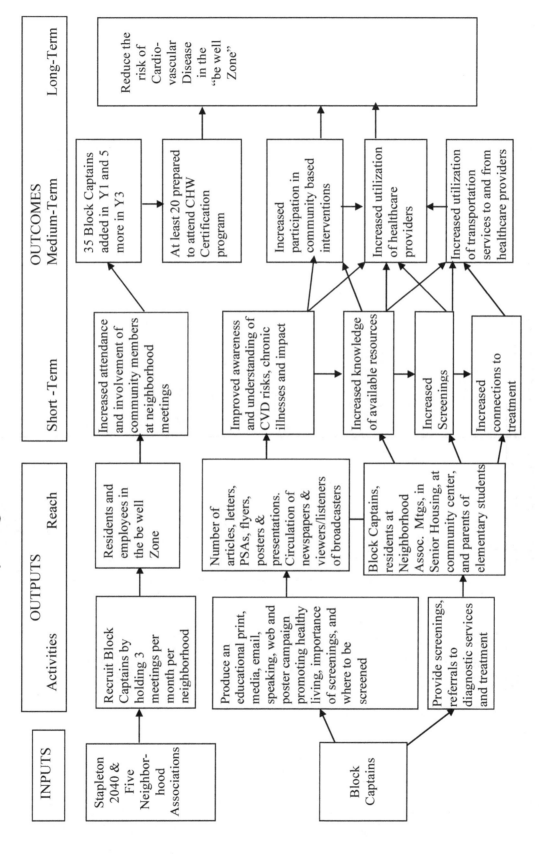

Sample Logic Model 4 – Additions to Traditional Model

Culinary HELIX Logic Model

Situation	Inputs	Activities	Outputs	Outcomes — Knowledge	Outcomes — Actions	Conditions
Description of challenge or opportunity:	What we invest:	What we do (Activities):	Products, services and events that are intended to lead to the program's outcomes:	Occurs when there is a change in knowledge or the participants actually **learn**:	Occur when there is a change in behavior or the participant's **act** upon what they've learned and:	Occur when a **societal condition** is improved due to a participant's action taken in the previous column:
- Lack of nutrition and food sciences courses	- Subject matter experts for curriculum design	- Design four new nutritional science courses	- Four nutrition and food science courses designed	- Increased knowledge of career opportunities in agricultural fields	- 25% of students in the Culinary HELIX program will declare intent to transfer to a bachelor's program	- Better use of indigenous species and sustainable production technologies as part of food production in the community
- Lack of experiential learning experiences for students	- Culinary Faculty	- Hire Project Director	- Four culinary arts courses redesigned and updated			
	- PCC-DV staff	- Install solar panels, cisterns and storage shed in garden	- Project Director hired and trained	- Increased knowledge of solar power & water harvesting practices	- Hispanic students see themselves as "college material"	- Increased number of Hispanic students obtaining a Bachelor's Degree in Nutritional Sciences
- Lack of clear pathway for articulation into a 4-year degree program	- Grants Compliance Office support	- Develop student recruitment materials	- Webpage developed			
	- External Partners: Bee Research Center, Fox Restaurant, Pascua Yaqui tribe	- Construct garden instructional space	- 35 students recruited into Culinary HELIX program	- Increased awareness of culturally relevant food production and preparation	- Increased employability of program participants because of skills and knowledge acquired	- Better retention of Hispanic students in the agricultural field
- Poor recruitment of Hispanic students in culinary arts		- Develop an articulation agreement between PCC-DV and UA	- More Hispanic students enrolled in the Culinary HELIX program			
	- Campus Garden	- Publish scientific article	- Completed articulation agreement between PCC-DV and UA	- Improved knowledge and skills in nutritional and food science	- Qualified, knowledgeable, and diverse culinary arts and nutritional sciences workforce in the community	- Vibrant and competitive agricultural workforce
- Insufficient number of trained and diverse students entering agriculture field	- Facilities	- Recruit and enroll students in Culinary HELIX program	- Clear pathway established for student transfer			
	- In-kind support	- Develop project webpage	- Campus garden enhanced with solar power and water harvesting sustainability elements	- Support USDA strategic goals and objectives	- Use of a campus garden as a model for student experiential learning	- Better quality of life for youth and adults in rural Pima County
	- Students	- Update existing culinary courses	- Partnership established between PCC-DV and local USDA agency			
		- Conduct field trips		- Campus garden enhances student skills & knowledge	- Use of a campus garden as a model for student experiential learning opportunities is adopted by other 2-year institutions	- Reduced obesity and improved nutrition and health
		- Present at educational meetings	- More Student experiential learning opportunities offered: field trips, guest lectures and campus garden activities & projects			
		Who we reach:	- Data is being collected, tracked and analyzed	- Increased awareness of the "garden to table" process		
		- Students				
		- Faculty				
		- Community Partners				
		- Agricultural Industry				
		- Conference attendees				

ASSUMPTIONS – Developing stronger curricula in nutrition and food science will provide students with greater educational and transfer opportunities leading more students to seek a Bachelor's Degree in Nutritional Sciences. This will lead to a more qualified workforce in the nutritional and food sciences arena. Experiential learning is an important factor in student learning, retention, and future career success and incorporating it into the culinary curriculum will attract more students.

EXTERNAL FACTORS – Things beyond the control of PCC-DV might include the University deciding to not sign the articulation agreement. This is unlikely as precedents are in place. Other external factors could be a weather disaster that destroys the Campus Garden, also unlikely.

Additional Resources

Fortunately, there are many resources available to help you learn more about logic models. We provide links to three of best and most comprehensive resources here:

◆ The Administration for Children & Families has an online logic model builder (toolkit.childwelfare.gov/toolkit) that may be helpful to you.

◆ The Innovation Network (innonet.org) offers a free online logic model builder.

◆ The W.K. Kellogg Foundation's "Logic Model Development Guide" (wkkf.org/knowledge-center/resources/2006/02/wk-kellogg-foundation-logic-model-development-guide.aspx) is one of the best free resources out there.

Tools for Guiding Project Design Discussions

Experienced grant professionals often use a logic model format to guide their program design, even if they're juggling the outcomes, activities, and inputs only in their heads. You can also use logic models to facilitate team discussions about program design.

If your project planning team is new to grants or new to grants jargon, you can remove some of the intimidation factor by stripping away all of the logic model column titles and just using questions to fill in columns on a whiteboard. Or you can dedicate one flip-chart sheet to what will become each column of a completed logic model.

We call this brainstorming program elements (see the next four pages). The term "brainstorming" is chosen carefully, because it frees participants to throw out ideas at the initial stages without worrying if they are giving a "wrong" answer.

It can be helpful to have groups practice completing a "program elements" table for a project that has nothing to do with your own mission and services. This distance from what you usually do can help free people from preconceived notions and opens the discussion up to all participants. Project ideas we've used in the past include (1) building a road to link Nigerian farmers to an urban center, (2) offering rehabilitative services to victims of sex trafficking, and (3) providing screening mammograms to low-income women.

 practical tip

When introducing these concepts to others, take a few moments to explain what sorts of items go in each of the columns. Then list the project to be brainstormed above the columns. Once you have agreed on a project, such as after-school tutoring, begin at the right-hand side of the table and brainstorm the long-term impacts on your community of a successful tutoring program.

Work your way "backward," from right to left, filling in the columns as you go. Once everyone agrees on the elements in each of the columns, fold the paper as instructed on the pages below, place the program element columns onto the blank "Logic Model" page, and your team has created a logic model.

Program Elements Brainstorming

Project:

What resources will you need to implement your project? Funds, yes, but what else?	How will you implement the project? What will you actually do?	Project Measurement When your project is complete, what will you be able to report has been done? What can you count?	Project Results (Outcomes) What will change in the community or in people's lives as a result of your project?	What kind of long-term positive impacts could this have?

Program Elements Brainstorming

Project: *Provide screening mammograms to low-income women in our service area*

What resources will you need to implement your project? Funds, yes, but what else?

- Mobile mammography unit
- Locations to perform screenings
- Marketing plan
- Nurses/techs to staff unit
- Volunteers
- Permission from selected locations

How will you implement the project? What will you actually do?

- Take mobile mammography unit to selected employers / plants
- Obtain permission from managers for women to be screened on breaks or lunch hour
- Take mobile mammography unit to farmer's market
- Promote free screening services via flyers, radio announcements and billboards

Project Measurement
When your project is complete, what will you be able to report has been done? What can you count?

- Number of women screened
- Number of women referred to diagnostic services
- Number of counseling sessions provided
- Amount of materials distributed
- Total number of participants served

Project Results (Outcomes)
What will change in the community or in people's lives as a result of your project?

- More women will understand the value of regular screenings
- Cancers identified earlier
- More women receive treatment
- Improved health

What kind of long-term positive impacts could this have?

- Longer lives
- Lower incidence of deaths from cancer
- Low-income recipients more financially stable
- Better quality of life

When you have completed the Program Elements, fold the document at dotted lines, top and bottom. Lay on top of a copy of the next page.

Transforming Your Program Planning Elements into A
LOGIC MODEL

Lay folded program elements columns on this page between the title and the boxes at the bottom of the page.

| Resources/Inputs | Activities | Outputs | Outcomes | Impact |

Your Planned Work

Your Intended Results

Sample Completed Logic Model from Program Elements Brainstorming Exercise

Project: *Provide screening mammograms to low-income women in our service area*

Resources/Inputs

What <u>resources</u> will you need to implement your project? Funds, yes, but what else?

- Mobile mammography unit
- Locations to perform screenings
- Marketing plan
- Nurses/techs to staff unit
- Volunteers
- Permission from selected locations

Activities

How will you <u>implement the</u> project? What will you actually do?

- Take mobile mammography unit to selected employers / plants
- Obtain permission from managers for women to be screened on breaks or lunch hour
- Take mobile mammography unit to farmer's market
- Promote free screening services via flyers, radio announcements and billboards

Outputs

Project <u>Measurement</u> When your project is complete, what will you be able to report has been done? What can you count?

- Number of women screened
- Number of women referred to diagnostic services
- Number of counseling sessions provided
- Amount of materials distributed
- Total number of participants served

Outcomes

Project <u>Results</u> (Outcomes) What will change in the community or in people's lives as a result of your project?

- More women will understand the value of regular screenings
- Cancers identified earlier
- More women receive treatment
- Improved health

Impact

What kind of <u>long-term positive</u> impacts could this have?

- Longer lives
- Lower incidence of deaths from cancer
- Low-income recipients more financially stable
- Better quality of life

Your Planned Work

Your Intended Results

To Recap

◆ Logic models are a brief overview of your program.

◆ Logic models may also be called other names, such as a theory of change model, logical framework, program matrix, to name a few.

◆ While we understand the temptation to do a logic model last, if you do it first, it can help you develop your narrative.

◆ Logic models often include short-term, mid-term, and long-range outcomes. These can be a reality check for your project planning.

get Narratives

budget categories

rting a federal budget

g checklist

e great consternation. Maybe that's because a lot of us were once
ught we had seen the last of any math more complicated than
we left college. Or maybe it's because we spend so much time and
that we are tired when we get to the budget.

ot falling into the
program, writing
ting on the budget
eginning your
egin project
asy to design a
you are allowed to
on.

different tools

plan a complete budget, create easy-
to-update line-item budget spreadsheets, and
track commitments of in-kind and matching
contributions. In addition, a complete budget
narrative is included with Annotated Proposal 2
in **Part Two**.

> We haven't overlooked how to write winning budget narratives. The companion *Writing to Win Federal Grants* book gives step-by-step instructions for creating a strong budget narrative clearly linked to your budget line items. But be aware that many agencies are very prescriptive as to the form and content of the budget narrative. Some even provide samples of successful budget narratives on their websites. Always follow the funder's requirements and suggestions.
>
> **Dig Deeper**

But first, we provide a quick overview of the federal budget categories so that we are all on the same page. This text is excerpted from the companion *Writing to Win Federal Grants* book.

EXCERPT...

Using Federal Budget Categories

Fortunately, most federal grants use standard budget categories that you will quickly learn. These categories are drawn from the budget form SF-424A from **Chapter Three**. Here is our non-federalese explanation of the budget categories:

- *Personnel.* This includes salaries/wages of grant-funded personnel, but not independent contractors or consultants.

- *Fringe benefits.* This includes insurance, retirement, payroll taxes and worker's compensation taxes. Fringe benefits are usually presented as a percentage of salaries.

- *Travel.* Can include airfare, hotels, meals, parking, mileage, and taxis or public transportation. We usually recommend basing estimated lodging, and meals on the federal per diem tables for that year (gsa.gov/perdiem) if your organization does not have its own per diem rates. Public agencies and state institutions of higher education may be required or allowed to use alternate state rates, especially for mileage reimbursements.

- *Equipment.* The federal definition of equipment is any item that has an individual purchase price of more than $5,000. As strange as this may seem, since computers go into inventory at most organizations, most computers and other technology are considered supplies (not equipment) for budgeting purposes.

- *Supplies.* Consumable supplies such as paper or pens, but also any item with a single purchase price of less than $5,000. Therefore, you include in the supplies category any items such as computers, printers, furniture, books, or brochures.

- *Contractual.* Includes costs associated with hiring independent contractors or consultants. It sometimes includes contracts for services such as web design or maintenance contracts for copiers. Some RFAs direct applicants to put no items in this category, so always double-check the rules pertaining to your application.

- *Construction.* For those programs that allow construction or renovation expenses, those expenses go into this category.

- *Other.* Place into this category any item that does not clearly fall into the previous categories. Some RFAs direct applicants to include no items in "Other." Some RFAs instruct you to place a seemingly random assortment of items in "Other." As always, follow the specific instructions in your RFA.

Getting Started

Organizations new to federal grants or those beginning new types of programs sometimes ask, "How do we know what our program is going to cost?" We know it can be a little scary, but the truth is that you are the only one who can answer this question. It takes a little legwork, a lot of thinking, and maybe some lucky guessing.

Start by trying to determine the one or two things in your budget that will cost the most. For many programs, personnel make up the largest expense. By the time you budget for all of the people you think you are going to need to deliver program activities, sometimes there is not much grant money left to go around.

It's usually in your best interest to have as few items as possible classified as "equipment" and as many as possible classified as "supplies." As soon as something becomes a piece of equipment, lots of additional federal rules become attached to it. You will have to tag and inventory each item of equipment, know its location in case of a surprise audit, and follow federal rules on disposing of equipment after the grant period closes.

practical tip

We recommend two tools that can help you get your budget off to a strong start. The first is a detailed budget planning checklist. It's an awful feeling to get the grant and then find out you missed a big expense or cost of delivering your program. Using a checklist can help you remember lots of small details that you might overlook when designing your budget. We tried to cover just about every eventuality in the checklist that we have provided on the following pages. You can likely adapt a simpler version for your own use.

If you are new to developing grant budgets, the companion *Writing to Win Federal Grants* book provides lots of information about how to budget for staff costs, in-kind contributions, and matching funds.

Dig Deeper

No single budget will ever include every item on this checklist. Rather, the checklist is designed to ensure that you don't forget possible expenses related to grant activities. If your organization tends to apply for similar types of projects all the time (and never will have a utilities expense, for example), then adapt this document to include only the types of expenses your organization will likely incur.

In addition, always follow the rules of the particular funding agency or competition to which you are applying. Just because something is listed here does not mean it will be an allowable expense for every type of grant.

Federal Budget Planning Checklist

Personnel Expenses

- Common Categories of Personnel
  - Full-time salary
  - Part-time salary
  - Full-time hourly
  - Part-time hourly
- Other Categories Unique to Higher Education – (some institutions budget these in Personnel, Contractual or Other; check your RFA)
  - Student employees (work study, graduate assistants, interns)
  - Adjunct faculty
  - Faculty release time or overload
- Possible "surprise" personnel costs, usually increases in existing personnel required because of your project activities (some may be recoverable as indirect costs)
  - Security
  - Custodial
  - Drivers
  - Grounds
  - Bookkeeper/Accounts Payable
  - Human Resources/Payroll

Fringe Benefits

(May have different rates for different categories of personnel. Amount may even vary from person to person due to family size, tenure, etc. Calculate an average per category.)

- FICA - 6.2%
- Medicare -1.45%
- Unemployment Insurance - ___%
- Workers Compensation - ____%
- Retirement (state pension, 403B, teachers' retirement, etc.) - ___%
- Insurance (health, dental, vision, etc.) - ___%
- Life Insurance - ___%

Travel Expenses

- Conference/workshop registrations
- Domestic airfare and baggage fees
- Mileage (for out-of-town travel or among local grant site locations)
- Meals and lodging on days traveling (use your organization's per diem rate/policies, or look up federal per diem rates for the destination city; these are updated annually by the General Services Administration at www.gsa.gov/perdiem)
- Parking
- Taxis, airport shuttles, or public transportation

- Rental car
- Entrance fees (e.g. for a national park)
- International travel, if allowed (airfare, visas, etc.); follow all federal regulations pertaining to international travel

Equipment

(Unless your organization has another rule in writing, the federal rule is that to qualify as equipment, an item must have an individual purchase price of more than $5,000. Any items that costs less than $5,000 each (like most computers) are supplies.)

(If you will purchase an item outright, list it in equipment. If you will lease the item or if there is an annual membership or subscription fee, some organizations choose to budget those expenses in contractual.)

- Major computer or networking equipment, such as servers, routers, or disk arrays
- Research instrumentation
- Science equipment
- Major software systems (such as software to support electronic medical records, student information systems, or distance learning)
- Vehicles (when allowed, such as for emergency services)
- Photocopier
- HVAC or other building systems (when allowed for construction or renovation projects)
- Educational equipment, such as simulators
- Potential "surprise" costs associated with purchasing some equipment (while these items may be budgeted in Contractual, Supplies or Other, or may not be allowed, consider the "total cost of ownership" for major purchases):
  - Delivery
  - Installation
  - Training
  - Inspections/licenses
  - On-going maintenance contract/subscriptions for updates
  - Warranty/service contract
  - Repairs
  - Insurance
  - Updating wiring, plumbing, or exhaust system
  - Consumables used by equipment item (e.g. tires for vehicles, gas canisters, etc.)

Supplies

(Almost anything else that you buy, other than services, can be considered supplies. Items you rent, such as tents and tables, may go in Supplies, Contractual, or Other. Check your RFA.)

- Consumable office supplies (paper, toner, file folders, notebooks, etc.)
- Training/board supplies (flip charts, highlighters, books, etc.)
- Computers, projectors, printers, and tablet devices

- Most standard office and productivity software
- Phones (purchased, not cell contracts, which are usually considered Contractual or Other)
- Supplies for events (decorations, handouts, signs/banners/posters, etc.)
- Furniture (allowed by some programs, not by others; check your RFA)
- Food (allowed on some projects, under specific circumstances, often not allowed)
- Tools
- Volunteer management supplies
- Cleaning supplies
- Uniforms, safety attire, turnout gear (for firefighters)

Contractual

(Almost any service that you pay someone else to do for you. Some competitions forbid any items be placed in contractual, which usually means that even though the costs are allowable, you have to list them in a different category. As always, follow your RFA.)

- External evaluator
- Strategic, business, or fundraising planning (cannot spend federal funds to conduct fundraising, but may develop your fundraising skills/capacity)
- Maintenance contracts
- Rent/lease of facilities (long-term for the organization's space; may need to pro-rate based on amount of space used by grant activities)
- Rental of facilities and supplies for special events (venue costs, tents, tables, sound system, etc.)
- Web or database design/updates (if not done by your personnel)
- Consultants
- Accountant/auditors
- Cell phone/smart phone/data plan contracts
- Surveys/research/community needs assessments
- Marketing and/or design services
- Billboards, bus shelters, other ad spaces (for public awareness campaigns)

Other

(Sometimes RFAs get persnickety about what they do or don't want listed in Other. If there are no guidelines telling you otherwise, these are the types of things you usually put in Other.)

- Printing (brochures, posters, flyers, billboards, banners, handbooks, etc.)
- Hiring costs (employment ads, physicals, drug screening, employment verification, license verification, background checks, etc.)
- Advertising (promoting services or events)
- Utilities (gas, electricity, water, Internet, cell phones, long distance)
- Dues, memberships, subscriptions
- Postage, shipping, delivery, courier
- Insurance (Director and Officer's, on vehicles, property/renter's)

Budget Templates

Next we provide two budget templates that are formatted slightly differently. Pick the one you understand the best or that best aligns with the type of project you are going to implement, and then adjust it within your own software.

These are both spreadsheets, with rows set up for each federal budget category and columns set up for multiple project years. If you are planning a budget for a three- or five-year project, it is essential to plan out the budget for every year. Even when you are required to submit the budget only for the first year of your program, you want to ensure that you will have enough funds to cover all planned activities for all years.

> If all or part of a person's time on a grant is being supplied by the applicant as an in-kind contribution, don't forget to calculate the value of the fringe benefits on that person's compensation as part of the match as well.
>
>
> important

This is especially important if the total amount of your budget in each subsequent year cannot change from the amount you requested in year one. If costs for anything in one category go up in subsequent years, you will have to reduce the price of items in another category to keep the budget in balance. For example, annual cost-of-living increases for personnel can have a major impact on the amount you have left to spend on other items after year one.

Remember, you usually enter only category totals onto forms like the SF-424A. However, we often use our detailed, line-item budget spreadsheet as the springboard for our budget narrative.

Also remember that the budget will guide program implementation over the next several years. The more detail and documentation you can provide while you are developing the budget, the easier it will be for program staff to adhere to the budget and successfully implement the planned project.

Budget Template 1

Template 1 includes some sample line items in each category. Text in several of the cells shows how to present details about line items in your budget narrative so that a reviewer can understand how you arrived at your totals. Text in italics describes what formula should be used in that cell.

Notice that we said these templates are spreadsheets. It can be tempting to just put numbers into cells. But after the initial setup, formulas can be a real time-saver. Budgets typically have to be changed frequently before they are finalized, and formulas to add up subtotals or calculate annual cost of living increases can help you avoid errors. That is, if you enter the formulas correctly!

Federal Grant Budget Template 1—No Matching Funds Required

Text in italics explains what formula should be in that cell.

Personnel	Year 1	Year 2	Year 3	Total
Project Director _____ % FTE x $_____ base salary				*Sum of Columns*
Program Coordinator __% FTE x $_____ base salary				*Sum of Columns*
Project Staff Person $____/hour x ____ hours/week				*Sum of Columns*
Administrative Assistant $____/hour x ____ hours/week				*Sum of Columns*
Sub-Total Personnel	*Sum of Rows*	*Sum of Rows*	*Sum of Rows*	*Sum of Columns*
Fringe Benefits	**Year 1**	**Year 2**	**Year 3**	**Total**
Fringe Benefits rate for full-time/salaried staff = ____%				
Fringe Benefits rate for part-time or hourly staff = ____%				
Sub-Total Fringe				
Travel	**Year 1**	**Year 2**	**Year 3**	**Total**
Sample Conference Calculation: Travel for ___(#) staff to attend ABC conference (airfare: $___; lodging: $___/night x __ nights; per diem: $___/ day x ___ days; Airport parking/ground transport $___/ day x ___ days; Mileage to airport ___ miles x $.__/mile)				
Sample Local Mileage Calculation: Local travel for ___ staff to ___ sites __ times per week/month/year; ____ miles per round trip x $.___ per mile				
Sub-Total Travel				
Equipment*	**Year 1**	**Year 2**	**Year 3**	**Total**
XYZ Brand server				
ABC Brand software				
Sub-Total Equipment				

*Remember that for an item to be "equipment," it must have an individual purchase price of greater than $5,000.

Federal Grant Budget Template 1 — Page Two

Supplies	Year 1	Year 2	Year 3	Total
Staff desktop computers: Qty. __ ABC Brand/Model x $____/each				*Sum of Columns*
Laptop and projector for training: XYZ brand laptop at $_____ plus ABC model projector at $____				*Sum of Columns*
Office Supplies (avg. $___/month x 12 months)				*Sum of Columns*
Sub-Total Supplies	*Sum of Rows*	*Sum of Rows*	*Sum of Rows*	*Sum of Columns*
Contractual	**Year 1**	**Year 2**	**Year 3**	**Total**
External Evaluator: ___ days x $ ____/day				
Vendor Training on ABC Software				
Maintenance Contract on ABC Software				
Sub-Total Contractual				
Construction	**Year 1**	**Year 2**	**Year 3**	**Total**
Remodeling of Rooms 102 and 104 into distance learning classroom: ___ sq. ft. at $_____/s.f.				
Building outdoor gathering space: ___ sq. ft x $___/s.f.				
Sub-Total Construction				
Other	**Year 1**	**Year 2**	**Year 3**	**Total**
Printing Marketing Materials: _____ brochures at $____/ea				
Advertising for Staff Positions				
Postage				
Sub-Total Other				
Totals	**Year 1**	**Year 2**	**Year 3**	**Total**
Total Direct Costs (Sum of all Sub-Totals)				*Sum of Columns*
Indirect Costs of ___% - (If allowed)	*Direct Costs x Percent*			*Sum of Columns*
Total Project Costs (Sum of Direct and Indirect Costs)	*Sum of Rows*	*Sum of Rows*	*Sum of Rows*	*Sum of Columns*
Maximum Grant Amount Allowed	From RFA			
Amount Left to Spend/Over Budget	*(Max Allowed Minus Total Project Costs)*			

Budget Template 2

The second budget template offers a more streamlined example. While it includes space for a five-year project, it also includes columns in which to indicate matching funds in each year of the project.

Another reason we usually use formulas in our budget spreadsheets is that we often use a sheet like the one in the next template as a summary page. It captures in one place all of the major expenses.

Behind the summary page are typically several other tabs. The tabs may be organized by project year, or they may be organized by a major category, such as supplies. You can use the supporting tab to supply extensive detail that will help you and the program team remember what you intended when you begin to implement the program. The detail also provides rich content for your budget narrative.

> If you feel a little intimidated by all this talk of formulas and linking cells, do as much as you are comfortable doing. But every now and then, take a moment to follow a simple online tutorial on how to link cells or calculate percentages using formulas. It won't take you long to master a few techniques that will save you loads of time in the future.
>
>

Microsoft's Excel not only allows you to put formulas into cells to add up numbers for you, but it also allows you to insert a simple command in a cell to tell that cell that its content should come from another cell, another tab, or even another spreadsheet entirely. We find this incredibly useful to link line items on our summary page to more detail on a subsequent tab.

As just one example of how this technique can save you enormous time, think of a project in which you will be purchasing multiple computers or a variety of instructional supplies for multiple classrooms or labs over several years. If you enter all of the detail on a supplies tab and link the total of those supplies to a cell on the main page, any change to a per-item cost or the quantity of items will automatically update all of your totals for you and let you instantly understand the impact of that change on your bottom line.

Federal Grant Budget Template 2—Includes Matching Funds

Add (or delete) rows to each category as necessary to contain all of your line items.

Salaries	Year 1	Match	Year 2	Match	Year 3	Match	Year 4	Match	Year 5	Match
Subtotal Salaries										
Fringe Benefits	Year 1	Match	Year 2	Match	Year 3	Match	Year 4	Match	Year 5	Match
Subtotal Fringe										
Travel	Year 1	Match	Year 2	Match	Year 3	Match	Year 4	Match	Year 5	Match
Subtotal Travel										
Equipment	Year 1	Match	Year 2	Match	Year 3	Match	Year 4	Match	Year 5	Match
Subtotal Equipment										
Supplies	Year 1	Match	Year 2	Match	Year 3	Match	Year 4	Match	Year 5	Match
Subtotal Supplies										

Federal Grant Budget Template 2 (Matching Funds)—Page Two

Contractual	Year 1	Match	Year 2	Match	Year 3	Match	Year 4	Match	Year 5	Match
Subtotal Contractual										
Other	**Year 1**	**Match**	**Year 2**	**Match**	**Year 3**	**Match**	**Year 4**	**Match**	**Year 5**	**Match**
Subtotal Other										
Total Direct Expenses	Sum of All Sub-Totals									
Indirect Costs (____%) (Calculated on Federal Contribution Only; Not on Match)		XX		XX		XX		XX		XX
Total Costs	Direct Plus Indirect Costs									
Total Direct Expenses (All Five Years)	$									
Total Matching Funds (All Five Years)	$									

Suggestions for Using the Budget Templates

Which budget format you choose or develop for yourself is not as important as the budget being organized by federal budget categories and being easy to read. While you usually don't simply attach your budget spreadsheet to an application, it can form the foundation of your budget narrative.

You can also add a sheet to the front of your workbook that summarizes each project year so that numbers are ready for easy entry into the SF-424A form. That sheet would look something like the excerpt below. A summary sheet like this is one place where we really like to use that ability to link one cell to another so that we don't risk introducing an error by retyping the numbers.

EXCERPT...

Budget Summary for SF-424A				
	Year 1	Year 2	Year 3	Total
Personnel	$ 64,342	$ 66,273	$ 68,262	$198,877
Fringe Benefits	$ 17,372	$ 17,894	$ 18,431	$ 53,697
Travel	$ 1,938	$ 5,403	$ 5,403	$ 12,744
Equipment	$ 0	$ 0	$ 0	$ 0
Supplies	$ 21,683	$ 29,980	$ 29,950	$ 81,613
Contractual	$ 30,902	$ 16,664	$ 14,164	$ 61,730
Construction	$ 0	$ 0	$ 0	$ 0
Other	$ 13,760	$ 13,760	$ 13,760	$ 41,280
Total Direct Costs	$149,997	$149,974	$149,970	$449,941
Indirect Costs				
Total Costs	$149,997	$149,974	$149,970	$449,941

Following this paragraph is an excerpt from a budget narrative. It includes real budget figures for a three-year grant. In this example, personnel and fringe together comprise more than 50 percent of the project budget each year. This is normal and perfectly acceptable in certain grants. Pay attention to any guidance from your funding agency regarding caps on any budget categories.

EXCERPT...

PERSONNEL	FEDERAL	MATCH	TOTAL
Project Director (1 FTE)	$44,000		$44,000
Member Services Coordinator (1 FTE)	$28,000		$28,000
Administrative Assistant (.5 FTE)	$11,000		$11,000
Media Relations Coordinator (.25 FTE)		$ 6,760	$ 6,760
Subtotal Personnel	$83,000	$ 6,760	$89,760

FRINGE BENEFITS	FEDERAL	MATCH	TOTAL
Project Director Fringe (Rate - 28.08%)	$12,355	$ 0	$12,355
Member Services Coordinator (@ 28.08%)	$ 7,862	$ 0	$ 7,862
Administrative Assistant (@ 19.94%)	$ 2,193	$ 0	$ 2,193
Media Relations Coordinator (@ 19.94%)		$ 1,348	$ 1,348
Subtotal Fringe	$22,410	$ 1,348	$23,758

Budgeting Matching Funds

You will also notice the excerpt includes a column for matching funds. An unspecified amount of match was expected in this grant program. In the personnel and fringe categories, the applicant is counting the value of time spent on delivering or supporting project activities as part of its match. This is considered an in-kind match, because the contributor was not giving $6,760 in cash to the grant applicant but merely providing services valued at $6,760.

If matching funds are required, you will list these funds in your budget and allocate them toward certain items, just as you allocate your grant funds. You are often allowed to meet all or part of your match through in-kind contributions rather than cash. The guidelines for the program to which you are applying should be clear about (1) whether a match is required or suggested, (2) the amount of the match, and (3) whether all or part of the match must be in cash rather than in-kind.

In the same grant application, another consortium member agreed to subsidize part of the cost of one of its staff members to travel on behalf of the consortium. That contribution counted as a cash match, because the contributor would be spending its own money to advance the grant's project activities. See the next excerpt to see how this was accounted for in the budget.

EXCERPT...			
TRAVEL	FEDERAL	MATCH	TOTAL
2 Staff to DC Grantee Workshop & Training			
Airfare (2 tickets x $500 x 2 trips)	$1,500	$ 500	$2,000
Meals @ 2 staff x $65 per day x 3 days x 2 trips	$ 585	$ 195	$ 780
Lodging $180 x 3 days x 2 rooms x 2 trips	$1,620	$ 540	$2,160
Ground Transport/Airport Parking ($45/day x 3 days x 2 conferences/workshops)	$ 270	$ 0	$ 270

Most of the time, one cannot tell only from looking at a budget whether a matching item is a cash contribution or will be supplied in-kind. If we have space, we usually explain the source of all matches in our budget narrative. For example, in the personnel category, our accompanying narrative will say something such as, "XYZ Hospital is providing as in-kind the salary and fringe of a 0.25 FTE media relations coordinator."

Documenting Matching Funds

Your accountant or bookkeeper can help you set up a system in your software to track matching funds and to document the value of in-kind contributions that should count toward your match. As far as the funding agency is concerned, once it gives you a grant, matching funds become as much its money as the grant money is. The matching funds are no longer your money. So they should be set aside in a restricted account, and all of the same procedures you follow to document grant expenditures should be followed when accounting for matching funds.

Aside from this bookkeeping to track the money through your accounting system, it can also be a good idea to create a record of each commitment by a contributor of matching funds. People change jobs. Companies get bought and sold. Miscommunications and misunderstandings occur. If you are claiming matching funds in your grant application and are depending on other people or organizations to provide those funds (or in-kind value), you want to be able to "collect" from those contributors.

To help with this, we created a simple in-kind contributions tracking form. On the next page is an excerpt from a tracking form you can use for your own projects. This includes some of the entries from an actual form used to track more than twenty-five contributions to one grant project. We recommend attaching copies of the emails in which the promises were confirmed. If you receive a verbal promise, get it in writing. Getting a match commitment confirmed in a signed MOU or letter of commitment is the best protection against faulty memories or changes in leadership. (See **Chapters Six** and **Seven**.)

Sample Completed In-Kind Tracking Form

Contributor	Item	Value	Budget Line #	Year(s) of Grant	Source of Info
XYZ Hospital	Media Relations Person .25 FTE	$8,108	10 & 16	1-3	
	Waiver of Fiscal Agent fee	$2,400	64	1 Only	Mr. Brown e-mail 8 Oct
	Including us in Audit	$1,000	64	1 Only	
Chamber of Commerce	Use of Conf. Rm. and LCD projector; $50/ea x 12 (once per mo.)	$600	47	1 Only	Ms. Jones e-mail 10 Oct
ABC Business	Laptop Computer	$2,000	47	1 Only	Mrs. Smith e-mail 11 Oct
	Member travel to 1 conference	$1,770	43	1-3	
Attorney	Legal documents review	$1,000	64	1-3	Board e-mail 27 Sept
Landlord	Office space (2 offices)	$7,200	71	1-3	e-mails with Office Manager, 10 Oct & other
	2 office Desks + 2 desk chairs	$1,400	49	1-3	
	Internet, phone & long distance	$1,800	48	1-3	
A#1 Business	Cubicles (2)	$500	49	1-3	Verbal conversation w/ Mr. Owner 9 Oct; e-mail from Assistant 11 Oct
County Dept of Health	Health Educational Materials	$1,000	51	1-3	Letter of Support from County Health Department Office
	Area Director and Educator time	$6,000	56	1-3	
	Research	$1,000	57	1-3	
State Office of Rural Health	Research	$5,000	57	1-3	Estimated value of their time for completing Need for Assistance
Community Foundation	Board and Staff Training	$8,600	62	1-3	Foundation's training web site: "Full Value" to organizations of subsidized trainings
Misc. Sponsors	Printing (Referral Guide)	$5,000	51	1-3	To be secured
Network Members	Member Travel to Conference	$1,770	43	1-3	Per Mr. Rich 5 Oct; Member will be asked to pay at time of travel
	Miscellaneous Office Supplies	$200	50	1-3 (amt. varies)	Per Network Memorandum of Agreement

To Recap

◆ Begin your budget planning with the most important and the most expensive items, then work your way down.

◆ Putting budget figures in a spreadsheet instead of a word processor is a great way to double-check your calculations and make quick changes.

◆ It's important to track and document matching contributions.

Chapter Six

Partnerships and the ABCs of MOUs

IN THIS CHAPTER

···→ Documenting informal partnerships

···→ Talking about partners in your proposals

···→ Formalizing relationships with a memorandum of understanding

···→ A build-your-own MOU template

In the companion *Writing to Win Federal Grants* book, we talk about how working with other organizations can be a lot like marriage. So think of a memorandum of understanding (MOU) as being like a prenuptial agreement.

It serves many of the same purposes: Preventing arguments. Spelling out roles and responsibilities. Being very specific about how two or more organizations will interact with one another—in good times and bad. Sometimes making clear who owns what when the relationship dissolves.

We both advocate strongly that organizations should have MOUs in place whenever they depend on someone else to help deliver their essential services. On the other hand, we know many of you have developed informal collaborations over the years. Few, if any, of these are likely to have an MOU. So that's where we start.

Documenting Informal Partnerships

Many funders expect or require you to partner with other organizations to deliver services. Sometimes the only eligible applicant for a grant is a multimember consortium. Funding agencies want us to focus on our core competencies. They also hope we achieve efficiencies and reduce duplication of services by working together.

Many of you thrive on informal partnerships. Such relationships may be no more structured than two people who pick up a phone and say, "I heard your students need fifty hours of community service to graduate. Well, I need babysitters for my parenting program. Let's talk!"

We love to see organizations collaborating like this. But we also know from experience that programs can be thrown into chaos if any of the individuals holding the partnership together fall ill or leave the organization. That is why we recommend that you document all partnerships for your internal records, at the very minimum.

You may have noticed that we talk about partnerships and consortia without really distinguishing among them. The word "consortium" usually implies something more than partnering but less than merging. Most consortia have multiple members. These members typically come together for a long-term purpose, such as reducing homelessness in a community. On any particular project or grant, some members may play larger or smaller roles, but they all remain members who are committed to the larger goal.

Everyone is busy, and it can be hard to find time to fill out forms that someone else wants you to complete. But ask your colleagues what would happen if suddenly the teenaged babysitters who make it possible for the parents in their program to come to their workshops stopped showing up or if the church group that picks up fresh fruits and vegetables for the food pantry stopped coming.

So we recommend using a simple, nonthreatening partnership roster like the one below. We developed this for our own use in-house. It's not a dissertation on the ins and outs of each partnership on which your organization depends. But it is an invaluable record that could save a project from disaster if the only person at your organization who knows how the project really works is unexpectedly not available.

Sample Partnership Roster

Program Area	Activity	Provider	Where	Contact Name	Ph #
Children's Services	Art Therapy				
Children's Services	Babysitting for Mom's Group				
Children's Services	Dental Services				
Children's Services	Tutoring				
Food Pantry	Transportation				
Food Pantry	Boxes for Distribution				
Adult Services	Mental Health Services				
Adult Services	Dental Services				

Talking about Partners in Your Grant Proposals

Sometimes you do need to include your partners in a grant proposal, even if no MOU is required. In that case, we usually use a table such as the one below that is drawn from the companion *Writing to Win Federal Grants* book and is excerpted from an actual proposal.

EXCERPT...

ROLES OF PROJECT PARTNERS				
Who	What	When	Where	Purpose
Smith County Schools	- transport students to Lead Hill Community Center	- 2 days/week	- From Mt. Peak Elementary	- To transport students safely
	- nutritious snacks for all project students	- every day	- All Centers	- Improve nutrition
	- invite staff and volunteers to trainings	- district staff development	- All Centers	- To train tutors
Clinton Methodist Church	- provide a location for project activities	- 4 days/week	- Serves Polk Elementary	- To provide a safe location for student services
Family Services Network	- provide anti-drug/anti-violence training materials for sessions	- entire project	- All Centers	- To deter students from drug use and violence
Adult Basic Ed.	- provide parents with educational classes	- entire project	- Hope High School	- To increase parent success
Montfort College	- provide college students as volunteer tutors	- entire project	- All Centers	- Role models - To tutor students
Chamber of Commerce	- provide business professionals to deliver entrepreneurial training	- quarterly	- All Centers	- To develop entrepreneurship skills

The table in the excerpt above was placed directly into the project narrative. This was done in response to RFA prompts that asked about how project services were going to be delivered, by whom, and where. Other proposals may want only a roster of partners or consortium members. An additional example of an informal partnership list that shows each partner's level of commitment appears in Sample Proposal 2 in **Part Two** of this workbook.

Formalizing the Relationship with an MOU

A memorandum of understanding (MOU), memorandum of agreement (MOA), or other such document makes the cooperative relationship among those who execute it more formal. Usually the executive director or president signs an MOU because that person has the authority to commit the organization and its resources to the partnership.

An MOU is a positive document. It demonstrates the strength and commitment of partners who will be working together. It memorializes an intent to work together, provide services, and work out any problems that may arise. Well-crafted MOUs should accomplish the following:

◆ Articulate a shared vision or understanding between the partners

◆ Specify the roles and responsibilities of the partners

◆ Spell out how the organizations intend to resolve problems

◆ Define the period of agreement

◆ Identify the primary point of contact at each partnering organization

◆ Provide a space for signatures, which affirms the agreement of the partnering organizations.

Write your MOUs in plain language, without the legalese. Leave the *shall*, *henceforth*, and *whereas* statements to the lawyers. Just say what you mean as clearly as possible. It's much easier for nonlawyers to interpret and far less threatening.

Cheryl often starts a new page at the end of the MOU so that the signatures appear on their own page or pages. This is a time-saving trick that's really important when you have to drive around a service area obtaining in-person signatures from several partners. This way, if you need to make any edits or corrections to the MOU that might change the last page or cause a new page break, you can send the revised version via email for approval without having to collect all of the signatures again.

 practical tip

Three sample MOUs appear on the following pages. They progress from simple to more complex. We did not create all of them, so they may not all follow the list above. But, each was acceptable to the partners and the reviewers for the particular grant proposal to which they were attached.

Sample MOU 1 was written as an agreement between two partnering organizations. Sample MOU 2 documents an agreement among the members of an existing consortium, mostly to spell out the roles of consortium members in the upcoming grant project. The third MOU (alas, in legalese) documents a relationship between a lead applicant (who will have additional duties) and other partners.

Many times, the quirks of individual MOUs develop because someone is worried about a particular aspect of working together. Maybe they were part of a previous unsuccessful relationship. It's not worth fighting about the quirk. If members want language that says organizations will not attempt to hire away staff from each other (as in Sample MOU 3), put it in.

Finally, you will notice that none of the MOU samples discusses payment arrangements in detail. If the lead organization will be paying any of its partners for providing services, payment terms and conditions are usually handled in an actual contract (sometimes called a subrecipient agreement) that is executed separately—and after the grant proposal is funded.

Sample MOU 1

MEMORANDUM OF AGREEMENT BETWEEN
Community-Based Organization ABC and
Local Middle School

This document sets forth the agreement between Community-Based Organization ABC (CBO ABC), at 1234 Anystreet, City, USA, represented by Ms. Program Director, and Local Middle School (LMS), represented by Ms. School Principal. Local Middle School agrees to contract with the Community-Based Organization ABC Training Center to implement the following program:

Community Based Abstinence Education for Family Life Education

Section 1: Responsibilities of the parties:

1.1 <u>CBO ABC</u> will be responsible for the following:

  a) Operate overall program – including materials, curriculum and presenters

  b) Training of presenters

  c) Adherence to the school's classroom schedules

  d) Maintenance of program results (evaluation and comments)

1.2 <u>Local Middle School</u> will be responsible for the following:

  a) Provide facilities for CBO ABC to meet _____ days until program is completed

  b) Teacher input on students' needs

  c) Teacher evaluation, to be completed on both the presenter and the program content and returned to CBO ABC office

  d) School representative to provide current classroom bell schedule prior to program presentation

Section 2: Duration

2.1 This Memorandum of Understanding will remain in effect for the duration of the grant project, as agreed by the parties, beginning October 1, 20xx.

_____   _____

(Name, Title Organization)   Date

_____   _____

(Name, Title Organization)   Date

Sample MOU 2

MEMORANDUM OF AGREEMENT
Name of Healthcare Network

The Members of the **XYZ Rural Healthcare Network** (hereinafter "Network" or "XYZ") execute this Memorandum of Agreement in order to reconfirm their long-standing commitment to continue to partner together in helping to meet the health care needs of rural northwest State #1 and northeast State #2.

Commitment to Delivering Health and Wellness Services

XYZ Members herein reaffirm their commitment to jointly achieve Network health care goals and objectives. For the purposes of the proposed Rural Health Network Outreach project, Members commit themselves to supporting Network strategies to provide increased access to, education about and encouragement to engage in physical activity and to make healthy food choices.

The Members' previous collaborative efforts since 2006 and the demonstrated community need for increased physical activity and nutritious eating habits are such that Network Members remain committed to working together to increase access to and the quality of rural health care. Therefore, even though this Agreement shall be an integral part of current and future funding applications, the Members are committed to pursuing the goals of the Network prior to or in the absence of grant funding. The scope of services may be affected by the availability of financial resources, but the institutional commitment of the Members is without condition.

Goals

At planning meetings, the Members have agreed to work toward the following goals during the Network Outreach grant project period:

 Goal #1: Increase Physical Activity
 Goal #2: Improve Healthy Eating Habits

Confirmed Member Commitments to *Grant-funded Project* Activities

1. All members shall continue to attend monthly Network meetings, participate on relevant Network committees and publicly support and promote Network activities and services, especially *Grant-funded Project.*

2. *ABC Hospital* hereby commits to providing reduced-rent office space for two offices for Network staff through April 30, 20xx. The hospital, with prior approval, will partner with XYZ allowing a registered dietician to conduct training for the nutrition peer educators and jointly marketing *Grant-funded Project.* to hospital constituent groups such as Healthy Woman and Senior Circle.

3. *Local healthcare provider (ABC)* hereby commits to enrolling employees into *Grant-funded Project*, obtaining *Project* participant permission to share health indicator data with the project (whether these are ABC staff or patients), and providing aggregate pre- and post-health indicator data on staff who are not participating in the project as a quasi-control group.

4. *Local private university* hereby commits to enrolling interested employees into *Grant-funded Project*, marketing *Project* activities and services to its various constituent groups (including students, faculty, staff, and local alumni), obtaining *Project* participant permission to share health indicator data with the project, and sharing results of staff health assessments and blood work with the Project.

Signatures of all Network Members appear below:

_____   _____   _____

_____   _____   _____

_____   _____   _____

Sample MOU 3

Program Name
Memorandum of Understanding
between Organization A and Organization B

This agreement is made this 5th day of March, 2013 by and between Organization A and Organization B. This document shall reflect, when signed, an understanding of this agreement being in effect until the completion and evaluation of the funded project titled, Program Name with the intent of pursuing funding from the Agency/Foundation.

Background: Program Name was developed based on the belief 1) consumers likely have undiagnosed mental health issues and episodes of trauma; 2) consumers would benefit from having co-located mental health services that are culturally competent and convenient; 3) Motivational Interviewing, which is successfully used in other venues to support change, should have similar successful outcomes with a homeless population in supporting consumer's efforts to change. To that end, Organization A and Organization B decided to build on the strengths of each agency and partner to provide services.

<u>Organization A</u> provides emergency shelter, transitional housing and access to permanent housing for homeless women, women with children, men with children and families. Organization A operates the largest 24-hour emergency shelter for women, children and families in the State, providing shelter to more than 1,500 households annually.

<u>Organization B</u> provides mental health services to underserved families through evidence-based, trauma informed interventions, and provides training for other community providers. In this project, Organization B will provide co-located mental health services to adult clients. Additionally, Organization B will provide training to Organization A's staff to improve outcomes, including decreasing recidivism rates.

To that end, Organization A and Organization B agree to implement the project according to the scope discussed in the sections that follow.

Scope of Project: Both of the collaborating entities agree that the target population served will consist of homeless female, adult family leaders. Both Organization A and Organization B agree that:

- Each consumer participating in the program will meet the definition of homelessness as established by HUD, and will be appropriately referred to the program;

- Each consumer participating in the program will be assigned a case manager at Organization A. The Organization A case manager will provide, directly or through referral, supportive services including, but not limited to: training and education in budgeting, housekeeping, community living, accessing mainstream resources, transportation, and problem solving skills;

- Each consumer will be screened for the potential presence of mental health issues using the Depression, Anxiety and Stress Scale-21 (DASS-21) which will be administered by the Intake Specialist who will have been trained in the delivery and feedback of results from the DASS-21 using a Motivational Interviewing approach.

- Organization A will identify consumers in need of and will schedule them into pre-defined slots identified by Organization B.

- Approximately 10 adults will be treated by Organization B in each 17 week period. The total hours provided by Organization B will be 6 clinical hours per adult client per week. Additionally, Organization B will provide 10 hours of administrative work per week on case notes and meetings related to the program.

- Both Organization A and Organization B will be named on and issue a certificate of insurance naming the other agency as an additional insured.

- The program will enroll 300 individuals over the course of the project with 90 individuals completing the program. Those who complete the program will: 1) report positive changes in their depression, anxiety or stress symptoms or changes in interpersonal relationships and/or social role functioning; 2) Report achieving one or more goals identified in their comprehensive case plan; 3) Articulate quality of life changes, improved decision making abilities, and, as necessary will be linked to on-going mental health services.

To that end, it is agreed that Organization A and Organization B will work together to implement the program according to the roles described as follows:

Organization A will:

1. Serve as the lead agency for purposes of the submission and, if awarded, manage grant-related activities relative to the funded project;

2. Designate a staff member to serve as the primary point of contact;

3. Maintain confidential records associated with the program;

4. Maintain all financial records associated with the program;

5. Manage project activities collaboratively with Organization B to ensure objectives are met;

6. Participate in joint orientation and training of all personnel assigned to the project;

7. Coordinate activities in planning and implementation and facilitate project meetings; and,

8. Share data, facilitate and support the evaluation of the project.

9. Reimburse Organization B for services rendered on a monthly basis with payments of an equal amount (1/12th of the annual contract).

ORGANIZATION B will:

1. Coordinate all activities with Organization A;

2. Participate in joint orientation and training of all personnel assigned to the project;

3. Provide a designated staff member to serve as the primary point of contact;

4. Share programmatic expertise with Organization A to implement programmatic elements of the program;

5. Share programmatic expertise with Organization A to implement Motivational Interviewing;

6. Provide mental health services to consumers;

    a. Organization B staff member will meet the Organization B minimum hiring qualifications and will be appropriately credentialed to provide services;

    b. Provide evidence to Organization A about consumers' progress to specified outcomes;

    c. Provide consumers with appropriate linkages to other needed community services;

7. Manage project activities collaboratively with Organization A to ensure outcomes and objectives are met, and work with Organization A to provide necessary reports to the Mental Health Board;

8. Share data, facilitate and support the evaluation of the project;

9. Submit appropriate billings with all required documentation to Organization A for the project by the 5th of every month;

10. Maintain confidential records of all consumers referred for services; and,

11. Will provide documents to Organization A detailing written information the clients will receive about the program.

Program Design

Organization B is responsible for contributing the mental health components of the unique program design, including the model for training staff as well as the services delivered to the consumers of Organization A, and as such are proprietors of these components of the program.

Key Personnel and Advisory Committee: Each staff person listed below, by agency, will provide day-to-day oversight of the project activities and monitor adherence to this agreement.

- **Organization A:** The Executive Director will serve as the primary point of contact.

- **Organization B:** The Executive Director will serve as the primary point of contact for administrative issues, with the Clinical Director as the backup contact.

- Additionally, both parties acknowledge that the funding agency may want to periodically meet with the agencies to assess and support the project.

Marketing and Promotion: It is understood that each agency, individually, may issue publications including, but not limited to, journal articles and agency newsletter articles based on this project for educational, promotional, or historical purposes. In all instances, the agencies agree to appropriately cite the other partner for their collaborative work. Further, as the primary grantee it is understood that Organization A bears the primary responsibility for the implementation of this program, and, as such, Organization A must approve all communications regarding the project. Finally, it is understood that the partners may collectively issue publications of the type previously listed.

Training Materials: All training materials and manuals developed jointly as part of the program (notwithstanding existing materials) are the property of Organization A and Organization B.

Modification, Problem Resolution, and Termination: As the project grows and evolves, it is understood that this process may result in the need to amend this MOU. Any amendments will be added as appendices to this agreement and shall be signed by designated representatives from both organizations.

Both Organization A and Organization B agree to not approach, solicit, or hire employees involved in the project for purposes of delivering any component of the project, both during the grant period and after without permission from the partnering agency.

Each organization signing this agreement understands that from time to time, disagreements may arise. Each organization, believing in the principles of partnership (shared success, shared failure, shared problem-solving, shared input and shared commitment to the project and each other) agrees to address problems through negotiation or consensus. Further, it is agreed that Organization A and Organization B agree to a regular review of the MOU to ensure it continues to reflect the operations of the project. Regular review will, at a minimum, mean at least twice per year.

Finally, it is understood that circumstances may sometimes result in challenges that cannot be overcome. In those instances Organization A and Organization B agree that either party may terminate this agreement with 60 days written notice to the other. Such termination will be undertaken so as to cause the least amount of disruption possible to the consumer and the program. Should either party terminate this agreement, Organization B agrees to provide all documentation regarding the program, data and outcomes, to Organization A in a timely fashion (defined as within 10 days of the final termination date). It is understood that clinical case files will remain the property of the consumer and will not be released to Organization A without the consent of the consumer.

Term of Agreement: This Memorandum shall commence on the date of its signing and shall remain in force for a period of up to three (3) years that coincides with Organization A's execution of an agreement with the funding agency. Both parties agree that upon the execution of Organization A's agreement with the funding agency, Organization A and Organization B will execute a separate sub-contracting agreement that shall specify the terms and conditions related to the financial arrangements of implementing the program.

Organization A and Organization B have agreed to the terms outlined in this agreement, as indicated by the signatures of the authorizing agents below.

_____   _____
NAME   NAME

_____   _____
Executive Director   Executive Director

_____   _____
Organization A   Organization B

_____   _____
Signature   Signature

_____   _____
Date   Date

A Build-Your-Own MOU Template

If you search the Internet for "MOU samples," you will find a wide range of examples. We developed the template that appears on the following pages. It has formed the basis for dozens of successful MOUs over the years. We've provided it as a sample for you to use and adapt as you need. Of course, if your RFA requires your MOU to have certain content or headers, you follow those guidelines. This template is offered for circumstances in which you have no guidance.

Be prepared for the "quirky" requests from your partners, and accommodate them whenever you can. The first time you execute an MOU among partners or members of a consortium, leave plenty of time for everyone to review it. Expect edits. They may even bring in their attorney. Just smile. It may help to share the examples from this workbook to let them see that your MOU does not have to be written like a contract.

There are some particular elements in the template that begins on the next page that we wish to point out:

◆ Notice that the first paragraph mentions evaluation.

◆ This version indicates a lead agency. You can adapt to two equal partners or a consortium by replacing this language with language from Sample MOUs 1 and 2.

◆ The agreement specifically agrees to maintain confidentiality. (See item 8 under Agency 1.)

◆ There is a place to list and provide the value of any in-kind contributions. (See item 5 under Agency 2.)

◆ A primary point of contact is listed for each signee (key personnel section).

◆ Provision is made (on the second page) for modifying the terms of the agreement, if necessary.

Finally, all of the sample MOUs and the template provide space for signatures.

Insert Title Here

Memorandum of Understanding between
Insert Organization Name
and
Insert Organization Name

This agreement is made this __ day of _[month]_ 20xx by and between Organization 1 (herein referred to as *acronym*), and Organization 2, (herein referred to as *acronym*). This document shall reflect, when signed, an understanding of this agreement being in effect until the completion and evaluation of the funded project titled _____.

The agreements adopted presently by the parties are defined below.

SCOPE OF PROJECT:

Define project scope here.

To that end, Organization 1 agrees to:

1. Serve as the lead Organization thereby managing grant related activities.

2. Manage project activities to ensure objectives are met.

3. Coordinate activities in planning and implementation and facilitate project meetings.

4. Provide _____.

5. Provide_____.

6. Share _____.

7. Share_____.

8. Maintain confidential records of _____.

9. _____.

Organization 2 agrees to:

1. Share information with Organization 1 for the purposes of _____.

2. Act as a referral source to the project.

3. Schedule ____.

4. Provide space for the valued at $_____ per training.

5. X staff will participate in each training and will receive no compensation from Organization 1. The staff time will be an in-kind contribution to the project totaling $_____ per training.

6. _____.

7. _____.

KEY PERSONNEL:

Organization 1 will provide administrative oversight of the project. (Insert named staff person here) will provide day-to-day oversight of the project activities and monitor adherence to this agreement.

_____ will serve as the primary point of contact for Organization 2.

MARKETING AND PROMOTION:

Organization 1 and Organization 2 may issue publications and/or photographs based on this project for educational, promotional, or historical purposes.

TRAINING MATERIALS:

[Note to reader: Sometimes training materials (or other materials) are developed as part of the collaborative work. In this section you may want to insert language that discusses ownership of materials. For example, if materials are collaboratively developed, you may want to indicate that the organizations signing the MOU agree that materials are jointly owned and may be used by either organization.

In other situations, one organization may be using existing materials they've developed and are sharing. In this case, you may want to indicate that the materials are the intellectual property of the organization and may not be used without written permission. Insert anything, if appropriate here.]

MODIFICATION:

Organization 1's President and CEO and Organization 2's President and CEO may modify or cancel this agreement in writing with 30 days written notice. Any amendments will be added as appendices to this agreement and shall be signed by representatives from each organization.

TERM OF AGREEMENT

This Memorandum shall commence on the date of its signing and shall remain in force for a period of ____ years. *[Note to reader: Here you can either specify either a specific period of time or you can indicate that it will automatically renew after a certain time period.]* Unless one of the parties notifies the other party in writing of its desire to terminate this Memorandum at least three months prior to the termination of any such ___-year period, this Memorandum shall renew automatically for another ____ years.

Organization 1 and Organization 2 have agreed to the terms outlined in this agreement, as indicated by the signatures of the authorizing agents below.

_____   _____
INSERT NAME   INSERT NAME

_____   _____
Organization 1   Organization 2

_____   _____
Signature   Signature

_____   _____
Date   Date

Each of the sample MOUs provided in this chapter is a little different from the others. Yet they all accomplish the same purpose. They all communicate that those signing the MOU desire to work together on a specific project. They lay out roles and responsibilities. And they are all signed, which indicates the approval of the partnering organizations.

> The companion *Writing to Win Federal Grants* book devotes an entire chapter to developing, strengthening, and documenting partnerships and collaborations.
>
> **Dig Deeper**

Have the confidence to adapt any of these to fit your needs. There is no right or wrong way (unless your RFA tells you there is). It's almost always just about what will keep all of your members happy.

To Recap

◆ Formalizing partnerships supports the sustainability of your services and perhaps even your organization.

◆ MOUs can take on many different forms, but they should always reflect the intent and nature of the partnership.

◆ Some funders require that formal MOUs be included in the application package. Others require only a statement that you have an MOU executed and on file. Either way, a formal MOU assures reviewers that your partners are committed to delivering the services indicated in your grant proposal.

Chapter Seven

Organizational Charts and Letters of Support

IN THIS CHAPTER

···→ Attachments other than federal forms

···→ Suggestions for creating organizational charts

···→ Letters of support/commitment

The number and variety of the types of attachments you may be asked to include in your grant application are as varied as the number of funding agencies. In this chapter, we don't try to think of every possible attachment you will ever encounter. Instead, we focus on two of the most common types of attachments.

We include organizational charts for several reasons. First, they frequently require lots of time maneuvering text boxes or fighting with office productivity software that wants to "help" you format your organizational chart. Frequently, someone else may provide you with an organizational chart that needs major reformatting to comply with the font and margin sizes prescribed by the RFA. In addition, it's common for partnership and consortium applications to include more than one organizational chart. So we give you a few models.

We also include copies of letters of support and letters of commitment indicating varying levels of commitment to a project. Letters of support can be an application's Achilles' heel. You are often at the mercy of important people who are doing you a favor. You need the letters quickly, and you need them to say certain things. Unfortunately, letters that fail to meet the RFA's minimum standards for their content can jeopardize an entire project.

Other items that you may typically include either in your proposal or as an attachment—such as abstracts, timelines, staffing plans, and work plans—appear in the annotated sample proposals in **Part Two** of this workbook.

Organizational Charts

Maybe it's just us, but we get frustrated by the automatic formatting features of word processors and presentation software that want to dictate to us how our organizational charts should look.

> The companion *Writing to Win Federal Grants* book discusses how to create strong timelines and work plans. It also includes samples of each.
>
> **Dig Deeper**

Many organizations do have good luck creating charts with software just for this purpose, such as Microsoft's Visio. One of us uses this software all the time. The other usually prefers the simple lines and boxes that are available in Word or PowerPoint.

When an organizational chart is required to be a separate attachment, we may have the freedom to dedicate an entire page to the chart. That's great. Sometimes, however, we are stuffing an org chart into a document that's already bursting at the seams, and we need to compress it as much as possible. In these cases, we sacrifice beauty for saving a few more lines of text.

Take a look at this chart below. It probably wins the prize for the ugliest org chart, but the reviewers aren't scoring it on its looks. In this particular instance, we were allowed to go as small as a ten-point font in charts and illustrations, which we reluctantly did. We usually try not to use text that small because it's much harder to read.

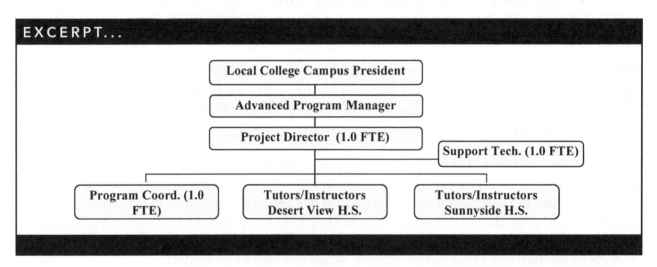

EXCERPT...

Since we drew this chart ourselves, we were able to put the boxes much closer together and make the lines between charts shorter than they would have been in a preformatted chart. Of course, if you have a more complicated project structure to chart out, it will take more space.

Project-Specific Organizational Charts

The chart above listed the staff to be assigned to the grant project and showed how the grant project would fit into the applicant's overall organizational structure. Usually, if an RFA only asks for an organizational chart without specifying exactly what is to be contained in that chart, you are being asked to do something similar.

A good example of a project organizational chart appears in Sample Proposal 2 in **Part Two** of this workbook.

Organization-Wide or Consortium-Wide Organizational Charts

Other times, you are asked to include the applicant's organizational chart in addition to the project-specific chart. This makes the most sense when the applicant is a solo applicant not applying as part of a consortium or partnership. Usually it's best to use a separate page for each chart.

When you are submitting a proposal as the lead applicant in a consortium or partnership, you often are requested to provide one chart that illustrates your own organization's structure. A second chart would illustrate the structure of the partnership. Partnership charts list the lead applicant or fiscal agent at the top, with all partners or consortium members listed below the partner. These charts are designed to show whether partners are equally represented. Sometimes each partner's name and tax ID is listed. It all depends on what your funding agency requests.

If the RFA does not specify exactly what it's looking for but only requests an organizational chart, we sometimes try to do a hybrid version. The chart below was built from the applicant's "official" chart of its existing personnel. We then added the proposed project personnel (in italics). We also made sure to indicate when existing personnel were going to spend some time on the grant, whether in-kind or charged to the grant. (Note: The words "be well" appear in lowercase in the organizational chart because the be well program is always presented in lowercase by the applicant.)

EXCERPT...

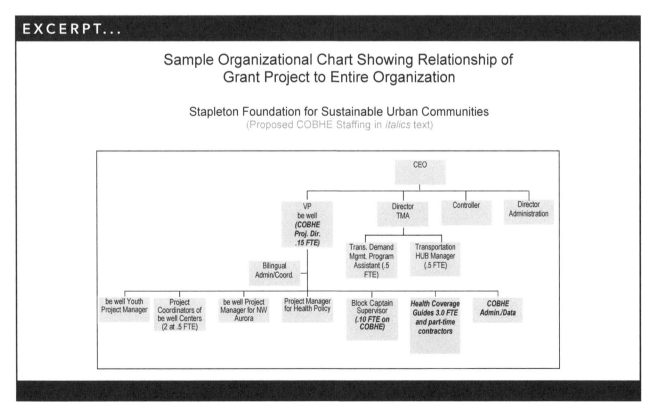

Both of us have a personal preference to remove the names of individuals, leaving only position titles in org chart boxes whenever possible. Sometimes, however, there is no time to edit the chart or it is important to the applicant that names be listed. Occasionally, reviewers for some programs want to see individuals named. Clearly there is no right or wrong to this decision.

 practical tip

In our experience, large organizations like hospitals or universities can have extremely complex and detailed organizational charts. Sometimes they stretch to more than one page or use very small fonts.

Our preference is usually for simplicity. That is why we recommend that you obtain such documents early in the application process. If you need to edit them, you don't want to be rushed at the last minute.

However, think about the type of project for which you are applying and what reviewers might be most interested in when they scrutinize your organizational chart. If your grant proposal is for a multi-million-dollar project lasting for several years, you may want to present the large, detailed organizational chart.

Why? Because in that instance, it may be more important to demonstrate that your organization is large enough, with enough depth of expertise and personnel, to successfully implement something that large.

Or what if your project includes funds in the budget to train two hundred employees but you include an org chart that makes it look as if your organization has only two departments, with only a few staff members each? The organizational chart on the next page accompanies Sample Proposal 1 from **Part Two** of this workbook, which was just such a project.

As long as you can meet the font-size restrictions of the RFA, including a complex chart detailing as many staff members as possible is sometimes a smart strategy.

Ozarks Medical Center
Organizational Chart

Sample Organizational Chart 1 – Large Organization

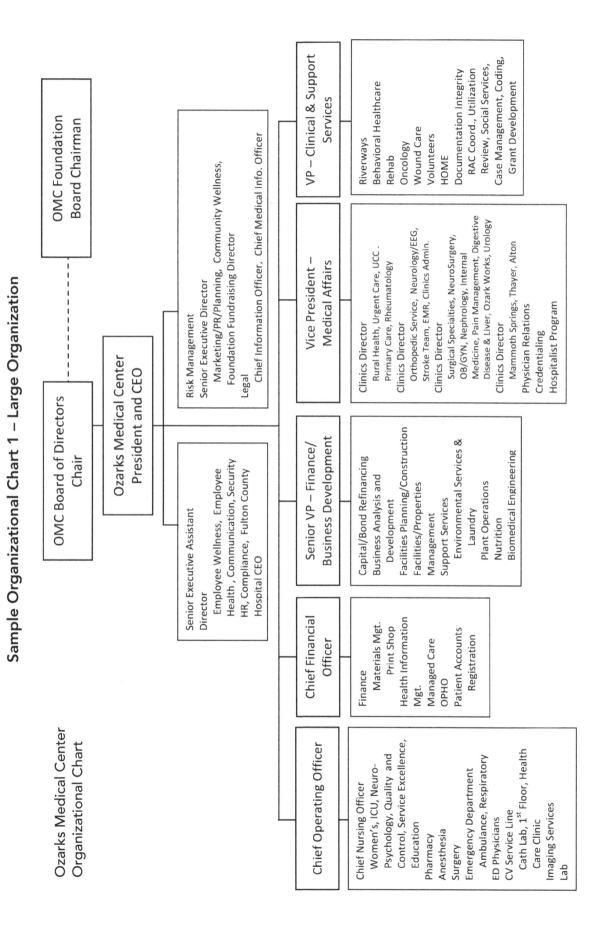

Charts Emphasizing Functions Instead of Personnel

The organizational charts we have provided up to this point were focused on personnel. That is usually what is required. For less complex projects, there is usually room to list each person's full-time equivalency (FTE) on the project and to indicate who is charged to the grant and who is in-kind.

In these instances, the purpose of the chart is partly to serve as a visual snapshot of the personnel plan for reviewers. They want to see that enough people have been allocated to each task, that you have a clear reporting structure, and that the project is placed highly enough in the organization to be effective at accomplishing its mission or to receive enough attention from senior leadership.

However, sometimes your purpose is to illustrate that your staffing plan or partnership structure will enable you to provide all major services or activities required by the RFA. If that is the case, you will probably be responding to RFA text that tells you how to lay out your chart.

The organizational chart excerpted on the next page is an example of a chart structured by function rather than by individual job positions. This grant project required the collaboration of several community organizations and public agencies to accomplish all of the services required by the funding agency.

Sample Organizational Chart 2 – Multi-Partner Function Emphasis

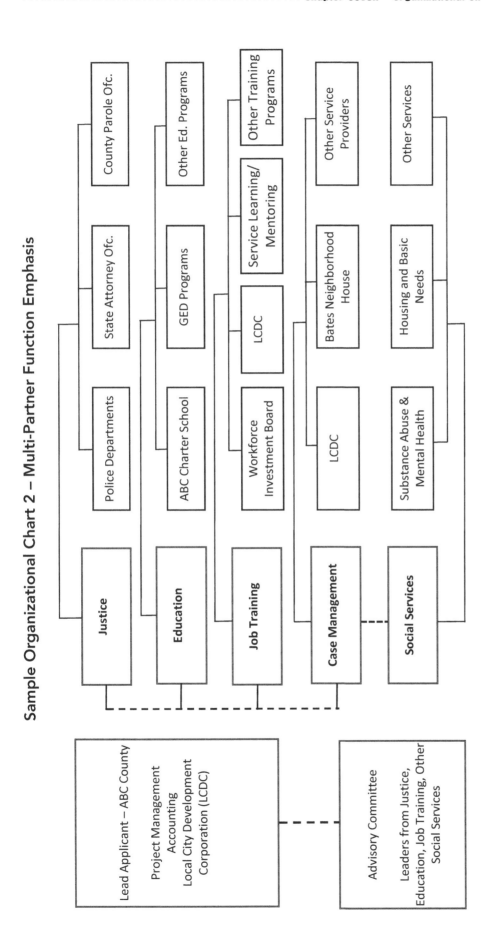

Letters of Support

Letters of support are popular, although they are becoming less and less persuasive with reviewers. In fact, many funding agencies now explicitly forbid you to include letters of support. Why is this? Usually because a letter of support often does not have substantive content. It only says, "We like the applicant and think they should receive this grant."

Some applicants request such letters from their federal delegation, and the letters are sent directly to the funding agency instead of included in the application package. If there are several applications coming from the same congressional district, however, the letters from most legislators will exhibit the same level of support for each applicant.

In spite of these issues, we still recommend that you include such letters whenever you are allowed to do so. Letters from federal legislators may have some impact, because these people serve on committees that affect your funding agency's budget. In some situations, such as building affordable housing, having a letter of support from a legislator helps the funding agency be assured that the funding and program are actually wanted in the applicant's community. (This is not always the case.)

Other good letters could be from your governor or mayor, a key foundation, or community partners. When we submit state grants, we get letters of support from other state agencies saying our project is a priority for them too.

Offer to provide some or all of the content to the person from whom you have requested a letter. Inform the author of any page limits or required phrases. It may seem obvious, but it's a good idea to remind the letter writer to print the letter on organizational or office letterhead and sign it. Depending on the requirements of your RFA, you may need the author to scan a copy and email it to you for you to submit with your application or to keep on file. Or the author may need to print the letter, sign it, and mail it directly to the funding agency. Provide the address, of course. Sometimes, despite all of your precautions and the guidance you provide to your letter writers, you still get something completely different. In one case, Karen was told that the mayor's office could not write a letter of support but could issue a "proclamation" instead.

On the following pages are two examples of letters of support and a copy of the mayoral proclamation that was used in lieu of a letter of support. Sample Letter of Support 1, on the next page, says little more than the letter writer likes the applicant, is in support of the idea of a grant, and would like to "partner" on implementing the grant. There are no specifics, however, and no promises are made. Sample Letter of Support 2 is a little stronger, since it comes from a highly placed elected official. The state senator urges the funding agency to give the application "every consideration."

If your RFA asks for "letters of support," then the proclamation or sample letters that we have included here are usually sufficient.

Sample Letter of Support 1

LETTERHEAD OF ORGANIZATION SENDING LETTER

DATE

Ms. Project Director
Community-Based Organization
Address
City, State ZIP

Dear *Ms. Project Director*,

It is our pleasure to endorse your application for funding from the Department of Health and Human Services, Administration for Children and Families, Community-Based Abstinence Education Program. The programs you offer through *Project One* and *Project Two* are a major credit to the schools, agencies and communities you serve within *our region in our state*.

ABC Organization would like to partner with you to assist us in addressing abstinence and associated risky behaviors for our in-school pregnant/parenting teens, resource mothers, empowered girls, and Reach programs. We are fully aware of the contributions made by your organization that have served thousands in *our region in our state*.

Thank you for the work you are doing in the community, and we look forward to collaborating to best serve the *ABC* participants.

Sincerely,

Mr. Program Coordinator
ABC Organization

Sample Letter of Support 2

LETTERHEAD OF THE ILLINOIS STATE SENATE

DATE

Mr. Brandon Bodor
Executive Director
Serve Illinois Commission
Office of Governor Pat Quinn
100 W. Randolph Street, Suite 16-100
Chicago, Illinois 60601

Re: Lessie Bates Davis Neighborhood House
     School Turnaround AmeriCorps Application, FY 13
     For East St. Louis Senior High School,
     NCES School ID: 171332004975

Dear Mr. Bodor;

On behalf of the East St. Louis community, I am pleased to write this letter in support of the AmeriCorps School Turnaround grant proposal submitted by Lessie Bates Davis Neighborhood House.

In 2013, East St. Louis High School was awarded a School Improvement Grant (SIG) designed to improve the educational outcomes for children in East St. Louis. The SIG grant was our way of saying as a community that graduation rates must improve and that our community is focused on improving educational outcomes for our children. The AmeriCorps School Turnaround grant program would certainly compliment the efforts of the SIG by deepening the level of service, provided by AmeriCorps members, to the students of East St. Louis High School.

My understanding is that the program, designed by the Neighborhood House, the District and community partners focuses on improving reading skills and scores, improving persistence and graduation rates and improving the chances that students from East St. Louis will go on to college and post-secondary training.

Each of the elements described to me is a critical need for the community and its children commend the Neighborhood House's application to you and that you give it every consideration.

Sincerely,

James F. Clayborne, Jr.
Majority Leader
Illinois Senate
57th District

OFFICE OF THE MAYOR

City of East St. Louis, Illinois

PROCLAMATION

Recognizing

AmeriCorps-East St. Louis

WHEREAS: AmeriCorps engages more than 75,000 men and women in intensive service each year at more than 15,000 locations including nonprofits, schools, public agencies, and community and faith-based groups across the country; and,

WHEREAS: AmeriCorps members help communities tackle pressing problems while mobilizing millions of volunteers for the organizations they serve; and,

WHEREAS: Members gain valuable professional, educational, and life benefits, and the experience has a lasting impact on the members and the communities they serve; and,

WHEREAS: AmeriCorps members make our communities safer, stronger, healthier, and improve the lives of tens of millions of our most vulnerable citizens. AmeriCorps' impacts are proven and measurable.

NOW THEREFORE, I, ALVIN PARKS, JR. MAYOR OF THE CITY OF EAST ST. LOUIS AND THE CITY COUNCIL, DO FIND IT APPROPRIATE AND SIGNIFICANT TO HEREBY RECOGNIZE **AMERICORPS-EAST ST. LOUIS MEMBERS ON THEIR DEDICATION TO THE EAST ST. LOUIS /METROPOLITAN COMMUNITIES.**

IN WITNESSS WHERFORE, I HAVE HEREUNTO SET MY HAND AND CAUSED TO BE AFFIXED THE SEAL OF THE CITY OF EAST ST. LOUIS ON THIS 1ST DAY OF APRIL, 2014, WHICH IS THE SECOND-ANNUAL MAYORS DAY OF RECOGNITON FOR NATIONAL SERVICE.

ALVIN L. PARKS, JR. MAYOR

Letters of Commitment

Most of the time when letters are allowed or required, they must be letters of commitment. A letter of commitment has an essential difference from a letter that is only a letter of support. Letters of commitment must include in them a "commitment" from the letter writer.

Obtaining such commitments is always a bit of a balancing act. You want to get the largest, firmest commitment possible out of your potential partners. They typically want to minimize what they promise to do.

If your RFA requires that you obtain letters of commitment from consortium members or from potential community partners but does not tell you what that commitment must entail, you can usually get letter writers to agree to one or more of the following low-risk commitments:

◆ Full participation in the partnership/coalition

◆ Attendance at meetings

◆ Free use of a conference room or meeting space

◆ Refreshments for meetings (may be as simple as a coffee pot)

◆ Promoting your services via their newsletter, website, or social media

These types of commitments rarely cost the letter writers money. At most, they may require that they let a staff member go to some meetings.

But reviewers know that too. So you are usually trying to get more specific commitments from partners. If your project will require you to have access to students or faculty in a public school or to patients or patient records at a health care provider, reviewers will expect to see letters stating you have secured this access, which is protected under federal law. That is because many well-intentioned projects have failed because this important step of securing written permission from an essential partner was overlooked.

Letter of Commitment 1 on the next page is a good model of making clear the writer's specific commitments. We provided her with the content as a guide. She, of course, edited the text until she was comfortable with it. The second letter of commitment includes several specific commitments from the employer partner. The employers who were asked to write letters of commitment were provided a list of possible contributions to which they might be able to commit and then selected from among that list.

Sample Letter of Commitment 1

LETTERHEAD OF ORGANIZATION SENDING LETTER

DATE

Cynthia Ryan
Director, Discretionary Grants Division
Office of English Language Acquisition

Dear Ms. Ryan:

As Superintendent of the *Our Town* School District, it is my pleasure to give my wholehearted support to the proposed LEARN project. This project will enable the partners to further expand an already positive relationship. The *Our Town* School District is fully committed to collaborating with *XYZ University* to achieve ESL endorsement for at least 60 of our dedicated teachers over 4 years. Their endorsement will enhance the learning environment we provide to the over 4600 ESL students in our district each year.

Our Town Public Schools specifically commits the following resources to the LEARN project:

- After-hours classroom space for conducting 2 classes per semester for the life of the project

- Commitment of 60 participants

- Commitment of allowing participants to attend a one day ESL conference/symposium

- Time and compensation for the *Our Town* School District site director

- SIOP training for LEARN personnel

The *Our Town* School District looks forward to participating in this valuable project and is fully committed to its success.

Sincerely,

Molly Leader, Ed.D.
Superintendent

Sample Letter of Commitment 2

LETTERHEAD OF ORGANIZATION SENDING LETTER

DATE

Dear Mr. Project Director:

Flight Technologies is pleased to collaborate with *Applicant* to implement proposed activities of the TAACCCT grant proposal funded through the US Department of Labor, Employment and Training Administration.

Flight has a strong interest in developing a pipeline of qualified and credentialed aviation individuals. We see this accelerated licensure program as a means to quickly get experienced but non-credentialed individuals qualified and promotable in the aviation work force.

As a project partner we will:
- Serve on the project's leadership team and/or help implement program strategies and goals
- Identify and map the necessary skills and competencies for the program
- Assist with development of national industry-recognized credentials if needed
- Assist with curriculum development and courses, as applicable
- Provide potential internship/on-the-job training/apprenticeship opportunities for participants enrolled in the TAACCCT program over the course of the four year grant
- Loan equipment, facilities or materials to support the curriculum
- Hire, promote, and/or retain qualified participants in our company
- Donate materials
- Encourage Trainers to the extent workloads permit

We regard the ability to have credentialed employees as crucial to our operations in *state*. We compete on a world-wide basis, and our competitors in foreign countries have significant advantages over *Flight* due to free or low costs state provided educational opportunities.

Flight has a strong history of supporting and fostering education and training of employees.

Regards,

_____

President

Sometimes you do not have to actually attach letters of commitment in your application. You merely have to state in your application that you have obtained such letters or MOUs and that they are on file in your office.

We shouldn't have to say it, but we will. Don't lie about this! If you are required to have signed letters on file in your grant project's office, they had better be there. Funding agencies frequently make surprise visits to their grant recipients to make sure they are complying with all rules and regulations.

Sample Annotated Proposal 2 in **Part Two** of this workbook includes a table listing community partners and the level of commitment that had been obtained from those partners at the time of application. Project staff kept copies of the written commitments on file.

Letters of Commitment from Vendors or Consultants

There is another type of letter of commitment you may be required to include in your application. If your project expends budget money on external consultants or large contracts with external service providers (such as marketing or research firms), you sometimes are required to include a letter of commitment from any such potential vendor/consultant.

If so, you will want to be sure the letter spells out the agreed-upon scope of work for the services that will be provided, length of service to be expected, and perhaps even compensation. Follow what your RFA says, and don't be shy about sending a letter back to the author if it is missing a required element.

To Recap

◆ Provide enough information in your organizational charts that reviewers are confident that you have staffed your project adequately and that the project will receive attention from senior leadership at your organization.

◆ Request letters and any other documents that you depend upon others to provide as soon as you start working on your grant proposal. You often need time to ask for revisions (letters) or to edit documents (charts) to meet proposal requirements.

◆ Whenever possible, offer content to the writers of letters of support and letters of commitment to help ensure the content meets your RFA's requirements.

Chapter Eight

Postaward Policies and Tools

IN THIS CHAPTER

····➔ Postaward processes

····➔ Tracking grant awards internally

····➔ Basic forms for good grants management

Winning a federal grant can be an exhilarating yet frightening experience all at the same time. You definitely should celebrate! You succeeded against some tough competition. But what happens next?

If you work in a large organization staffed with grant accountants and grants managers, there is probably already an extensive grants management handbook that sets out all of the processes to follow to hand the grant over to those who must manage it once it has been awarded. The grant has now moved from the preaward stage (the application stage) to the postaward stage (the implementation and management stage).

We recognize that you may not have the luxury of walking into an organization with a ready-made grants handbook and clear postaward procedures established. You may even have to be creating them as you go along, one grant at a time.

Even if your process is nothing more complicated than a short bullet list, it helps to get it in writing and then tweak it as necessary as you get the next grant and then the next. So here are some things to think through:

◆ *Notification.* Who should I notify about this grant, and when should I allow someone else to do the notifying?

◆ *Execution.* If you are required to execute a grant contract or award notice, who has the authority to do that (should match your Grants.gov and SAM registrations)?

The companion *Writing to Win Federal Grants* book goes into more detail about each of the bulleted items that appear below and covers additional topics.

Dig Deeper

◆ *Negotiation.* If the funder wants to negotiate changes to your budget or scope of work, who has the authority and responsibility to negotiate on behalf of your organization?

◆ *Implementation.* If you have to conduct a search for the project director, who is responsible for implementing the grant until that position is filled?

These are some of the first decisions to make when you learn of your grant award. We recommend that for the first few federal grants you submit, you create for yourself a postsubmittal form. It doesn't have to be complicated, but it can help avoid a panicked scramble when you get the award. You can use the model below as a jumping-off point for your own plan.

Federal Grant Post-Submittal Record		
Name of Proposal Submitted:		
Project Period If Funded:	Start Date:	End Date:
Project Director:	☐ To be hired ☐ On Staff: _____	
Signer of Contracts:		
Authorized Budget Negotiator:		
Who Gets Notified (and in what order)?	☐ Me/Grant Contact ➡ ⬇ ☐ Director of Development ⬇ ☐ President/Exec. Dir. ⬇ ☐ Board Chair	After leaders notified, I also notify: ☐ Project Director/PI ☐ Partners ☐ Budget Office/Treasurer ☐ Human Resources ☐ PR/Communications ☐ Other:_____

Let's talk about each of the positions or offices listed in the notification row. If you are listed on the grant application as the contact, you may be the first person at your organization to receive notice that the grant has been funded. In your excitement, you may pick up the phone or run down the hall to tell the project director the great news.

But wait a minute. This may work fine at your organization. On the other hand, we've both worked at organizations where if we did not let our boss know first, so our boss could notify his boss, things could get a little tense. So be attentive to your organization's hierarchy and culture. You should probably let your executive director notify the board chair about the grant before a jubilant press release goes out.

After you have notified the people in your organization who need to know about the grant, you will probably have to route some paper (or email files) around to help everyone do their part to make sure the grant is implemented and managed properly. While this list is not exhaustive, it does give you an idea of the steps you should take when the grant award becomes official:

◆ *Executive director/president.* Send any grant contracts that need to be signed.

◆ *Project director/principal investigator (PI).* Send a copy of the entire grant and budget.

◆ *Partners.* Send a copy of the finalized MOU, grant outcomes, reporting requirements, and/or any subrecipient agreements (if applicable) regarding disbursements if the partners are to receive some of the grant funds.

◆ *Development office.* Depending on the type of organization you are in, the grant may need to be recorded in the same database into which donor gifts are recorded, but make sure your standard donor receipt is not accidentally issued to a government funding agency.

◆ *Business office/treasurer.* Send a copy of the entire grant budget and information about any matching requirement. Request that grant account numbers be created or that other systems to track grant funds and matching funds separately from other organization funds be implemented.

◆ *Human resources.* Send a list of grant personnel with their percentage of effort on the grant to the personnel office. Include any job descriptions or information about which staff will perform which tasks related to the grant.

◆ *Communications/PR.* Provide information for a press release. Notify your communications team if the funding agency has a requirement that its contribution and/or logo be included on all informational and promotional materials related to the grant project (such as brochures, websites, programs, etc.).

Once you have been through this process a few times, you may feel as if you do not need to maintain a postsubmittal record or send the same information every time to the human resources department. However, people can forget, and staff change positions. The postsubmittal record could save your organization from failing to follow through on an important detail that could cost it the grant.

Saying Thank You

In the midst of celebrating and then chasing down all of the paperwork and fine print for the grant, don't forget to say "thank you" as well. Of course, you are not sending off a thank-you letter to the funding agency as you would to a foundation.

However, your executive director or board chair might want to call or email members of your congressional delegation to thank them for the grant. They probably know it has been awarded. Senators and representatives pay pretty close attention to federal dollars being spent in their districts. While they may not have actually had anything to do with your grant, it's still a nice touch to thank them as if they had.

Don't forget to thank anyone who wrote letters of support or letters of commitment for your project. We know the list can be long in some cases. That's why you need a good method to keep track of those letters. But the people who wrote letters for you did you a favor. A favor you might need repeated someday. At the very least, send nice thank-you notes and let them know you got the grant thanks to their help.

The same principle goes for your colleagues who hustled to get you the stats you needed, or to pull together a workable budget, or to proofread your application at the last minute. In addition to saying "thank you," recognize these people loudly and repeatedly whenever the grant gets mentioned. We sometimes send flowers or a treat to someone who really went above and beyond to help us win a grant.

The Postaward Meeting

If you've read the companion *Writing to Win Federal Grants* book, you know that we recommend holding a postaward meeting with as many people who will be impacted by the grant as possible. We know that if you are at a small organization, you may not even have this many staff members, but someone is performing all of these roles. They may be board members, or each staff person may do three jobs. At larger organizations, these are people from different departments:

◆ Project director/PI

◆ Your boss, if possible

◆ Finance office/bookkeeper

◆ Human resources department

◆ Communications department

In addition, you may need someone from your facilities department if your grant application promised office or other space to be set aside for the grant project. Other times, you may need someone from your IT department if your project has a significant technology component.

You may wish to have your internal meeting first and then another meeting with your external

> If your organization is new to federal grants (or has managed many but has had challenges), it's a good idea to develop a system for keeping all grant documentation together and calendaring report due dates. Review each of the postaward reporting tasks (and due dates) with your management team, and be sure that tasks are assigned. Trust us, unless a task is assigned to a specific person, it won't get done, and then you'll have to jump in at the last minute and do it (while digging up needed records).
>
> Karen is a bit old school and uses a hard-copy binder system where she keeps a paper copy of the RFA, proposal, and award notice; a reporting checklist; and copies of materials that may be needed for audit. This same information can be kept in an electronic file. Just make sure it's backed up. Program officers and auditors are completely unsympathetic if your computer crashes and information is lost.

 practical tip

partners, since your internal meeting will cover a lot of minutiae about accounting, forms, budget numbers, and job openings.

So you've gotten everyone together. What are you there to talk about? Especially if this grant is one of the first grants for most of the people in the room, you have everyone there to emphasize the serious nature of their responsibility to properly manage the grant activities and grant funds.

During the meeting, you will cover these important topics:

◆ Celebrating and thanking everyone for their role in winning the grant

◆ Overview of the grant

◆ Major grant activities

◆ Allowable and unallowable costs and policies to be followed to ensure all expenditures are reasonable and documented

◆ Matching funds requirement, if any

◆ Any other resources promised in the application as leverage (office space, computers, staff time not charged to the grant, etc.)

◆ Grant staff (to be released from other duties or hired)

◆ Time and effort reporting

◆ Required grant outcomes

◆ Data/statistics that will need to be tracked for evaluation and reporting

◆ Report deadlines, required content of reports, and who is responsible for completing and submitting reports.

Summary of Grants under Management

It may be hard to imagine a time when you have so many federal grants coming in that you won't be able to keep them all straight. But you can always dream! It does happen.

We've worked in organizations where a decision whether to pursue the next grant was partly based on whether there was a required match. This is especially true if the organization is already committed to raising matching funds for one or more other grants. It may also depend on the space available at your organization to house new staff or deliver services. Sometimes you have to say "no" to a funding opportunity that is a mission fit if it might strain your finances or your fundraising capacity.

To help our organization's leaders keep track of grants under management, we created a one-page document that summarized each grant that was currently being managed. In the excerpt on the next page, you will see that the summary lists the grant's project period, award amount, any matching dollars required, and any other in-kind services or things we had promised as part of our commitment to the project. It also lists reporting requirements.

You, of course, can modify this form however necessary to meet your needs.

Sample Completed Summary of Grants Under Management

Grant	TRIO Student Support Services Grant
Project Director:	Ms. Project Director
Budget Account Number(s):	20-6670-xxxx; 10-6670-xxxx
Total Amount of Award:	$1,100,000 ($220,000/yr)
Awarding Foundation/Agency:	US Dept of Education
Date of Award:	April 2009
Award Period:	July 1, 2009 – June 30, 2014
Multi-Year Grant:	Yes – 5 Years
Renewable:	Yes
Indirect Costs:	Capped by Dept. at 8%
Recipient Obligations:	
Budget Match—	$34,068 (annual) $37,317 (one-time, start-up)
Release Time—	n/a
Space—	Yes
Equipment—	4 computers (one-time, start-up)
Other—	Performance objectives (see attached)
	Presidential Reception (annually)
	Discount for SSS students at ropes course (annually)
	Furnishings and remodeling (one-time, start-up)
	ITS: data assistance (on-going)
	Acad. Aff.: oversight of SSS; memberships in SWASAP & COE, professional dev't for SSS staff, 10% director's salary
Certifications and Assurances:	State Office Review (Executive Order 12372) – done
	Std. Form 424B – signed by VP of Finance, rev'd by Pres
	Std. Disclosure of Lobbying Activities – signed by VPFA
	ED 80-0014 – Debarment, Suspension – signed by VPFA

Reporting Obligations:	Annual Report via Dept's website
	A-133 Audit
Disbursement Procedures:	GAPS – reimbursement only

Travel Report Forms

We hope that your organization already has clear spending and travel policies. These should include a requirement that all purchases be supported by proper documentation. However, you may need to update or modify some policies and procedures for better record keeping now that you have a federal grant. For example, on the next few pages, we have provided four sample travel report forms.

The first two are simpler and are focused more on what was learned at the conference attended and how that conference related to the purpose of the grant. Often it is a good idea to attach copies of meeting agendas or handouts to file with the report.

> Especially if your organization is new to federal grants, it's better to "overdocument" all grant expenditures rather than not have enough documentation. Travel expenses seem to garner extra scrutiny during audits. So pay extra attention when documenting them.
>
> practical tip

The third and fourth travel report forms are more focused on a detailed financial record of all travel expenses. Those traveling on grant-related business collect their receipts, attach them to the trip report form, and document any expenses for which there are not receipts (such as cash tips).

The detailed financial trip report forms can easily be modified to suit your organization's travel policies, such as whether your staff members:

◆ are given petty cash that they must account for;

◆ use their personal credit cards and request reimbursement;

◆ use an organizational credit card;

◆ are reimbursed for mileage based on the federal IRS rate, a state-mandated rate, or an organizational rate; or

◆ receive a per diem or are reimbursed for direct expenses only. (Note any limits on such expenses.)

Sample Travel Report Form 1

_____ Grant

Travel Report Form

Employee Name: _____

Title of Workshop/Conference: _____

Dates of Workshop/Conference: _____

Location of Workshop/Conference: _____

Major Topics Addressed (please attach copies of schedules/agenda):

_____

_____

_____

_____

Benefits you attained by attending:

_____

_____

_____

_____

Employee Signature: _____ Date: _____

Project Director Signature: _____ Date: _____

Sample Travel Report Form 2

Brief Trip Report

Date: _____

Person/s Traveling : _____

Purpose: _____

Destination: _____

Signature of Traveler: _____

If you are requesting reimbursement for expenses charged to your personal credit card
or out-of-pocket cash, please attach receipts or record amounts of tolls, parking, etc.

Expenses (provide totals for each category)

Mileage:

    Miles Driven Round-Trip: _____ x   Mileage Rate of _____   = $_____

Parking: $_____

Tolls: $_____

Meals (incl. tip): $_____

Other: _____ $_____

_____

Total to Be Reimbursed to Traveler: $_____

Account Number/Line Item: _____   Check #: _____

Authorized by: _____

(Cannot be signed by person seeking reimbursement)

Sample Travel Report Form 3

Travel Expense Report

	Name						Date Submitted	
	Dates of Travel						Purpose of Trip	
	Mileage Rate						Duration of Trip	

Date	Description of Expense	Airfare	Lodging	Ground Transport (Gas, Rental, Taxi)	Meals & Tips (Receipt Method)	Conf / Workshops	Miles	Totals
Cash Expenditures								
Charges Placed on Personal Credit Card								
Charges on Organization Credit Card								
Totals in Each Category								

		Total Expenses	
		Less $ Charged to Comp. Credit Card	
		Total Reimbursement	
		Paid by check #	

Sample Travel Report Form 4

Travel Expense Report

Submitted By: _____ **Date:** _____

Business Purpose For Travel: _____

	Date:	Sun	Mon	Tue	Wed	Thu	Fri	Sat	Total
Auto Mileage: Number of Miles:									
x xx.x cents/mile		0.00	0.00	0.00	0.00	0.000	0.00	0.00	0.00
Airfare									$0.00
Taxi									$0.00
Hotel									$0.00
Breakfast									$0.00
Lunch									$0.00
Dinner									$0.00
Per Diem									$0.00
Tips (Excluding Meals)									$0.00
Parking									$0.00
Other:									$0.00
Total		$0.00	$0.00	$0.00	$0.00	$0.00	$0.00	$0.00	$0.00

Total Expense (reimbursable) $0.00

Less Travel Advance Amount $0.00

Balance due from (to) Organization $0.00

CERTIFICATION

I hereby certify that the foregoing account is correct, and that I have paid out the amounts shown above.

APPROVAL

_____
Signature of Traveler/Date

_____
Budget Officer/Date

Time and Effort Reports

One aspect of federal grants that can take new grantees by surprise is the need to track the time that your personnel spend on grant activities. This is especially true of personnel who are paid from the grant and who may be splitting their time among multiple grants. It can also apply for personnel whose time you promised as an in-kind contribution to a grant budget.

This is called documenting time and effort. Notice that it's more than simply time. Usually you should provide some evidence of the work that was done during that time.

Even though time and effort reports may not be officially required under the new Council on Financial Assistance Reform (COFAR) uniform guidance, staff from the Office of Management and Budget advised us that it may still be a good idea to complete them, at least for some funding agencies. Every funding agency has different expectations (sometimes unofficial). Read the fine print of your Notice of Grant award and any grants management handbooks published by your agency. Ask fellow grantees what they do, or ask what your program officer's preference is.

> We cannot promise you that if you use one our forms it will be deemed sufficient by your particular funding agency. They are a great starting point, but do your homework too.
>
> **watch out!**

Although the practice of keeping time and effort reports is not limited to institutions of higher education, they have developed good systems by which to do so. This is probably because they have faculty and administrators whose salaries may be drawn from multiple budget lines. Some faculty may be paid 50 percent by one grant, 25 percent by another, and only 25 percent by their institution.

You can see why it would be important to develop some way to keep track of how grant-funded personnel spend their time in the "real world." Some funding agencies even expect work samples, calendars, or other documents to be attached to the time and effort report to prove how individuals are spending their time.

On the pages that follow, we provide two sample models of time and effort report forms.

Sample Time and Effort Report Form 1

Monthly Time/Effort Report

Employee Name: _____

Month and Year: _____

Grant Name: _____

Dates Worked	Hours Worked	Grant-Related Work Completed

Total Hours Worked:	
Employee Signature:	Date:
Project Director:	Date:

Sample Time and Effort Report Form 2

XYZ Organization

Employee Time and Effort Report

_____, _____
(Month)   (Year)

Employee Name: _____

GRANTS
Please report the hours worked for each Grant. (Please use a separate line for each Grant.)

Grant Name	Tasks Performed	Hours
Grant #1 (xx% effort)	Week 1:	
	Week 2:	
	Week 3:	
	Week 4:	
Grant #2 (xx% effort)	Week 1:	
	Week 2:	
	Week 3:	
	Week 4:	

Employee Signature: _____

Supervisor/Board Chair Signature: _____

Closing Thoughts and Tips

While we have barely scratched the surface with the resources we've provided you in this chapter, you now have a good start on some of the things that sometimes trip up new grantees. Managing a federal grant properly is a skill you can learn, and there are many resources out there to help you do just that.

First, don't forget your program officer. Program officers want their grantees to succeed. They are usually available for questions and advice.

Here are some other resources you can tap:

◆ Attend any grantees' workshops that are offered by the funding agency. Some funding agencies require that at least one person attend.

◆ Sign up for any technical assistance offered by your funding agency.

◆ Check out training and other resources offered by the National Grants Management Association (NGMA).

◆ Once you are managing more than one grant, you may consider adding grants management software. Check with professional associations such as the Grant Professionals Association (grantprofessionals.org) or the NGMA (ngma.org) for vendor partners they recommend.

To Recap

◆ Develop a process by which you notify the appropriate people, partners, and offices about grants when they are awarded.

◆ Hold a postaward meeting with relevant personnel to review the terms of the grant.

◆ Develop or update financial management procedures if necessary to meet federal expectations.

◆ Document, document, document. Keep copies of all documents pertaining to your grant, especially financial records.

Part Two

Annotated Sample Proposals

Part Two contains four complete federal proposals for you to use as models and examples. We are deeply grateful to the three applicants who gave us permission to share their successful proposals with you. Pursuing federal grants is a competitive business. Yet, each organization generously allowed us to share their content with you. A fourth applicant was not reachable to obtain permission. That application has had all identifying information removed.

Both of the authors contributed proposals for this section, giving you insight into the writing styles of two successful proposal writers and the organizations with whom we collaborated. We have different writing styles and like to format some things differently. However, we think you will also be struck by how many successful strategies we both use. We did not collaborate with each other on these proposals.

The annotations on the proposals highlight why a paragraph or sentence or table was presented in a certain way. Annotations may point out an example of something we recommended in the companion *Writing to Win Federal Grants* book, or they may explain something that could be confusing.

We selected the proposals for inclusion in the workbook because of the variety of types of information included in them. Upon reflection, we realized, purely accidentally, that three of the applications were for organizations based in small communities or rural areas. These have annotations that point out how the service areas were described to reviewers. But other than that detail, the principles of quality proposals would apply to applicants both urban and rural.

The original RFAs to which the sample proposals were responding will be available on the bookstore page for this book at CharityChannel.com. Look under the tab for Resources.

Dig Deeper

What's Included in Each Annotated Proposal

Annotated Proposal 1—Ozarks Medical Center, Project IMPACTS

- ◆ Abstract

- ◆ Request for funding preference

- ◆ Footnotes

- ◆ How maps were used

- ◆ Data tables

- ◆ Graphic to illustrate proposal content

- ◆ Extensive work plan, which also serves as a timeline

- ◆ Evidence-based program model

- ◆ Sustainability narrative

- ◆ Most attachments

  - ❖ Staffing plan

  - ❖ Biosketches

  - ❖ Organizational chart

  - ❖ Request for funding preference

  - ❖ Staff Office of Rural Health letter of support

  - ❖ Logic model

  - ❖ Evaluation plan

  - ❖ Applicant's history with funding agency

  - ❖ Consortium members letters of support

Annotated Proposal 2—John Brown University, Healthy Marriages Initiative

- ◆ Abstract

- ◆ A page budget

- ◆ Footnotes and in-line citations

- ◆ Tables that summarize program content

- ◆ Data tables

- Graphic to illustrate proposal content

- Cross-referencing to address repetitive RFA prompts

- Evidence-based program model

- Logic model

- Timeline

- Partner table

- Organizational chart

- Budget narrative

- Request for bonus points

Annotated Proposal 3—Unnamed Applicant, EPA Regional Indoor Environments Grant

- Evaluation criteria from RFA

- Condensed abstract

- Graphic to illustrate proposal content

- Logic model/outcomes table

- Past performance section (describing previous grant awards)

Annotated Proposal 4—Sabine Volunteer Fire Department, FEMA Assistance to Firefighters Grant

- Extremely abbreviated project narrative to be pasted into website application system

- In-line citations

- World's shortest budget narrative

- Request for priority points

We introduce each proposal in more detail on the following pages.

Annotated Application 1—Using Diagrams, Maps, and Tables Effectively

US Department of Health and Human Services (HHS) Health Resources and Services Administration (HRSA), Office of Rural Health Policy (ORHP)

Funding Opportunity Name

Small Health Care Provider Quality Improvement Grant Program

Background of Application

The application for the Small Health Care Provider Quality Improvement Grant Program was submitted in January 2013. Despite the fact that we regularly advise you to begin your projects early and not wait until the RFA is released, this proposal was completed in less than thirty days.

This was possible for several important reasons: (1) the organization had a very solid project idea, (2) the organization had a point person assigned to the project who was exceptionally organized, (3) the grant writer and the point person created a timeline with specific assigned tasks, (4) the author had a prior working history with the organization, (5) the author was familiar with the data elements needed to illustrate need, and (6) the organization had selected evidenced-based practices that were consistent with the funder's desires.

The grant recipient is a small rural health care organization in southern central Missouri. Eligible for a funding preference, the applicant stated its eligibility and provided the documentation of eligibility as required.

Finally, we include most of the attachments associated with this application.

ABSTRACT

Project Title	***Project IMPACTS*** (Improving and Monitoring Positive and Active Cardiac Team Services)
Applicant Organization Name:	Ozarks Medical Center, Inc.
Type of Entity:	Rural Hospital/Rural Health Clinic
Address:	1100 Kentucky Ave. PO Box 1100; West Plains, MO 65775
Project Director Name:	Mary Dyck, Vice President of Clinical Services
Contact Phone Numbers (Voice, Fax):	(000) 555-1212
E-Mail Address:	xxxxxxx@xxxxxxxxxxx.com
Web Site Address, if applicable:	www.ozarksmedicalcenter.com

The Model: Using an evidenced-based model for Quality Improvement called the Model for Improvement, which is widely used and recommended by the Institute for Health Care Improvement, Ozarks Medical Center intends to implement a redesigned discharge process for individuals admitted with a cardiac diagnosis. Called ***Project IMPACTS*** (Improving and Monitoring Positive and Active Cardiac Team Services), the newly re-designed discharge process we intend to implement is based on best-practices adapted to meet local needs and situations. ***Project IMPACTS*** will identify patients at high-risk for readmission, based on an assessment using the LACES tool, and will provide special supports to decrease the hospital readmission rate for cardiac patients (defined as readmitted within 30 days of original discharge). The new discharge process will include a Discharge Advocate who will focus on making the transition from hospital to home a smooth one. The process will focus on patient and caregiver education (development of health literacy), understanding the patient and caregiver's needs for support, providing and reviewing detailed discharge instructions as early as possible (avoiding the day of discharge rush), carefully reviewing medications prescribed, providing follow-up supports including home health visits and/or follow-up phone support, supporting patient follow-through on medication protocols and follow-up appointments, and auditing readmissions.

Goals and Objectives: 1) Reduce hospital readmissions for cardiac patients. 2) Improve patient satisfaction with regard to care. 3) Improve patient and/or caregiver health literacy. 4) Improve OMC staff knowledge with regard to implementing evidenced-based practices. Objectives include: 1) 100% of evaluation team will be trained on the implementation of the Model for Improvement; 2) 100% of cardiac care team members will be trained to use the LACES tool for assessing patients at high-risk for readmission; 3) Hospital readmission rates will decrease by 10% over baseline in year one, 20% over baseline in year 2 and 30% over baseline in year 3 for patients originally admitted with a cardiac diagnosis; 4) 30% of

> The RFA gave specific guidance for the content of the abstract and requested that the contact information be at the top like this.

> The funder indicated a clear desire for evidence-based models and practices. So we began our abstract with a statement emphasizing the evidence basis for our program design.

patients in year one, 45% in year two, and 60% in year three will make and complete follow-up care visits with their physician or clinic as indicated on discharge orders; 5) 100% of patients will receive follow-up phone calls or home visits (if high-risk as determined by LACES) within 2 days of discharge; and 6) 70% of patients/ family members/ caregivers will report feeling more confident and informed about the patient's condition and care.

Staffing: Project Director (.25 FTE), a data specialist (.5 FTE), and a Discharge Advocate (1.0 FTE) staff from our information technology department who will help resolve problems with health information technology applications (in-kind), and an external evaluator (grant funded)

[A Table of Contents Appeared Here in the Application Package]

PROJECT NARRATIVE

1. INTRODUCTION

Ozarks Medical Center (OMC), a 114-bed, non-profit medical center, located in Howell County, provides comprehensive medical care to more than 130,000 residents across its rural service area in south central Missouri. Services provided include ambulance transportation, behavioral healthcare, cancer treatment, cardiology, emergency department, heart care services, imaging services, nephrology, neurology, orthopedics, pain management, pulmonary rehabilitation, general rehabilitation, rheumatology, sleep lab, surgical, obstetrics and gynecology and wound care services. OMC is accredited by the Joint Commission on Accreditation of Healthcare Organizations. Ozarks Medical Center is requesting a Funding Preference and has provided evidence of HRSA Shortage Designation in Attachment 5.

Some RFAs request an introduction, even if there are no points attached to it. The content here varies from the content in the abstract. Even if the RFA does not request an introduction, taking a bit of space to orient reviewers and lay the groundwork for your project can pay off. It's also a good place to state if you are requesting a funding preference.

The target population served by *Project IMPACTS* (Improving and Monitoring Positive and Active Cardiac Team Services) will include approximately 200 patients who have been admitted to Ozarks Medical Center with a cardiovascular diagnosis. The typical patient admitted with a cardiovascular diagnosis at Ozarks Medical Center is male, generally age 65 or greater with Medicare as their primary source of insurance coverage. Secondary or supplemental coverage, if available, is likely to be Medicaid. Approximately 25% of the patients will score as being at high-risk for hospital readmission, scoring a 10 or greater on the LACES assessment tool.

The purpose of the proposed project is to decrease unplanned readmissions (defined as readmitted within 30 days of original discharge) for patients admitted with a cardiovascular diagnosis. This will be accomplished by changing the discharge processes to provide greater support and contact with the patients and caregiver(s) and working with a consortium of providers through existing provider councils.

In 2011, Ozarks Medical Center began providing cardiac services 24 hours per day, seven days per week. Previously, patients were stabilized and then sent to other hospitals for the complex care they needed. With the opening of round-the-clock cardiac services, OMC is beginning to see patients with more complex needs making a higher acuity level of care necessary.

The case mix, in terms of acuity of care, increased from a measureable acuity level of 1.3591 in 2010 to 1.4567 in 2012. Along with the increase in level of acuity, the number of admissions for cardiovascular reasons increased as well from 171 in 2011 to 214 in 2012. Decreasing hospital readmissions is essential to OMC who is expecting a $71,000 penalty this year from Medicare due to readmission rates.

Goals include: 1) Reduce hospital readmissions for cardiac patients. 2) Improve patient satisfaction with regard to care. 3) Improve patient and/or caregiver health literacy. 4) Improve OMC staff knowledge with regard to implementing evidenced-based practices.

Objectives include: 1) 100% of evaluation team will be trained on the implementation of the Model for Improvement; 2) 100% of cardiac care team members will be trained to use the LACES tool for assessing patients at high-risk for readmission; 3) Hospital readmission rates will decrease by 10% over baseline in year one, 20% over baseline in year 2 and 30% over baseline in year 3 for patients originally admitted with a cardiac diagnosis; 4) 30% of patients in year one, 45% in year two, and 60% in year three will make and complete follow-up care visits with their physician or clinic as indicated on discharge orders; 5) 100% of patients will receive follow-up phone calls or home visits (if high-risk as determined by LACES) within 2 days of discharge; and 6) 70% of patients/ family members/ caregivers will report feeling more confident and informed about the patient's condition and care.

Quality Improvement efforts will follow the Model for Improvement from the Institute from Healthcare Improvement. The Model for Improvement follows a common sense approach: Plan – Do – Study – Act while focusing questions around three central themes; 1) what are we trying to accomplish? 2) How will we know that a change is an improvement? And 3) what changes can we make that will result in improvement? Results will be measured using an electronic health records system with data collected and analyzed by a Data Specialist and external evaluator.

With Project IMPACTS, OMC anticipates providing services to an estimated 200 patients per year. Approximately 25% of those patients (or

This particular application allowed single-spaced text in the narrative. In addition, the author of this narrative followed the old typing rule of including two spaces after a period that ends a sentence. However it is perfectly acceptable (and sometimes necessary) to use only one space.

50 patients) will be assessed as high-risk for readmission using the LACES evaluative model. Implementing programmatic changes through a redesign of the discharge process – overlaid with the Model for Improvement – is expected to promote patient/family/caregiver health literacy, decrease hospital readmissions, increase patient follow-through with discharge orders, and improve patient care and health outcomes.

2. NEEDS ASSESSMENT

a. Target Population

The target population served by *Project IMPACTS* will include patients who have been admitted to Ozarks Medical Center with a cardiovascular diagnosis. The typical patient admitted with a cardiovascular diagnosis at Ozarks Medical Center is male, generally age 65 or greater with Medicare as their primary source of insurance coverage. Secondary or supplemental coverage, if available, is likely to be Medicaid. Their health is impacted directly by a variety of socio- economic factors including income, age, educational attainment and health literacy discussed in the sections that follow.

Social and Economic Factors

The Ozarks region served by Ozarks Medical Center (OMC) includes Douglas, Howell, Ozark, Oregon, Shannon, Texas and Wright counties in south central Missouri. The OMC service area encompasses an astonishing 6,140 square miles nestled in the rolling hills surrounded by the beautiful Ozark Mountains. The seven counties in the region, with a combined population of 130,000 residents, are designated as Health Professional Shortage, Mental Health Care Professional Shortage, and Medically Underserved Areas (see **Attachment 5**) and are located in the 11 poorest Congressional Districts in the Nation.   The area is consumed by poverty with high levels of unemployment.

Figure 2.A: Persistent Poverty Counties in United States. (Arrow highlights OMC service area.)

A publicly accessible map from the U.S. Census Bureau that displayed "persistent-poverty counties" was included here. The proposal author drew an arrow with word processing software to indicate the applicant's service area.

The required section headers did not match the review criteria exactly. In such cases, we base our outline on any required headers. Then we make sure to weave in all material from the review criteria. This differs from our regular advice and practice, which is to build an outline from the review criteria, but it is important to follow the directions provided in the guidance as closely as you can.

Locator maps can be very helpful for reviewers, who are probably unfamiliar with your state. Fortunately, you can sometimes obtain maps like the one that was used here from online sources and add simple embellishments like arrows to direct the reviewer's attention.

According to the Missouri Department of Labor and Industrial Relations the average unemployment rate of 11.2% in the area is substantially higher than the statewide average of 6.7% as of December 2012[1]. Shannon County with a December 2012 unemployment rate of 11% has the highest unemployment rate in the project area and Howell County with an unemployment rate of 6.6% has the lowest.[2]

Figure 2.B: Income and Education Data for Region (2010 Census Data)

County	Percentage of persons below poverty	Median Household Income	Percent of persons age 25+ with high school diploma	Percent of persons 25+ with bachelor's degree or higher
Douglas	21.1%	$32,300	80%	9.7%
Howell	20.7%	$35,625	83.4%	15.7%
Oregon	25.2%	$27,885	77.2%	9.4%
Ozark	17.3%	$31,992	78.3%	10.1%
Shannon	23.3%	$31,748	76.4%	12.6%
Texas	20.2%	$33,128	80.1%	11.6%
Wright	26.1%	$29,212	77.3%	11.6%
Missouri Statewide Average	**14.3%**	**$47,202**	**86.8%**	**25.4%**

Notice that the table provides data on each county in the service area. The data are then compared to state rates to illustrate the obvious disparities in the service area. The text following the table interprets the table for readers and builds upon the data to further develop the case for need in the target area.

Poverty in the area, at an average of 22%,[3] is also significantly higher than the statewide average of 14.3%.[4] Poverty ranges from a high in Wright County at 26.19% and a low of 17.37% in Ozark County. Unfortunately, according to Ozarks Action, Inc., (the Community Action Agency that serves the area) much of the poverty is intergenerational requiring multiple interventions at both individual and systemic levels, and is often correlated with lower levels of education and literacy. In fact, five of the seven counties are listed as persistent-poverty counties meaning the residents have been defined as living in poverty for at least the last 30 years.

The text following the data table illustrates how it's important to layer different items of data that, when combined, build a stronger picture of need than any one fact would on its own.

Educational attainment is also substantially less than statewide averages as shown in Figure 2.B, above. According to the Robert Wood Johnson Foundation's Commission to Build a Healthier America, "People with more education are likely to live longer, to experience better health outcomes and to practice health-promoting behaviors such as exercising regularly, refraining from smoking, and obtaining timely health care check-ups and

The author of this proposal chose to use footnotes to indicate the sources of her data. In other proposals, we use simple in-line citations. We select the format of our citations based on what works best and fits in our space limits.

---

[1] www.labor.mo.gov/des

[2] www.missourieconomy.org. Missouri Economic Research and Information Center

[3] Region G Assessment. May 2011. A Community Needs assessment, providing an overview of current communications for Carter, Douglas, Howell, Oregon, Ozark, Reynolds, Shannon, Texas and Wright counties in Missouri.

[4] Ibid.

screenings."[5]   Poor educational attainment also impacts health literacy.

Health literacy, defined as the degree to which individuals have the capacity to obtain, process and understand basic health information and services needed to make appropriate health decisions and adhere to sometimes complex disease management protocols, increases with educational attainment. "The proportion of American adults with below basic health literacy ranges from 3 percent of college graduates to 15 percent of high-school graduates and 49 percent of adults who have not completed high school.[6]"

Understanding the impact of poor educational attainment is particularly significant to this project as the region, generally, suffers from poor educational attainment – particularly in the senior population as demonstrated in figure 2.C, below. Providing services which address health literacy – both while a patient in the hospital, as well as immediately following discharge when so many questions occur, is vital.

There is a logical progression in this section of poverty and low educational attainment leading to poor health literacy, which lays the groundwork for the project activities to be proposed.

Figure 2.C: Educational Attainment of Seniors in Service Area

	% of Seniors with no High School Diploma	% of Seniors with High School Diploma or GED	% of Seniors with Some College, No Degree	% of Seniors with College Diploma or Professional Degree
Douglas	56.4%	27.2%	9.2%	6.9%
Howell	49.4%	29.3%	14.6%	6.7%
Oregon	48.3%	38.2%	9.7%	3.8%
Ozark	48.6%	30%	12.9%	8.4%
Shannon	54%	29.8%	10.3%	5.9%
Texas	49.1%	30.1%	12.9%	7.8%
Wright	50.3%	31.1%	14%	4.6%
Missouri Statewide Average	**37.3%**	**33.9%**	**17%**	**11.8%**

Age
From a health perspective, 2010 census data, as compiled by the Missouri Office of Social and Economic Data Analysis (OSEDA) based at the University of Missouri, indicates that there are 97,918 adults over the age of eighteen living in the identified service area, and, as shown in the table below, nearly 15 to 20% of adults living in these counties are age 65 and over. The number of individuals age 65 and greater is important, as age

---

[5] Robert Wood Johnson Foundation, Commission to Build a Healthier America. Issue Brief
   6: Education and Health, September 2009. www.commissiononhealth.org.
[6] Ibid.

often plays a role in heart disease and cardiovascular issues. As demonstrated in the table below (Figure 2.D), the percentage of adults, age 65 and over in the service area is much higher than the Missouri statewide average, and the percentage of adults age 85+ is also substantially higher than the Missouri statewide average.

Figure 2.D: Elderly and Advanced Elderly Populations in Service Area

County	Douglas	Howell	Oregon	Ozark	Shannon	Texas	Wright
Population 65+	2,279	6,928	1,844	1,858	1,328	4,391	3,385
Percent Population 65+	16.9%	17.8%	18%	20.1%	15.8%	17.9%	18.4%
Population 85+	309	1,014	257	212	177	110	88
Percent Population 85+	2.3%	2.6%	2.5%	2.3%	2.1%	2.5%	2.6%
Missouri Population 65+	755,837						
% of Missouri Population 65+	13.5%						
Missouri Population 85+	99,473						
% of Missouri Population 85+	1.8%						

Health Factors

A Comprehensive Community Needs Assessment completed by Ozark Action, Inc. (the Community Action Agency serving the region) reported that 67.3% of the residents in the identified counties can be classified as having fair to poor health (based on individual self- reports). Of those surveyed in the Community Assessment, 53% indicated that Medicare and Medicaid were their primary forms of insurance and most indicated that they either used Community Health Centers or Federally Qualified Health Centers as their primary care providers. The self-reports of health status correlate to statistics from the Missouri Department of Health and Senior Services that focus on the rates of hospitalizations and emergency room ER) visits. Specific rates of hospitalizations and ER visits for Heart issues in the OMC service area are shown in the figure below:

The author used varying data sources including federal Census data, statewide data, and local reports. Using multiple data sources helps provide solid and convincing support of the point you are making.

Figure 2.E: Hospitalizations & ER Visits for Heart Issues in Service Area

County	Hospitalizations & ER Visits for Heart Issues per 10,000 seniors by Missouri County		Missouri Hospitalizations & ER Visits for Heart Issues per 10,000 seniors	
	2000 Base Year	2012 Current Year	2000 Base Year	2012 Current Year
Douglas	691.7	616.0		
Howell	1,305.3	1262.8		
Oregon	1,037.4	1161.3		

Highlighting important pieces of data through shading, as the author did in this table, can help draw reviewers' attention to the data you want to emphasize.

In the original application, the table appeared all on one page.

Ozark	829.1	805.5	1,071.5	1,022.6
Shannon	1,497.7	1345.3		
Texas	1,239.5	1150.0		
Wright	925.5	919.0		

In rural Missouri, largely due to the socio-economic challenges, chronic health conditions in the elderly tend to be more disabling, more difficult to manage and more costly to treat than the conditions in younger age groups. As demonstrated in the data tables above, elderly individuals and their caregivers in the area served by OMC have lower rates of educational attainment and lower levels of health literacy. These two factors require health care providers to spend more time explaining care and treatment protocols and require special supports that allow the patient and their caregivers to feel comfortable with managing care at home.

The author chose to end this section with a summary paragraph. While this isn't always possible, it's a great idea when wrapping up a long section.

b. Barriers/Challenges

Barriers and challenges the project plans to overcome include:

Barrier/Challenge:
Possible Resolution:
Limited health literacy of patients and their families. Discharge Advocate will improve patient and caregiver understanding of health conditions by directly asking questions regarding understanding of conditions, medications, discharge orders and follow-up care and services.

Barrier/Challenge:
Limited financial capacities of patients create challenges with adherence to discharge orders.
Possible Resolution:
Discharge Advocate will work with the hospital's social work staff and community agencies to ensure that the patient has access to follow-up medical care through a private physician or clinic. The Discharge Advocate will work with the social work staff to ensure the patient has information regarding medical insurance (Medicare, Medicaid). The Discharge Advocate will work with hospital staff and community agencies to ensure the patient can fill prescriptions.

Barrier/Challenge:
Community partners and consortia members have a limited familiarity with Quality Improvement models.
Possible Resolution:
OMC leadership is committed to providing training and information to support QI processes and measures.

<u>Barrier/Challenge:</u>	Significant cost-pressures due to public policies regarding Medicare and Medicaid reimbursement rates.
<u>Possible Resolution:</u>	OMC will continue to work with the community, legislators and hospital associations to educate the public and legislators about the risks and challenges associated with further reductions in reimbursement rates – particularly as it relates to negatively impacting small rural health care hospitals and medical facilities.
<u>Barrier/Challenge:</u>	Limited organizational experience in implementing evidenced-based practices with fidelity.
<u>Possible Resolution:</u>	OMC will use the services of an external-evaluator to support the implementation of the evidenced-based practice with fidelity to the identified model.
<u>Barrier/Challenge:</u>	Achieving buy-in from staff not involved in the decision to implement evidence-based practices
<u>Possible Resolution:</u>	OMC will transparently implement the use of the evidenced-based practice and will, through staff training and supervisor modeling, emphasize the importance of the practice and how it has led to improved patient care and health outcomes.

> Using this Barrier/Challenge and Possible Resolution layout can help reviewers zero in on each element more easily than if each had been presented in a long narrative paragraph.

The consortium has spent a great deal of time identifying, discussing, and evaluating the barriers and challenges that may be encountered during the project. Each barrier has been addressed in the Resolution of Challenges section with an approach to resolve each challenge.

c. Geographic Details of Service Area

The area serviced by this project includes the Missouri counties of Douglas, Howell, Oregon, Ozark, Shannon, Texas and Wright, covering 6,140 square miles, nestled in the rolling hills of the Ozarks. Ozarks Medical Center, located in West Plains, Missouri (Howell County), lies approximately 100 miles south of the nearest interstate (Interstate 44 in Rolla, MO). St. Louis, MO lies approximately 198 miles to the northeast; Springfield, MO is approximately 111 miles to the northwest. The terrain across the service area is rolling hills that run largely through farmland, the Mark Twain National Forest, the Ozark National Scenic Riverways and other smaller streams and rivers. A map is provided below, labeled Figure 2.F.

As the map on the next page indicates, the service area lies in the south central portion of Missouri. The largest geographic barrier of the service area is that of size and distance. The size of the area and its rural nature, combined with a lack of public transportation, makes it difficult for patients to access care. Often patients will travel one hour or more to obtain medical care at OMC.

Figure 2.F.: Map of Service Area

A large map of the service area was included here. Text boxes and word processing line drawing tools were used to delineate the boundaries of the project's service area and indicate its relationship to the rest of the state.

d. Health Care in Service Area

Our extreme rural seven county service region, in addition to being a Health Professional Shortage and Medically Underserved Areas, is also a Mental Health Professional Shortage Area (see **Attachment 5**). Access to health care is problematic in the area. "Although 38% of Missouri's population lives in rural areas of the state, only 18% of the primary care physicians are located in rural areas. This disparity in primary care medical practitioners is critical in assuring access to preventive and maintenance health services in rural Missouri.[7]"

Figure 2.G: Access to Healthcare in OMC Service Area

County	Primary Care Physicians per 10,000 people	Staffed Hospital Beds per 1,000 Residents
Douglas	6	0
Howell	71	134
Oregon	3	0
Ozark	3	0
Shannon	0	0
Texas	17	47
Wright	12	0

Other providers in the area include St. John's, St. Francis Hospital, located in Mountain View, Missouri and Texas County Memorial Hospital, located in Houston, Missouri.

---

[7] Missouri Rural Health Biennial Report, 2010-2011

St. John's, St. Francis Hospital lies approximately 25 miles (or 40 minutes by rural roads) north and east of OMC. Texas County Memorial Hospital is approximately 50 miles (or nearly one hour) north of OMC. All three hospitals routinely collaborate with one another on a variety of patient care issues and refer patients to each other for services.

St. John's, St. Francis Hospital, a non-profit hospital, is member of the Mercy health care system. The hospital in Mountain View is a 20-bed facility that operates an emergency department as well as a general medicine/surgical facility. The hospital is JCAHO accredited.

Texas County Memorial Hospital is an unaccredited 60-bed general acute care institution providing emergency services, surgery, obstetrics, laboratory, radiology, cardiac care and physical therapy. Its catchment area includes three counties served by OMC (Texas, Shannon, and Wright) in addition to Dent, Phelps, Laclede and Pulaski counties.

Project IMPACTS will provide both St. John's, St. Francis and Texas County Memorial hospitals with an example of a small rural hospital, implementing an evidence-based quality improvement model. OMC will share its experiences with both institutions, including the challenges experienced, and practical resolutions employed. OMC will also share the re-design of our discharge process and its evaluated impact on hospital readmissions. OMC will broadly share the knowledge it gains as a result of the project to support other rural institutions interested in implementing Quality Improvement activities.

e. Burden of Chronic Disease

In rural areas, Missouri residents tend to be older and have higher rates of chronic diseases, such as heart disease, cancer, diabetes and COPD, which are further complicated by a lack of access to primary care physicians.[8] The evidence supports the negative effects of lower socioeconomic status and decreased access to primary care health services. These factors contribute to the increased hospitalization rates for diseases in rural versus metropolitan Missouri.

Each year, heart disease accounts for more than 15,000 deaths in Missouri making it the leading cause of death in the state.[9] In the counties served by OMC, heart disease, as a cause of death, occurs at a rate greater than the statewide average, 1,356.8 per 100,000 for the OMC service area versus 1,308.6 statewide. When including all other contributing factors and cardiopulmonary diagnoses (atherosclerosis, COPD, essential hypertension,

The RFA asked respondents to discuss problems with access to healthcare in the service area. The author emphasized distance and how long it takes to travel over rural roads.

These types of details can help your reviewers better understand the local situation.

Whenever possible, interpret need data for your readers. Give a statistic or measure and then explain what that means in terms of your project. Link everything together for your reviewers. Don't make them work to make the connections you want them to make.

---

[8] www.missourihealthmatters.com. Missouri Hospital Association. "Primary Care Physicians: The Status in Rural Missouri." August 2011.
[9] Missouri Department of Health and Senior Services.

heart disease, and other cardiovascular/circulatory conditions), the rates of each are nearly double that of the statewide averages.

Heart disease, the leading cause of heart attacks, has controllable and uncontrollable risk factors. Uncontrollable risk factors include sex, age, race and family history. Controllable risk factors include smoking, high LDL cholesterol, high blood pressure, obesity, physical inactivity, and uncontrolled diabetes. According to the Missouri Department of Health and Senior Services, many of these risk factors are prevalent at rates higher than the statewide average among seniors in the counties served by OMC as shown in Figure 2.H, below.

Figure 2.H: Senior Population (65+) Cardiac Risk Factor Indicators as a Percentage of Total

County	Smoking in past 12 months	High cholesterol	High Blood Pressure	Obesity (BMI 30+)	Physical Inactivity in past 12 months	Diabetes
Douglas	10.3%	21.8%	42.6%	18.5%	32.8%	15.8%
Howell	8.0%	21.9%	43.7%	24.0%	42.1%	8.3%
Oregon	12.1%	24.6%	50.0%	32.6%	39.9%	21.3%
Ozark	10.6%	25.8%	45.8%	21.8%	37.8%	16.5%
Shannon	15.8%	30.2%	49.6%	28.3%	42.7%	21.1%
Texas	15.9%	23.4%	45.5%	25.2%	39.1%	19.4%
Wright	10.2%	24.5%	44.1%	28.2%	35.1%	16.4%
State of Missouri	**10.8%**	**25.1%**	**40.1%**	**25.2%**	**38.5%**	**19.3%**

Note: Shading indicates percentages greater than the statewide average.

Chronic health conditions, particularly those that require hospitalizations, are quite stressful for the patient, his primary caregiver(s) and family. "On the whole, the conditions that are most common among older age groups require more care, are more disabling, and are more difficult and costly to treat than the conditions that are more common for younger age groups.[10]" Further, it is generally accepted that people with lower incomes are more likely to have conditions that are more difficult or costly to treat. Between the costs associated with treatment and the disruptions to family life (economic and otherwise), individuals with chronic conditions also generally have higher levels of stress and often "indicate feelings of helplessness and hopelessness[11]" while their caregivers and family also report frustrations and stress.

---

[10] National Academy on an Aging Society. Chronic Conditions: A Challenge for the 21st Century. www.agingsociety.org.

[11] Depression and Chronic Illness: Which Comes First? www.clevelandclinic.com.

Recognizing this, OMC has deliberately chosen to involve the patient, caregiver(s) and family in the new process (Discharge Advocate) to ensure that concerns are addressed and that the patient, their caregiver(s) and family members feel empowered to provide care knowing that they have supports that are aimed at developing their health literacy and coping with challenges without returning to the hospital unnecessarily.

3. METHODOLOGY

a. Evidenced-Based Quality Improvement Model

Ozarks Medical Center intends to implement an evidenced-based quality improvement model called the **Model for Improvement**[12] (see figure 3.A.) that will support the hospital in reducing readmissions among cardiac patients. Using an evidenced-based quality improvement model, laid over a series of program improvements that are based on evidenced-based best-practices, OMC will reduce readmissions (defined as the same patient, readmitted within 30 days of the original discharge date) overall by 30% (from baseline of 2012) by the end of year three and by 20% among high-risk patients by the end of year three.

Patients will be assessed for risk using the modified LACES tool which measures length of stay in hospital; acuity of the admission – was it through the emergency department; comorbidity of the patient; and utilization of emergency room in the past six months, along with an added element of support systems at home. The addition of the support systems at home is an addition based on knowledge of the local population. Consistent with the tool, patients scoring a 10 or above on the modified numerical scale will be considered high risk for readmission.

LACE is being modified to become LACES due to local conditions. In the OMC service area, many of the high-risk cardiac patients either live alone or live with spouses that also have multiple medical conditions that make it difficult for them to

Figure 3.A: Model for Improvement from IHI

Wisely using figures, diagrams, and charts can help illustrate complicated processes and can appeal to visual readers. Diagrams rarely replace narrative content. They supplement it.

---

[12] Developed by Associated in Process Improvement and used by the Institute for Healthcare Improvement. www.ihi.org.

provide the care needed upon discharge.

Following the Model for Improvement, OMC has identified these key steps for implementing a Quality Improvement model as follows:

- **Step 1:** Hospital leadership has established a working group to identify an evidenced- based quality improvement model, focused on a specific care area.
  o <u>Progress:</u> OMC has identified potential funding and is working on a grant submission.
- **Step 2:** Hospital leadership, working collaboratively with community provider councils, educational partners and medical staff develops a practice improvement focused on transitions in care for cardiac patients.
- **Step 3**: The team identifies opportunities for improvement.
  o <u>Progress:</u> Cardiac care has been identified.
  o <u>Progress:</u> Team has completed literature reviews and has developed a transitions in care process.
- **Step 4:** The team develops an Aim statement.
  o <u>Progress:</u> The draft Aim statement of ***Project IMPACTS*** is to decrease the number of readmissions for cardiac patients annually by 10%. Readmissions are defined as a patient discharged from cardiac care who is readmitted to the hospital for any cause within 30 days of original discharge.

<u>Testing, Implementing, and Spreading Changes – Using the Model for Improvement</u>
- Step 1. Based on your existing process, select a place to start and identify the opportunities or failures in your current processes.
  o <u>Progress:</u> Underway
- Step 2. Use the Model for Improvement; test changes.
  o <u>Progress:</u> Pending fund availability.
- Step 3. Increase the reliability of processes.
  o <u>Progress:</u> Pending fund availability.
- Step 4. Use data, displayed over time, to assess progress.
  o <u>Progress:</u> Pending fund availability.
- Step 5. Implement and spread successful practices to other care areas.
  o <u>Progress:</u> Pending implementation and evaluation of program.
- Step 6. Disseminate results, share results with other services providers to encourage adoption of successful practices.
  o <u>Progress:</u> Pending implementation and evaluation of program.

The selection of the Model for Improvement is based on extensive reading and review of the various models presented by the Office of Rural Health Policy in the funding announcement. In reading through suggested evidenced-based models, the Institute for Healthcare Improvement's (IHI) citation of the Model for Improvement and how it was used to facilitate the quality improvement program focused on transitions in care soundly resonated with the Project Director. The transitions in care project described by IHI is similar in many ways to OMC's project – with community specific interventions or "tweaks" that will better support the population OMC intends to reach.

This section clearly links the selected approach with resources suggested by the funding agency. If resources are recommended in the RFA or on the funder's website, reviewers will be concerned if it seems you created your project in a vacuum.

New Care and Discharge Process
1. Patients admitted for cardiac care will be assigned to a Discharge Advocate at the time of admission who will act as the team leader for patient discharge planning.
2. The Discharge Advocate will participate in daily rounds with the physician, patient care nurse, communicating with the care team, patient and other care givers.
3. The Discharge Advocate will have daily "huddle" meetings with representatives from social services, rehab and pharmacy to identify concerns for discharge.
4. The Discharge Advocate will visit with the patient and care giver(s) to identify any discharge concerns. The Discharge Advocate will:
    a. Ensure the patient and care giver(s) receive education throughout their stay regarding their diagnosis and post hospital care plan;
    b. Facilitate nutrition education applicable to the patient's diagnosis and condition;
    c. Understand and communicate any new care guidelines including new medication plans;
        i.   Patients will be provided with "take home information packets" that are provided by pharmaceutical companies.
        ii. Patients will be provided with information regarding pharmaceutical programs that help to make prescriptions more affordable.
    d. Communicate the importance of appointments for post-discharge care;
    e. Communicate prescribed post-discharge services to the patient/family/caregiver.
5. Each cardiac patient will be assessed using the LACES tool which helps to determine which patients are at high-risk for readmission.
6. Patients who are identified as high-risk using the LACES tool (scoring 10 or greater) will:
    a. Receive a detailed review of any changes in medication;
        i.   Rather than handing prescriptions that need to be filled upon discharge, OMC will make every effort to fill the

The outline format helps break up what would otherwise be a page of almost solid text. Not only does white space help avoid reader fatigue, but a process that has steps that must be followed in order is a good choice for presenting in this fashion.

prescriptions in the hospital (unless the patient prefers another pharmacy) so that the medications can be reviewed with the patient and/or their caregiver(s) by a pharmacist.

   b. Be scheduled for a home health visit two days following discharge (unless they are transitioned to skilled nursing or other out-of-home care setting).

   c. The home health visit will include a health assessment as well as address any questions related to care. The home health visit will review discharge orders and work to ensure any follow-up medical appointments are scheduled. A student nurse from a nearby educational institution will accompany the home health nurse, providing an experiential learning opportunity for student nurses.

7. Patients who are identified as medium risk (scoring nine or less on the LACES tool) will receive a phone call from their Discharge Advocate within 48 hours following discharge. The purpose will be to determine if the patient or caregiver(s) have questions or concern, review discharge orders, and determine if patients have made their follow-up appointment.

   a. If the follow-up appointment has not been made, an additional follow-up call will be made within three days of the first phone call.

   b. If the follow-up appointment is still not made, a visit from a home health provider will be recommended to assess patient and determine what obstacles exist to making the follow-up appointment.

   b. Data Collection and Reporting

Data Elements
Data will be collected on each patient through electronic health records. Specific data elements will be aggregated that determine overall numbers of admissions for cardiac care as well as readmission rates for patients discharged within the previous 30 days for a primary diagnosis that is cardiac related. Additional data elements that will be collected include administration of the LACES tool, Discharge Advocate services, including follow-up elements such as home-health visits and/or follow-up phone calls as well as participation in follow-up care with physician or clinic of record.

For patients at high-risk of readmission (determined by LACES scoring), OMC will use tele- health monitors. These monitors will provide additional data elements that will allow the cardiac care team to reach out to the patient and make changes in the patient's care plan or medication regime. For example, through the tele-monitoring devices, daily measures of a patient's condition will be transmitted to the hospital including blood pressure, heart rate, oxygen saturation, weight, and other data that the patient's physician may want to capture. OMC has used tele-health monitoring since 2007 on a limited basis (with Medicaid patients) and has experienced a 40% reduction in hospital readmissions. Using them with the high-risk population, we believe, will help to reduce their readmissions.

Data Collection, Review and Reporting
Data will be collected and reviewed by the Data Specialist who will share it with the Project Director and External Evaluator. The Project Director will share the data with OMC's Leadership Team and Provider Councils (consortia). Provider Councils will examine data to identify areas of concern and if any identifiable "fixes" to process can be easily implemented to address identified issues.

Data results will, following the Model for Improvement, go through a continuous feedback loop to identify issues, develop resolutions, implement fixes and then re-evaluate results. As part of the data collection, evaluation, and reporting process, and consistent with the Model for Improvement, results will be measured against three key points: 1) What are we trying to accomplish? 2) How will we know that a change is an improvement? 3) What changes can we make that will result in improvement?

The Data Specialist, Project Director and External Evaluator will review the data elements prior to analysis to ensure validity and integrity. Any results outside the anticipated norm will be closely examined to ensure that mistakes were made.

Finally, consistent with OHRP guidelines, OMC will report on Clinical Measures six months after project start, and then quarterly thereafter. Additional data elements that will be collected and reported annually include the Performance Improvement Measurement System (PIMS) consistent with ORHP guidelines.

c. **Sustainability**

Primary Considerations for Funding
It is important to understand that in this fiscal year alone, OMC has a current readmission penalty that will total approximately $71,000. This means that if OMC is able to reduce hospital readmissions to a level that is acceptable by Medicare, OMC would gain an additional $71,000 in revenues (or more) going forward. Implementing the Model for Improvement and reducing readmission rates for cardiac patients would enable OMC to self-fund several important elements of *Project IMPACTS* without any additional funding and even expand the program.

> The plan calls for a designated staff person whose job is to ensure that data are collected and reported. It is also important to demonstrate that you will actually act upon what you learn from the data you collect. The entire point of collecting data is so that someone analyzes it and makes changes as a result.

> The author used this paragraph to tell the reviewer the applicant understands the reporting guidelines and is prepared to be compliant.

Sustainability Planning and Approach
The OMC Quality Improvement initiative is based on improvements in three areas of concern: 1) hospital readmissions (which can negatively impact Medicare reimbursement rates); 2) patient satisfaction with care (which can positively or negatively impact the likelihood that OMC will be the patient's provider of choice); 3) patient health literacy (which can positively impact the ability of the patient and caregiver to participate in aspects of care). Each of these areas has the potential to positively or negatively impact the organization's finances, community standing and reputation.

OMC is committed to the following elements of sustainability (established as best practices by IHI)[13]:

1. Supportive Management Structure
2. Structures to "Foolproof" Change
3. Robust, Transparent Feedback Systems
4. Shared Sense of the Systems to Be Improved
5. Culture of Improvement and a Deeply Engaged Staff
6. Formal Capacity-Building Programs

1. Supportive Management Structure
In order to support sustainability, OMC's leadership will continue to treat quality of care as a high priority, devoting regular attention to outcome measures, creating accountability systems for improvement, and recognizing the organization's successes.

2. Structures to "Foolproof" Change
In each of the intervention areas, OMC will build structures (e.g., IT systems, packaged materials that support a given intervention) that make it difficult—if not impossible—for providers of care to revert to old ways of doing things.

3. Robust, Transparent Feedback Systems
OMC leadership will regularly and routinely communicate performance on key indicators, reviewing information generated by a measurement system (that provides data to stakeholders at every level in the organization), comparing it to clear standards set by management, and taking part in improvements devised in response.

4. A Shared Sense of the Systems to Be Improved
OMC will engage all stakeholders (executives, managers, frontline providers of care) in clearly understanding the importance of improving the procedures and systems of care and their contribution to the sought-after improvements.

Sustainability is often one of the hardest sections to address. In this situation, the author was fortunate to be able to point to something very specific that would help with sustainability. This isn't always the case, but be as specific as you can.

In this section, the author admitted that change is difficult. Then she explained the plan to make the proposed changes more likely to be successfully implemented.

---

[13] www.ihi.org. How to Guide: Sustainability and Spread.

5. Culture of Improvement and a Deeply Engaged Staff
OMC shares a sense of pride regarding performance and improvement skill, and understands that providers of care enjoy their work in this area. OMC will ensure that staff are well aware of quality improvement initiative and feel invested in outcomes. OMC will implement specific changes in job descriptions and performance evaluations to include attention to quality improvement skills.

6. Formal Capacity-Building Programs
OMC will make the training of executives and staff a high priority, building skills in appropriate disciplines and building organization-wide skills in application of modern quality improvement methods with the aim of creating a culture where improvement work is seamlessly integrated into day-to-day activity in the unit or facility.

Sustaining Activities, Expanding to Other Areas
Once the ORHP grant expires, OMC intends to re-invest the proceeds realized from readmission reductions into quality improvement. With increased gross revenues of $71,000 or more, OMC will be able to retain the primary activities (with the exception of external evaluation) and intends to expand the model to other chronic diseases and areas of care. At this point, OMC is considering the expansion to institute a similar (with small adaptations) program to individuals with diabetes. We can certainly see how the Discharge Advocate program could be beneficial to diabetics admitted for a variety of reasons and will begin exploring this area in the near future.

Additionally, OMC intends to broadly share the outcomes of our Quality Improvement initiative with other rural health providers through a variety of avenues including 1) annual conferences such as the Missouri Hospital Association conference, the Home Care Association Conference, the Annual Frail Elderly Conference, and annual Long-Term Care Association conference. The Project Director, Mary Dyck, also intends to develop an article that she hopes to have published in nursing case management periodicals.

d. Health Care Redesign

Project IMPACTS incorporates specific values and elements of the health care redesign articulated in the Affordable Care Act. ***Project IMPACTS*** operates under a new paradigm – one that focuses on patient care and extends care in collaboration with the physician's and other community and health care agencies beyond the hospital's doors.

> The plan to disseminate project results is another area that sometimes gets short shrift in proposals. But this can cost you points. The author named specific events at which project results could be disseminated. This is always stronger than making only a general statement that you will disseminate through conferences and publications.

Under the "old" system, a hospital's role in patient care began when the patient was admitted to the hospital, and ended when the patient was discharged. Follow-up care was the responsibility of the primary care physician and/or a home health agency. ***Project IMPACTS*** puts into practice the principles articulated in the Affordable Care Act. ***Project IMPACTS*** delivers improved care, delivers better patient experiences and improves health outcomes.

The approach and tools used are based on common sense. By providing follow-up care after discharge, patients experience better transitions between health care providers, experience better health care delivery, and feel supported in their recovery. Key elements to ***Project IMPACTS*** include:

1. _Employing a research-based tool to identify patients at risk of readmission_

The Discharge Advocate will assess each cardiac patient using the modified LACES model. The best-practice LACE model of assessing patients at risk of readmission will be modified by OMC to account for local conditions – namely assigning a value for the existence and level of support systems at home. Patients with good support systems at home are, in OMC's experience, less likely to be readmitted to the hospital than patients who live alone or who have inadequate supports.

> Frequently when you plan to use an evidence-based practice in your program design, the RFA requires you to explain if you plan any changes to the model.

2. _Improving Patient Care Transitions_

As discussed previously, all cardiac patients will be assigned to a Discharge Advocate who will participate in rounds and "huddle" meetings with providers and discussions with the patient/family/caregivers to identify concerns and needs and resolve them. Transitions will be improved through this broad communication and supported by specific patient care enhancements.

3. _Patient Care Enhancements_

In addition to changing the care paradigm of our discharge process, specific tools will be provided to all patients with additional enhancements for identified high-risk patients.

Patients at low to moderate risk of readmission will receive follow-up services via the telephone within 2 days of discharge. The follow-up telephone call will determine if the patient or caregiver(s) have any questions or concern, to review the discharge orders, and determine if the patient has made their follow-up appointment. If the follow-up appointment has not been made, an additional follow-up call will be made within three days of the first phone call. Patients at high-risk of readmission will receive enhanced post-discharge services including:

- A home health visit two days following discharge (unless they are transitioned to skilled nursing or other out-of-home care setting). The home health visit will include a health assessment as well as address any questions related to care. The home health visit will review discharge orders and work to ensure any follow-up medical appointments are scheduled.
- Additional medical monitoring through tele-health monitoring.
  o Daily measures of a patient's condition will be transmitted to the hospital including blood pressure, heart rate, oxygen saturation, weight, and other data that the patient's physician may want to capture
- Additional equipment such as digital scales that will allow a patient to monitor their weight. Sudden increases in weight can signal that a patient is retaining fluids which can be an indicator of poor heart function.

4.   *Better Communication Between Providers*

The proposed model encourages and fosters communication between providers of care for the patient. With the use of electronic health records, combined with outreach services, the hospital is better positioned to act as focal point for communications that ensure the patient participates in follow-up care and follows discharge instructions. The Provider Councils will also help to foster communication and identify problems with service delivery.

5.   *Provider Councils Examining Evaluative Results*

The Provider Councils will also perform an important role in evaluating the program, monitoring quality improvement measures and tweaking service-delivery efforts to promote positive outcomes for patients.

> The workplan is an essential element for convincing reviewers that you can implement the project you have proposed. Some workplans are very short. Others, like this one, are longer. This funder prescribed the columns to be included, so the author had to follow the suggested format.
>
> Good workplans tie the objectives and/or outcomes to planned activities. They should also include time frames, who is responsible, and how you will document or evaluate results.

Goals for Year One		Measures of Success		
Objectives	Activities Planned to Achieve This Objective	Data	Time frame for Assessing Progress	Team Members Responsible
Additional staff (Discharge Advocate, Data Specialist) will be recruited, hired, oriented and trained.	1. Human Resources will place advertisements to recruit personnel. 2. Human resources will hire new staff. 3. Staff will be trained and oriented collaboratively by Human Resources and Project Director 4. Contract with evaluator will be signed.	Hiring log Time sheets Contract	Within 8 weeks of project award	Human Resources Director, Project Director
100% of evaluation team members will be trained on implementation of the Model for Improvement.	Team members will go through training.	Log in sheets	Quarter 1	Project Director, Data Specialist, and External Evaluator.
100% of cardiac care team members will be trained on the use of the LACES evaluation tool for assessing patient risk for readmission	Team members will go through training	Log in sheets	Quarter 1	Project Director, Data Specialist, External Evaluator; Vice President of Medical Affairs will also be involved
Hospital readmission rates will decrease by 10% over baseline in Year one.	1. Cardiac care team and Discharge Advocate along with Project Director will refine and implement redesigned discharge process 2. Patients will be assessed for readmission risk using LACES tool.	Meeting notes, electronic health records, documentation from home health nurse, case notes from Discharge	On-going	Discharge Advocate and Data Specialist with support from other cardiac care team members

In reference to the time frames in this workplan, this is a particular type of project. Some key activities taking place are tied to an event (in this case, patient discharge), instead of being tied to a certain month or quarter on a calendar.

3. Low to moderate risk patients will receive phone follow-up within two days of discharge.
4. High-risk patients will receive home health visit within 2 days of discharge.
5. High-risk patients will participate in tele-health home monitoring and be given other supplies such as scales to monitor health/risk factors.
6. All patients will be asked about follow-up visit with physician. Supports for making/securing appointments will be provided as needed.
7. Follow-up services end 31 days after discharge if patient is not readmitted.
8. If patient is readmitted within 30 days of discharge, the readmission will be audited to determine root cause and what steps can be taken to mitigate or eliminate the root cause of readmission.

	Advocate			
30% of patients will make and complete follow-up care visits with their physician or clinic as indicated on discharge orders.	Discharge Advocate will monitor patient files to ensure patient makes follow-up appointment as indicated on discharge orders.	Electronic health records	Within five days of discharge	Discharge Advocate
100% of patients will receive follow-up phone calls or home visits (as determined	Discharge Advocate will make calls and/or coordinate home health visit	Electronic health records	Within two days of discharge	Discharge Advocate

The evaluation and dissemination activities in the final two paragraphs of the second column show that the applicant is committed to using what it learns from its evaluation processes to contribute knowledge to the field.

appropriate by risk of readmission measured by LACES) within 2 days of discharge.				
70% of patients/family members/caregivers will report feeling more confident and informed about the patient's care and condition.	Patient/family members/caregivers will be surveyed. Questions will focus on satisfaction and health literacy issues.	Survey instrument	Just prior to discharge and again within two weeks of discharge	Project Director, Data Specialist and Discharge Advocate
Annual evaluation results will be completed and shared with OMC senior leadership, Provider Councils and other stakeholders.	Data Specialist, Project Director and Discharge Advocate will review and provide data to External Evaluator. External Evaluator will produce annual evaluation report. Once the report has been completed, the Project Director will distribute and review report with OMC leadership. Report will then be released and reviewed with Provider Councils and stakeholders. Annual evaluation results will also be assessed to determine if any developing trends may be beneficial for other rural health providers and hospitals. Presentations to conferences and journal articles will be reviewed and considered.	Annual report and meeting notes	Upon completion of the annual evaluation, ending by the end of Quarter 1 in Year 2	Project Director

When you assign the responsible parties for completing tasks, be sure to keep the workload looking reasonable for each position. Sometimes reviewers will worry that you are expecting one person to do too much, which can place the project in jeopardy. Other times, reviewers are looking to see if the "right" person or partner is assigned to certain tasks.

Sometimes the guidelines say that workplans for years following Year One are not required to provide as much detail as the plan for the first year. If the expectation for the workplan is unclear, or whenever page limits allow, we develop subsequent project years as fully as the first year, even if the plan becomes repetitive. More details make your project look more realistic.

Model for Improvement methodology will be employed to examine results of evaluation	Meeting notes	Beginning with the conclusion of the annual evaluation and ending by the end of Quarter 1 in Year 2	Project Director, Discharge Advocate, Data Specialist, External Evaluator and other stakeholders
Project team and other stakeholders will examine evaluation results and will use the three guiding questions of the model to determine what, if any adjustments are required to achieve goals of improved patient care, better health outcomes and reduced readmission rates. Review during QI will also be focus on identifying developing trends, causal relationship between intervention and results, and replication issues. Presentations to conferences and journal articles will be reviewed and considered.			
Goals for Year 2			
Hospital readmission rates will decrease by 20% over baseline in Year two.	Meeting notes, Electronic health records, documentation from home health nurse, case notes from Discharge Advocate	On-going	Discharge Advocate and Data Specialist with support from other cardiac care team members
1. Cardiac care team and Discharge Advocate along with Project Director will refine and implement redesigned discharge process 2. Patients will be assessed for readmission risk using LACES. 3. Low to moderate risk patients will receive phone follow-up within two days of discharge. 4. High-risk patients will receive home health visit within 2 days of discharge. 5. High-risk patients will participate in tele-health home			

> If you needed to save pages, you could say that Activities 1-8 in Year Two repeat Activities 1-8 from Year One instead of re-stating them. Or you might decide to make the Activities column very wide while making other columns narrower.

monitoring and be given other supplies such as scales to monitor health/risk factors.

6. All patients will be asked about follow-up visit with physician. Supports for making/securing appointments will be provided as needed.

7. Follow-up services end 31 days after discharge unless readmitted.

8. If patient is readmitted within 30 days of discharge, the readmission will be audited to determine root cause and what steps can be taken to mitigate or eliminate the root cause of readmission.

Activity	Outcome	Data Source	Timeline	Responsible Party
Discharge Advocate will monitor patient files to ensure patient makes follow-up appointment as indicated on discharge orders.	40% of patients will make and complete follow-up care visits with their physician or clinic as indicated on discharge orders.	Electronic health records	Within five days of discharge	Discharge Advocate
Discharge Advocate will make calls and/or coordinate home health visit	100% of patients will receive follow-up phone calls or home visits (as determined appropriate by risk of readmission measured by LACES) within 2 days of discharge.	Electronic health records	Within two days of discharge	Discharge Advocate
Patient/family members/caregivers will be surveyed. Questions will focus on satisfaction and health literacy issues.	70% of patients/family members/caregivers will report feeling more confident and	Survey instrument	Just prior to discharge and again within two weeks of	Project Director, Data Specialist and Discharge Advocate

informed about the patient's care and condition.			discharge	Project Director
Annual evaluation results will be completed and shared with OMC senior leadership, Provider Councils and other stakeholders.	Data Specialist, Project Director and Discharge Advocate will review and provide data to External Evaluator. External Evaluator will produce annual evaluation report. Once the report has been completed, the Project Director will distribute and review report with OMC leadership. Report will then be released and reviewed with Provider Councils and stakeholders. Annual evaluation results will also be assessed to determine if any developing trends may be beneficial for other rural health providers and hospitals. Presentations to conferences and journal articles will be reviewed and considered.	Annual report and meeting notes	Upon completion of the annual evaluation, ending by the end of Quarter 1 in Year 3	Project Director
Model for Improvement methodology will be employed to examine results of evaluation	Project team and other stakeholders will examine evaluation results and will use the three guiding questions of the model to determine what, if any adjustments are required to achieve goals of improved patient care, better health outcomes and reduced readmission rates. Review during QI will also be	Meeting notes	Beginning with the conclusion of the annual evaluation and ending by the end of Quarter 1 in Year 3	Project Director, Discharge Advocate, Data Specialist, External Evaluator and other stakeholders

	focus on identifying developing trends, causal relationship between intervention and results, and replication issues. Presentations to conferences and journal articles will be reviewed and considered.			Discharge Advocate and Data Specialist with support from other cardiac care team members
Goals for Year 3				
Hospital readmission rates will decrease by 30% over baseline in Year Three.	1. Cardiac care team and Discharge Advocate along with Project Director will refine and implement redesigned discharge process 2. Patients will be assessed for readmission risk using LACES tool. 3. Low to moderate risk patients will receive phone follow-up within two days of discharge. 4. High-risk patients will receive home health visit within 2 days of discharge. 5. High-risk patients will participate in tele-health home monitoring and be given other supplies such as scales to monitor health/risk factors. 6. All patients will be asked about follow-up visit with physician. Supports for making/securing appointments will be provided as needed. 7. Follow-up services end 31 days after discharge unless readmitted.	Meeting notes, electronic health records, documentation from home health nurse, case notes from Discharge Advocate	On-going	

8. If patient is readmitted within 30 days of discharge, the readmission will be audited to determine root cause and what steps can be taken to mitigate or eliminate the root cause of readmission.			
60% of patients will make and complete follow-up care visits with their physician or clinic as indicated on discharge orders.	Electronic health records	Within five days of discharge	Discharge Advocate
Discharge Advocate will monitor patient files to ensure patient makes follow-up appointment as indicated on discharge orders.			
100% of patients will receive follow-up phone calls or home visits (as determined appropriate by risk of readmission measured by LACES) within 2 days of discharge.	Electronic health records	Within two days of discharge	Discharge Advocate
Discharge Advocate will make calls and/or coordinate home health visit			
70% of patients/family members/caregivers will report feeling more confident and informed about the patient's care and condition.	Survey instrument	Just prior to discharge and again within two weeks of discharge	Project Director, Data Specialist and Discharge Advocate
Patient/family members/caregivers will be surveyed. Questions will focus on satisfaction and health literacy issues.			
Annual and project evaluation results will be completed and shared with OMC senior leadership, Provider Councils and other stakeholders.	Annual report and meeting notes	Upon completion of the final evaluation report (within 45 days of project close)	Project Director
Data Specialist, Project Director and Discharge Advocate will review and provide data to External Evaluator. External Evaluator will produce annual evaluation report. Once the report has been completed, the Project Director will distribute and review			

report with OMC leadership. Report will then be released and reviewed with Provider Councils and stakeholders. Annual and program evaluation results will also be assessed to determine if any developing trends may be beneficial for other rural health providers and hospitals. Presentations to conferences and journal articles will be reviewed and considered.				
Model for Improvement methodology will be employed to examine results of evaluation	Project team and other stakeholders will examine evaluation results and will use the three guiding questions of the model to determine what, if any adjustments are required to achieve goals of improved patient care, better health outcomes and reduced readmission rates. Review during QI will also be focus on identifying developing trends, causal relationship between intervention and results, and replication issues. Presentations to conferences and journal articles will be reviewed and considered.	Meeting notes	Upon completion of the final evaluation report (within 45 days of project close)	Project Director, Discharge Advocate, Data Specialist, External Evaluator and other stakeholders

5. RESOLUTION OF CHALLENGES

Challenges that are likely to be encountered in the design and implementation of the grant will be addressed as follows:

Challenge: Identifying and hiring appropriate staff.

Resolution: Recruitment, training, and orientation of project staff will be based on Ozarks Medical Center's current recruitment methodology that ensures an appropriate method of recruitment is in place. All training and orientation will be followed as stated in Ozarks Medical Center Human Resource Department.

Challenge: Limited familiarity of care staff with Quality Improvement models.

Resolution: OMC leadership is committed to providing professional development to support QI processes and measures.

Challenge: There may be resistance from care team members to participate in the QualityImprovement program.

Resolution: Through modeling by OMC's leadership, clinical care team members and other supervisors, OMC will experience a change in culture. The new culture will be focused on QI and program improvements. Information regarding QI initiatives will be shared transparently, including challenges. Successes will be broadly celebrated.

Challenge: There may be resistance from patients to participate in the re-designed discharge program.

Resolution: Through the coordination of care by the care team unit, these patients will be treated within the restrictions set by the patient. The patient will be encouraged to participate in the program and will be informed that the goal of the program is to improve his/her perceptions of quality of care and improve his/her health outcomes.

Challenge: Stability of health information technology.

Resolution: The hospital's technology team will make every effort to be aware of trends in electronic health records and other technology to make improvements in the gathering of data. Expenses for updating and maintaining electronic health records will be budgeted annually and reviewed every six months.

Challenge: Funding.

Resolution: Revenues should be positively impacted and with the stability of Medicare reimbursements as public

Another advantage to using the Challenge/ Resolution layout instead of presenting the content in long narrative paragraphs is that the author didn't have to spend a lot of space on the challenges. She referred to potential challenges very briefly and spent most of her valuable space on the resolutions.

perceptions of quality of care and patient concern becomes known.

6. EVALUATION AND TECHNICAL SUPPORT CAPACITY

a. Logic Model

A logic model and narrative is provided in **Attachment 7**. The logic model provides a brief overview of the program, including its intended impact and measurable outcomes.

b. Project Monitoring

The project will be monitored by an evaluation team which includes the Project Director, Data Specialist and external evaluation team. Data will be gathered daily, weekly and monthly and reviewed monthly by the Evaluation Team. Any data elements that appear to be outside the norm will be examined to ensure there was no data entry error. Progress on project outcomes will be examined monthly and shared with the project team, OMC leadership team and other
OMC units transparently to promote the culture of Quality Improvement throughout the hospital. All patient files and patient data will remain confidential.

c. Evaluation

[XYZ] Consulting & Evaluation Services, LLC has been selected by Ozark Medical Center as the external evaluator for the proposed *IMPACTS* program. Comprised of doctorate and Master's level researchers and evaluators, the *[XYZ]* staff has experience in collegiate teaching, project evaluation, and research at the university level. The memorandum of understanding between OMC and *[XYZ]* is included in **Attachment 12**. The *[XYZ]* team currently serves as an external evaluator for HRSA-funded Nursing Workforce Diversity grant- funded projects. The *[XYZ]* team has also evaluated three Partners in Nursing grant funded by the Robert Wood Johnson Foundation as well as two Healthy Start Eliminating Disparities grants. Moreover, *[XYZ]* has served as the Principal Evaluator on more than 125 federal and state funded projects within the past five years alone.

[XYZ] personnel will conduct and oversee the evaluation component, develop surveys as needed, provide project feedback to assure quality, prepare and disseminate findings and reports to staff and other stakeholders, and work in coordination with OMC to prepare all reports and documentation for federal authorities. Quarterly reports will include information on the use of cooperative agreement funding and an assessment of the program implementation, and lessons learned.

[XYZ] will work with the Project Director and team to gather, report, and analyze both qualitative and quantitative data. The evaluation plan is both formative and summative, providing an ongoing dialogue for continuous program improvement (formative), and an assessment of the project's effectiveness in meeting the ***Project IMPACTS*** goals and objectives (summative). Using both Objectives-based evaluation and Utilization-Focused Evaluation (Patton, 1997; Stufflebeam & Shinkfield, 2007), the evaluation team will follow Patton's six-part framework for clarifying program goals proceeding to determination of whether the goals and objectives have been adequately addressed. Throughout the evaluation process, focusing (Patton, 1997) will transpire through which the evaluation team and project team will carefully scrutinize programmatic aspects of the project which have been identified through various data to be problematic or have exceptional value. Focusing on intended use by intended users in a situational context will provide additional insights to both the project's intended and unintended outcomes. This flexibility will allow for the teams to explore issues as they arise while maintaining evaluation measures pre-identified to directly assess the project's stated goals. Along with the use of a variety of instruments (listed below), the evaluation and project teams will also use data triangulation surveys, interviews, and document and content analysis to examine procedures and processes. The evaluation design will seek to determine answers to the following questions: 1) In what ways and to what extent have the project's goals and objectives been met? 2) What unintended outcomes were revealed? 3) What adaptive elements were employed to improve low performing program aspects?

[XYZ] has a team of professionals with depth and breadth capable of serving on this project. Personnel include a Principal Investigator, a survey designer, database manager, SharePoint server administrator, administrative assistant, and a research assistant. The company maintains the following resources which will also be available for the project: 1) online surveying powered by Vovici, 2) SPSS v.17, 3) Scantron clarity 280i duplex scanner, 4) ParScore, ParTest, and eListen software suites, 5) SharePoint server, and 6) Windows Small Business Server 2008.

The key evaluation measures and the associated artifacts to be collected, responsible personnel, and method of analysis are addressed in the program *Workplan* and later in the *Logic Model*. Please refer to the Workplan and Logic Model when scoring this section.

Upon notification of the cooperative agreement award, *[XYZ]* staff and OMC personnel will meet to review and refine the evaluation plan with milestones and target dates to implement a systematic method for collecting, analyzing, and reporting performance and evaluation data. A primary goal will be to ensure that appropriate procedures are in place maintaining a feedback loop through which performance, periodic assessment of progress toward achieving outcomes, and continuous

The author was sure to say that the plan has both formative and summative elements and relies on quantitative and qualitative data. If these terms are unfamiliar to you, the companion *Writing to Win Federal Grants* book has a good chapter on evaluation plans that explains these concepts and more.

Clearly, much of the information in the evaluation plan had to come from the evaluator. But it has been edited and reformatted so that it flows with the writing style employed in the rest of the narrative and responds to RFA queries in the order in which they are asked.

improvement are incorporated.

A variety of instruments and evaluative methods will be employed to track progress toward goals and ascertain quality of services and learning activities provided. Working collaboratively with OMC, the *[XYZ]* Evaluation Team will use the following methods and instruments to track and record the number, type and quality of experiences of collaborating organizations, health professionals, nursing students, and patients. In addition, patient outcomes as related to the goals will be tracked. When available, the project team members will employ valid and reliable instruments that have been described in the research literature. Also, the Project Director will work with the evaluator to obtain IRB approval for the collection and analysis of data for the different components of the evaluation plan that includes patients, students, faculty, and healthcare providers.

Data will be stored on the company's Sharepoint server with hard copies maintained in the company's locked storage facility located within the office. The Sharepoint server is regularly maintained by the server administrator with routine security checks performed daily. All data entry will be checked at each stage in the analysis process. All evaluator-developed instruments will be reviewed by experts for content-validity. Through the use of valid and reliable instruments, reliability is assured. The evaluation team will also make considerations for power analysis, sample size estimation and effect size in order to ensure accuracy.

7. ORGANIZATIONAL INFORMATION

a. Organizational Information

Ozarks Medical Center (OMC) is located in West Plains, Missouri (Howell County). Throughout its half-century of operation Ozarks Medical Center has grown from a 42-bed hospital to a 114-bed complete health care system. *David Jones* is the current President and CEO is committed to making a healthy difference in the lives of those it serves.

OMC's Mission: "At Ozarks Medical Center, our mission is to provide high quality, compassionate health care and promote wellness in the communities we serve."

Our Vision is to be the best rural health care system in America. Our Core Values are:

- Respect: Having a regard for life, dignity and uniqueness of those served and serving.
- Compassion: Expressing care and concern for others through our attitudes and actions.
- Integrity: Maintaining the highest standards of behavior,

encompassing honesty, ethical practices and doing the right things for the right reasons.

- Superior Service: Providing the highest quality care, consistently exceeding our customer's expectations.
- Teamwork: having a unified commitment to demonstrate pride, responsibility and accountability in working together to achieve excellence.
- Enthusiasm: Inspiring others by displaying a positive attitude in all we say and do.

Ozarks Medical Center will serve as the lead organization. Ozarks Medical Center employs approximately 1,300 people and serves a population base of 130,000. Ozarks Medical Center's system includes an outpatient surgical center, an outpatient imaging center, a new 14 bed Emergency Department, outpatient rehabilitation services both centrally and in 3 outlying clinic locations, Cancer Treatment Center, an outpatient and inpatient Behavioral Health Service, a full complement of home care services, a durable medical equipment provider, and a clinics system including 8 rural health clinics, 8 specialty clinics which include, Heart Care Services, Neurology, Nephrology, Pain management, Internal Medicine, Surgery, Rheumatology and Orthopedics. An organizational chart for OMC is provided as **Attachment 4**.

b. Staffing Plan

The Project will be staffed by 0.25 FTE Project Director (Co-Principal Investigator) , 0.5FTE Data Specialist and 1.0 FTE Discharge Advocate. Additional supports to the project will be provided by the External Evaluator (grant funded), OMC's President and CEO who will serve as Co-Principal Investigator (Co-PI – in-kind) , and OMC's information technology department (in-kind). Evaluation will be completed by a team, supervised by OMC's Administrative Council (organizational leadership body) and reviewed with Provider Councils. Evaluation team members include the two Co-PIs: the President and CEO and the Project Director, along with the Data Specialist and Discharge Advocate working with our External Evaluator, *[XYZ]* Consulting.

Qualifications of Co-Principal Investigators (Co-PIs)
Mr. David M. Zechman, President and Chief Executive Officer and Ms. Mary Dyck, Vice President of Clinical Services will serve as co-Principal Investigators (PI) of *Project IMPACTS.*

Zechman holds a Masters in Public Administration (Health Care Administration) from Cleveland State University and has been President and CEO at OMC since 2008. The President and CEO at OMC provides senior leadership and executive management for a stand-alone health care system that includes a 114-bed acute care hospital, 10 specialty clinics, four satellite outpatient departments, nine rural health clinics, a managed

The staffing plan summarizes each key role and indicates clearly which are grant-funded and which the applicant will contribute at its own expense (in-kind).

25-bed critical access hospital, and a full service home care and hospice agency. OMC employs approximately 1300 employees, which includes 50 employed physicians on an active medical staff of approximately 100.

Zechman is an American College of Healthcare Executive (ACHE) Mentor, a Member of the Missouri Hospital Association Trustee Education Advisory Panel (2011), a member of the American College of Healthcare Executive Career Management Network a member and Secretary of the Missouri Hospital Association's Management Services Corporation Board, and a Fellow of the American College of Healthcare Executives. Zechman has presented at several conferences.

Dyck has been a leader within Ozarks Medical Center system for more than 30 years. As a medical center that is accredited by the Joint Commission, an independent, not-for-profit organization that develops standards of quality in collaboration with health professionals, Dyck participates in organizational Joint Commission Leadership Team, Corporate Compliance, and chairs the hospital ethics committee.

Dyck's 30 year career at OMC includes posts as an Infection Control Nurse, Nursing Supervisor, Director of Home Care Services, and now Vice President of Clinical Services. Dyck maintains an active nursing license with the Missouri State Board of Nursing. She serves on the Missouri Department of Health and Senior Services Hospice Advisory Council, is a past member Missouri Association of Home Care Board of Directors, a member of the Missouri Hospice and Palliative Care Association, and the Missouri Medicaid Hospice Advisory. Finally, Dyck serves as a member of the Community Interagency Council, coalition of community service agencies. Dyck's background is well suited to lead this initiative.

Key Staff and Roles
- Mr. Zechman, as a Co-PI, will focus his attention on the Quality Improvement process and evaluation and communication with the Provider Councils.
- As Project Director, Mary Dyck, will have day-to-day responsibility for the project, and will direct administrative and programmatic grant-funded activities. Ms. Dyck along with the Discharge Advocate will provide clinical technical expertise to the grant activities.
- The Discharge Advocate will work regularly with patients whose care is affected by quality improvement efforts.
- The Data Specialist will collect, analyze and report data including PIMS. The Data Specialist and Project Director will have oversight of the evaluation and external evaluator.

Position descriptions for each position are provided in **Attachment 2**.

Biographical Sketches of Key Personnel are provided in **Attachment 3**.

Role of Organizational Leadership
The Quality Improvement efforts will be monitored closely by OMC's senior leadership, also known as our Administrative Council. The role of each of the Administrative Council members is provided below:

- David M. Zechman, FACHE, President & Chief Executive Officer: Chairs all Provider Council meetings. Additionally Zechman will review the periodic and annual PIMS reports and evaluation of *Project IMPACTS* to ensure that goals and objectives are met. Zechman will serve as Co-Principal Investigator for this grant.
- Jeannie M. Looper, Chief Operating Officer: Looper ensures resources are available for the project and, as part of the Administrative Council, reviews the periodic and annual evaluation of the Project to ensure that goals and objectives are met.
- Kim Thompson, Chief Financial Officer: Thompson will be responsible, along with others in her department, for managing the financial responsibilities of the grant. Ms. Thompson will also review periodic and annual evaluation of the Project to ensure that the goals and objectives are met.
- Michael A. Gross, Senior Vice President of Finance and Business Development: Gross will be responsible for supporting and monitoring the sustainability plan. Additionally, Gross will review period reports and annual evaluations to ensure that project goals and objectives are met.
- Dr. Edward R. Henegar, Vice President of Medical Affairs: Henegar will facilitate medical staff adoption of *Project IMPACTS.* He will hold quarterly meetings with medical staff and addresses all Quality Improvement measures with medical staff. Henegar will also review period reports and annual evaluations to ensure that project goals and objectives are met.
- Mary J. Dyck, Vice President of Clinical Services: Dyck will act as the Project Director. As Project Director she will be responsible for supervising the day-to-day activities of the grant, working collaboratively across departments and with consortia members to review the results of data collection, and, using the Model for Improvement, will examine the outcomes and periodically ask the questions consistent with model to ensure that goals and objectives are met and that the project is having the intended impact.

c. Consortium

The consortium consists of established Provider Councils that meet quarterly to discuss transition of care issues. Consortium members include long-term care providers, acute care providers (home health and hospice) and physician practices and clinics (including the area FQHC).

The Provider Councils have played an important role in identifying care issues that have improved patient outcomes. For example, last year OMC noticed an emerging and problematic trend in infection rates among patients transitioned to a long-term care setting. In discussing care with consortium members, OMC learned that a dressing used by orthopedic surgeons that should not be removed until the patient sees the physician for the post hospital visit were being removed in the long-term care setting prior to the follow-up visit. Unfortunately, the long-term care facility did not understand that the dressing should not be removed, and would remove it upon receiving orders from the facility's physician to change the dressing. Now that the long-term care facility understands that OMC is using this new dressing, they are no longer changing the dressings and our rate is now down again.

In another Provider Council meeting, OMC had a staff psychiatrist talk about post hospital depression and how to identify when someone needs medical attention for depression with the Home Health and hospice provider group. As a result, patients are now being screened for depression and treated, as appropriate.

In *Project IMPACTS* the Provider Councils will help us gain community and provider understanding of Quality Improvement, what motivates OMC to adopt a Quality Improvement model and what the results and effects are on patient care and patient outcomes. Additionally, consortium members will help us to identify holes that exist in discharge planning, challenges with our newly re-designed discharge model, and provide us with an additional mechanism to measure increases in patient/family/caregiver health literacy and the result it has on health outcomes.

Provider Councils will meet quarterly. OMC will share evaluation data with the provider council and will engage them in the cycle of Quality Improvement – asking questions that focus on the Plan, Act, Do, Study model outlined in the Model for Improvement, ensuring that there is consistency of understanding surrounding 1) What are we trying to accomplish? 2) How will we know that a change is an improvement? And 3) What changes can we make that will result in improvement?

Results of our external evaluation will be shared broadly and transparently with our Provider Council members who will also be given time to reflect on the achievement toward outcomes and suggest additional modifications to our process that are respectful, inclusive and result in better patient outcomes.

OMC recognizes that our re-designed discharge process extends patient

Whenever possible, share specific examples of previous successes getting a group of partners or a large organization to implement changes in practice or culture. Based on their own experiences, reviewers are often skeptical that good ideas can be successfully implemented.

care beyond its doors and believes that working collaboratively with our Provider Councils will improve patient care, outcomes and create a healthier community.

Annotated Application 2—Faith-Based Applicant Delivering Community Services

US Department of Health and Human Services (HHS) Administration for Children and Families

Funding Opportunity Name and Number

Community-Centered Healthy Marriage and Relationship Grants—
HHS-2011-ACF-OFA-FM-0193

Background of Application

The application for the Community-Centered Healthy Marriage and Relationship Grants was submitted in 2011. The applicant had received a Healthy Marriages grant in a previous round of competition, but prior experience points were not awarded to any applicants. In other words, all applicants were reviewed equally.

The grant recipient is a faith-based organization, a Christian institution of higher education that has a separately funded but affiliated Center for Relationship Enrichment on its campus.

What is important about this fact is that reviewers are not likely to be able to discern a faith-based emphasis from the proposal content. The applicant is able to stay true to its faith orientation, but it is usually not wise (nor productive) for faith-based applicants to write their proposals in the jargon of their tradition.

Since many recipients of this grant are faith-based organizations, the funding agency provided guidance on properly implementing the grant. For example, speakers in programs funded by this grant are allowed to say that the principles they are teaching are drawn from a faith tradition, but they are not allowed to quote verses from sacred texts.

Many of the workshops delivered by this grant recipient take place in churches, because that is where the program leaders have relationships and where willing program participants can be found (and where there are facilities for meals and child care).

But the grant recipient is not allowed to require its clients to participate in any religious activities or identify as a member of a certain faith in order to receive services. The project narrative affirms that the program will be operated in this way.

This proposal also includes a brief budget narrative along with text narrative requesting the award of bonus points. A unique aspect of this proposal is that the applicant was required to provide an assurance that it would meet certain requirements or adhere to certain policies, but the RFA provided no guidance about where these assurances should appear in the document. You will find them at the end of the project narrative and at the end of the budget narrative, set off very clearly with their own subheadings to ensure that reviewers saw them.

We have not included the evaluation criteria to which this proposal was written. The narrative subheadings follow the RFA's evaluation criteria closely. Some comment boxes point out when we had to make a decision about where to put certain information.

Page Budget

We also included here an example of a document we call a "page budget." For this particular funding agency, there was not a page limit on the project narrative. There was a page limit on the total application. All required narrative documents and attachments combined could not exceed forty pages. Fortunately, in this case, the standard forms were not counted in that forty pages.

As we have said frequently, each competition is different. Even if you have applied for the same grant from the same agency in previous competitions, never assume that important details like which pages are counted in a page limit and which are not have not changed.

To help us monitor our application package and decide how many pages we could allocate to our project narrative, we put the page budget into a spreadsheet. The formulas are set up to automatically adjust if the second CV goes to a second page or if the budget narrative can be tightened up to cut a page. The formulas also automatically account for forms included in the total page count.

In this format, the page budget also can double as our application checklist. However, if you prefer, you can create a page budget that lists only documents that will be included in the page-count totals. The page budget is excerpted on the next page, and the annotated proposal begins immediately on the following page.

Sample Completed Page Budget

Contents of HMI Grant	Form Type	Est # of Pgs	In Page Count?	Running Total
Forms - required for all applications				
SF-424	Form	4	N	4
Additional Congressional District	Attachment	1	N	5
SF424a - Budget Form	Form	4	N	9
SF-424 Project/Performance Site Locations	Form	1	N	10
SF-424B Assurances for Non-Construction Programs	Form	2	N	12
SF-LLL Disclosure of Lobbying Activities	Form	0	N	12
Application Documents				
Abstract	Attachment	0	Y	12
TOC	Attachment	0	Y	12
Project Narrative (required)	Attachment	29	Y	41
Budget Justification (required)	Attachment	5	Y	46
Logic Model	Attachment	0	Y	46
CV- Project Director	Attachment	2	Y	48
CV- Other Project Person	Attachment	1	Y	49
SF-424 Other Attachments Form - only contains the attachment list (up to 15)	Form	0	N	49
501(c) 3 Letter	Attachment	2	Y	51
MOU(s)	Attachment	1	Y	52
Total Pages		52		
Less those not counted against max		12		
Total Counted Pages (must not exceed 40)		40		

Project Title: Healthy Marriages Initiative
Applicant Name: John Brown University
Applicant Address: 2000 W. University Street, Siloam Springs, Arkansas 72761
Contact Phone Numbers: (000) 555-1212 phone (000) 555-1212 fax
E-Mail Address: xxxxxx@jbu.edu
Web Site Addresses: www.liferelationships.com and www.nwamarriages.com

These headers to the proposal's abstract were required by the RFA.

Project Summary/Abstract

John Brown University's Center for Relationship Enrichment (CRE) proposes to significantly strengthen marriage relationships in our region through the *Healthy Marriages Initiative*. To meet the wide array of our target population's needs, CRE will implement six of the eight Allowable Activities—I. Advertising campaign, II. Education in high schools; III. Marriage and relationships skills education; IV. Pre-marital education; V. Marriage enhancement and skills training; and VII. Marriage mentoring. Our target population includes low-income (TANF/TANF-eligible residents) and Hispanic and Native American communities on the Arkansas/Oklahoma border. Marriages here are at high risk for divorce. Arkansas' divorce rate is second in the nation, while Oklahoma's is 7th. Both states have high rates of families in poverty. During the project period, CRE will engage, equip and empower 3,460 people in our nine-county service area to *build and sustain healthy, satisfying and lifelong marriages* by reaching the following measurable objectives:

The abstract's content was guided by RFA requirements. Its text is single-spaced as directed by the guidelines.

- Objective 1: At least 65% of participants who complete* Relationship, Pre-Marital, Marriage or Workplace education will demonstrate improved competencies in the target relationship and communication skills.
- Objective 2: At least 65% of single individuals who complete Relationship and/or Pre-Marital education will demonstrate increased competency in determining the health and safety of relationships.
- Objective 3: Couples who complete Pre-Marital, Marriage or Relationship education or mentoring will report an increased understanding of skills leading to higher marital satisfaction.
- Objective 4: Strategic marketing and recruitment efforts will result in more than 3,400 individuals receiving Marriage/Relationship education during the project period.
 * *Complete=attending 75% of a multi-week/multi-hour program's sessions or hours*

The abstract was only one page long in the proposal as it was submitted. In addition, the abstract and the table of contents were counted in the page limits. This is not always the case. Follow the rules of your particular RFA.

The Project will be delivered through free voluntary activities that implement marriage education services and skills-based interventions specifically designed to increase the likelihood that healthy marriages will form or that existing marriages will experience measurable long-term marital satisfaction and stability. To remove participation barriers and strengthen recruitment/ retention, CRE will offer all project event/activities free of charge and will provide wrap-around support services (e.g., childcare, meals, and transportation assistance), modest completion incentives, cultural/language-appropriate content tailored to Hispanic and Native American participants, job/career advancement services, case management, and referrals to outside community services.

[A Table of Contents was Included Here in the Application Package]

I. PROJECT APPROACH AND WORK PLAN

Consistency with Stated Purpose & Allowable Activities of FOA

Consistency with Stated Purpose. John Brown University (JBU), a

private university located on the Arkansas/Oklahoma border proposes to

deliver the *Healthy Marriages Initiative* through its Center for Relationship

Enrichment (CRE). CRE, a division of the university, has 14 years'

experience providing education and resources to cultivate healthy marriages

and relationships, regionally and nationwide. The project is consistent with

the FOA's stated purposes in that it will "offer a broad array of services

designed to promote healthy marriage at the community level." A

comprehensive marketing and recruitment plan targets TANF

recipients/TANF-eligible members of our community at local TANF

offices, Workforce Development offices, community-based/social services

organizations, churches, schools and community festivals. The proposed

marriage and relationship education efforts are combined with case

management and supportive services to reduce barriers to participation for

those with economic need. All Marriage or Relationship education services

The 29 double-spaced pages allowed for the project narrative gave the author barely enough room to respond to every item.

With such tight space restrictions, this narrative has no introduction. It launches directly into responding to the first evaluation criterion.

The opening paragraph also serves as a summary of project activities as a preview for the reviewer. The activities listed in the last sentence are required by the RFA. By re-stating them, the author linked the project to the "FOA's stated purpose."

contain elements of financial literacy/budgeting, stress and anger management, parenting skills, domestic violence and maltreatment in addition to communication skills, the benefits of marriage, and recognizing healthy relationships.

Consistency with Allowable Activities. To meet the wide array of our target population needs, CRE will implement six of the eight Allowable Activities—I. Advertising campaign (based on a community needs assessment), II. Education in high schools; III. Marriage and relationships skills education; IV. Pre-marital education; V. Marriage enhancement and skills training; and VII. Marriage mentoring. The table below summarizes the Marriage, Relationship and Workplace skills education that we will deliver and the relationship of these services to Allowable Activities. Please refer to the Logic Model and Timetable for numbers served, frequency, outputs and outcomes. Target Audiences include TANF/TANF-eligible residents, Hispanics and Native Americans, based on the community in which service is to be delivered.

Summary of Project Services/Events by Allowable Activity			
Services/Events	Target Audience	Format	Allowable Act.
Relationshipology	High School & Alternative School students (at-risk)	Two 4-hour sessions of content, role play, activities	#2
Within Our Reach	Couples	Eight weekly 2-hour sessions of marriage education/enrichment	#3, #5
Within My Reach	Single individuals; Low-income college students	Eight weekly 2-hour sessions of relationship education	#3
Valentine's Day Event	All – married or single	Seven hours of educational content; dinner-dance follows	#3, #5

The reviewers have not been introduced to the planned services yet. Since the author wanted to follow the outline suggested by the evaluation criteria, this table provided a quick introduction to the key services and explicitly linked each service on which grant funds will be spent with an allowable activity number from the FOA.

Pre-Marital Seminars	Unmarried Couples	Day-long educational seminar teaching marriage skills	#4
Pre-Marital Small Groups	Unmarried Couples	Eight weekly 1-hour small group marriage skills learning	#4
Marriage Mentoring	Married Couples	Nine monthly 2-hour sessions of couple-to-couple marriage strengthening	#7
Winning the Workplace Challenge	Employed, under-employed, and unemployed (different cohorts)	Day-long seminar on communication and other important workplace skills	#3
LifeSkills Classes	Any adult or youth over 16	Individual 90-minute classes on topical issues (budgeting, parenting, child safety, job and listening skills, etc.)	#3
Project Marketing	Adult residents of service area	Billboards, radio spots, news-paper ads, web and transit ads	#1

Need for Services and how Services Meet Need

Need for Services. Newspapers, blogs and television news report over and over again—Oklahoma and Arkansas have some of the highest divorce rates in the country. Arkansas is second highest (after Nevada), and Oklahoma currently seventh.[1] When the Pew Research Center analyzed the Census Bureau's 2008 American Community Survey (ACS), the resulting report led off with this opening salvo:

> *"In Arkansas and Oklahoma, men and women marry young—half of first-time brides in these states were age 24 or younger on their wedding day. These states also have above-average shares of women who divorced in 2007-2008."[2]*

Sometimes, you are allowed to single-space quotations, if the RFA explicitly states this is allowed. That was not the case for this application.

---

[1] Centers for Disease Control, National Vital Statistics Report, 2009
[2] "The States of Marriage and Divorce," Pew Research Center, 2009 http://pewresearch.org

Alarmingly, the same report revealed that 10% of all Arkansans and Oklahomans who have ever been married have had at least three spouses. People who marry that often clearly value marriage and desperately want it to work, but just as clearly, they are failing to build healthy marriages.

Target Service Area & Target Population. Ideally located in Siloam Springs, Arkansas—less than one mile from Oklahoma and one of the region's newest and largest tribally-owned casinos—we have selected nine counties immediately surrounding us as the project target area. They were chosen on the basis of existing relationships and the sense of "regionalism" that causes people to perceive the area as one far-flung community rather than two separate states. The border town of Siloam Springs (pop. 14,872), serves as a vital economic center. Hundreds of Oklahomans, as well residents of Benton and Washington County Arkansas, commute to Siloam Springs for work, education, health care, shopping—and gambling.

The service area was also selected because of the high population of TANF/TANF-eligible residents. Eastern Oklahoma especially is ravaged by high poverty rates, ranging from 20.1% to 25.5%, compared to 16.4% nationwide (US Census, American Community Survey [ACS], '09). The area is rural and agricultural, with few opportunities for employment. The Oklahoma counties encompass the headquarters of the Creek Nation and the Cherokee Nation, the majority of whose members live within a 45-minute drive of CRE. The two closest counties have Native populations of 34% and 37.9% (ACS, 2009). To our east, the Arkansas counties experience vast

> The second sentence of this paragraph goes beyond dry statistics and leads the reviewers back to personal emotions they can probably relate to.

> This paragraph attempts to paint a picture of a rural service area that the reviewers have no familiarity with and explain why the applicant believes its target participation numbers are reasonable.

disparities in wealth and a Hispanic population that jumped 780% between

1990 and 2000.[3] In one Arkansas county, the "Millionaire Effect" (incomes

of wealthy executives of Fortune 500 companies such as Wal-Mart and

Tyson Foods) obscures the fact that most of the rest of the population is

underemployed, earning low wages. Over the last few years, industry and

manufacturing have announced at least six major layoffs, with another 200

people losing their jobs at one plant this month. In Siloam Springs, the

poverty rate is 11.1%, compared with 9.9% nationally, and median family

incomes are almost $13,200 less than the national level (ACS, 2009). The

combined effects of these stressors on family life are revealed in the

divorce/ separation rates in our service area counties, as the table below

illustrates. (Please note: we list ethnic status only for those counties in

which our services target that ethnicity.)

> The text here introduces the table below. Both include some of the same information, but presented differently, to appeal to varied learning and communication styles.

Economic and Demographic Indicators of Target Population					
	Ark. Counties	**State: Ark**	**Ok. Counties**	**State: Okla.**	**US**
Separated/ Divorced	14%	15%	15%	15%	12%
Divorce rate per 1,000 people	5.2–7.3	5.7	4.1-7.0	4.9	3.5
Families in Poverty	7.8%*-15%	14%	15.2%-22.1%	12.2%	13.5%
Median Household Income	$39,131- $50,377*	$38,542	$28,100- $35,700	$41,700	$51,425
Hispanic	13.1%-14%	5.4%	n/a	n/a	15.1%
Native American	n/a	n/a	16.3%- 37.9%	6.6%	< 1%
Census: 2009 American Community Survey *County income skewed by Millionaire effect					

> Notice that the table compares data for the service area with state and national data to show a comparison.

Explanation of How Proposed Program will Meet Need. The proposed

---

[3] U.S. Census (1990, 2000), analysis by the Pew Hispanic Center, 2005

project will meet the need for accessible services that help couples who choose marriage to strengthen their marriages and that help single members to develop strong relationship skills. We will provide high quality, evidence-based education using trained facilitators to convey age-appropriate relationship skills to high school students, marriage education and relationship skills programs, pre-marital education and marriage skills training, marriage enhancement and skills training for married couples, marriage mentoring for at-risk couples, and marketing to recruit participants (Allowable Activities I, II, III, IV, V, VII). CRE is uniquely positioned to meet the need for marriage education, marriage skills, and relationship skills education. Leveraging existing relationships, CRE will maximize partnerships with local government, community, and faith-based organizations that maintain strong links among TANF recipients and other low-income persons. CRE will recruit low-income participants through its partner organizations, in many instances delivering services on-site at a social service agency or community center to make the education more accessible to low-income residents receiving services at those locations. The selected curriculum has been designed with the needs of low-income populations in mind and has proven successful with TANF recipients. We are committed to recruiting bi-lingual Latino/a facilitators, using Hispanic-centered curricula in the Hispanic community and using Native facilitators to lead culturally-appropriate curricula in classes targeting the Creek and Cherokee Nations.

> Since it has been a few pages since the activities were mentioned, the text reminds reviewers how the project's services align with the FOA's required activities.

> This sentence subtly anticipates potential reviewer concern about the ability to reach different ethnicities.

Specific Objectives for Achieving Meaningful Improvement for Participants

The four specific Objectives relate directly to the Allowable Activities. Objectives express overarching desired outcomes and drive specific, measurable performance targets (Outputs and Outcomes) for all services. Per-service targets and outcomes appear in the Logic Model (p.17). How Objectives are measured is described on the next page and in the Assessments section p. 9.

- Objective 1: At least 65% of participants who complete[4] Relationship, Pre-Marital, Marriage or Workplace education will demonstrate improved competencies in the target relationship and communication skills. (AA 2, 3, 4, 5, 7)

- Objective 2: At least 65% of single individuals who complete Relationship and/or Pre-Marital education will demonstrate increased competency in determining the health and safety of relationships. (AA 2, 3, 4)

- Objective 3: Couples who complete Pre-Marital, Marriage or Relationship education or mentoring will report an increased understanding of skills leading to higher marital satisfaction. (AA 3, 4. 5, 7)

- Objective 4: Strategic marketing and recruitment efforts will result in more than 3,400 individuals receiving Marriage/Relationship education during the project period. (AA 1)

> The first three objectives are outcome-based, with a specific performance target measuring a change in the people served.
>
> Notice we specified that we would measure changes among participants who complete the education program. This keeps us from being held accountable for changes among all participants, even those who drop out or do not attend all sessions.

> Objective 4 is an output measure, not an outcome, but this is outweighed by three strong outcome objectives.

---

[4] Complete=attending 75% of a multi-week program's sessions or 75% of the hours of a workshop

Objectives are Clear and Measurable

Objectives are clearly stated and clearly related to the FOA's purpose and intent. Objectives 1-3 are measurable because they indicate improvement on measurable and quantifiable skills . Objective 4 names a measurable, numeric output. Pre-/post-tests will be administered to participants in all Marriage/Relationship Education activities and will measure improvements in skills and knowledge appropriate to that activity and its target population. For example, while high school students and engaged couples in a pre-marital program will demonstrate improvements in "relationship and communication" skills, some results or skills measured will be different for these two populations. When these measurements are combined, they contribute to the overall improvement sought by the Objective. The figure below illustrates how such measurement works related to Obj. 2:

> Without room to go into similar detail for every single objective, the author chose to illustrate how what is measured differs among different populations using one objective as an example.

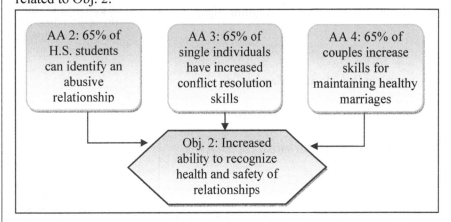

Detailed Description of How Proposed Services will be Implemented

1) Participant Recruitment/Retention & Considering Needs of Target Population. Strategies to recruit and retain participants are grounded in an understanding of the needs of our service area target populations. One

barrier to achieving project objectives is the public's lack of awareness of

marriage/relationship services. So a campaign of billboards, ads on radio

and in other media, and staffing a booth at select community/ethnic festivals

will promote Project Activities. Advertising materials tailored to reach

Hispanic and Native American populations will be disseminated via

Spanish language and tribal media. Other strategies include pro-actively

seeking referrals from social-service agencies and the TANF office;

offering services at no charge in accessible community locations; providing

flexible program schedules, childcare, and meals; and offering modest

incentives to participants to complete classes. Low-income college students

and high school students will be referred to our voluntary on-campus

services by their counselor. Recruitment/retention strategies for Hispanic,

Native and low-income populations include culture- and language-

appropriate materials, attending holiday festivals and community events,

assigning an individual Coordinator to recruit from each population, and

using class facilitators drawn from the target communities.

2) Program Access & Voluntary Participation Requirements. CRE is

committed to helping all individuals who wish to improve their relationship

skills and create healthy marriages. Therefore, project activities are open to

anyone desiring to participate, including mothers and expectant mothers.

We do not discriminate on the basis of the potential participant's race,

gender, age, disability, or religion in determining eligibility, benefits, or

> Marketing activities are a big budget expense. In this section, the author emphasized how marketing is essential to the project's success. It was good luck that the RFA asked how the applicant will recruit participants.

services provided, or applicable rules. Participation in any and all project activities is completely voluntary, which facilitators will emphasize at the beginning of class sessions. Registration materials will also state that activities are voluntary.

3) Screening & Assessments. Adequate but not intrusive screenings and assessments are performed when relevant and vary by population and the type of activity. All participants in educational activities will be screened for domestic violence issues, according to the protocol recommended by the Northwest Arkansas Women's Shelter. Any exhibiting domestic violence issues will be referred immediately to counseling or a shelter. Other screenings are minimal and generally performed by the agency/program referring participants to us. We do administer a client-intake form for participants in all activities except the 90-minuete LifeSkills classes. The intake form will determine possible need for supportive services. Assessments are administered to measure the effectiveness of project activities, allowing us to report on Outcomes to ACF and adjust strategies if targets are not being met. In a few instances, validated instruments are available commercially, and these are named. In other instances, we shall contract with an experienced contractor to design a psychometrically-sound assessment tool to measure changes in the targeted knowledge, skills and abilities of project participants. Screenings and pre-, and post-assessments are summarized here:

- High School students: identified as at-risk in some way by school

> Since the applicant seemed to be a little weak on screenings and pre-assessments, part of the author's strategy was to go into lots of detail about the ones they did have.

counselor and referred to voluntary program on campus; pre/post

instrument administered (to be designed)

- Low-Income single college students: screened and referred by their

  Student Support Services case manager; pre/post instrument

  administered (to be designed)

- Adults in marriage or pre-marital education: client intake form,

  referrals from other agencies when relevant; assessed by Couple

  Checkup (marriage and pre-marital only)

- Adults in workplace skills education: intake form; assessed by an

  instrument to be purchased or designed

In addition to client assessments, CRE will contract with a local firm to

conduct a community needs assessment in Year 1, which will gather

information about our community's awareness of and need for marriage and

relationships enrichment activities. It will identify services, gaps in services

and potential barriers to participation. The information received will inform

the project's marketing campaign as well other recruiting efforts and how to

deliver services.

Since the community needs assessment is a big line item in the budget, it is previewed here.

4) Allowable Activities. The *CRE Healthy Marriages Initiative* will

address six of the eight Allowable Activities, as was described on p. 1-2:

Activities 1, 2, 3, 4, 5, and 7. All services offered are directly related to one

or more Allowable Activity.

Because this item had already been answered more than once, a minimal response here was acceptable. However, don't ever just skip over a section that you think you've already answered.

5) Matching Participants to Program Components. In general, adults

self-select project activities (e.g. signing up for a one-time workshop or an

8-week marriage enrichment program). In some cases, the fit is obvious: high school students attend the high school program while engaged couples attend pre-marital workshops. However, facilitators will also recommend additional services or programs directly to participants on the basis of their interactions with them. In addition, the participant intake forms and on-going case management are designed to allow particular needs and issues to surface, such as a need for transportation assistance to attend classes or a need to be referred to Workforce Services for workforce education.

6) Support Services Provided, When Provided and Justification for Approach. Although the project's marriage and relationship programs are free of charge, low-income couples may still face certain barriers and obstacles to attending activities or events. Such barriers may include the time or resources to cook and serve meals, lack of affordable or reliable childcare, or high transportation costs. Also, many area residents still suffer from high unemployment rates, which can cause additional stress on relationships. Registration intake forms capture current income and ask participants to indicate if they fear childcare, transportation or other issues could prevent their participation. In response, the proposed project provides meals and childcare at many events, transportation assistance, and a range of job/career services. We have signed agreements with community agencies who have childcare programs to allow us to offer our multi-week programs at those facilities where childcare is provided. Class facilitators can provide small denomination gas cards (or transit passes) to eligible

> Basically, this paragraph says that the applicant has made an educated guess about what its program participants may need and has planned and budgeted accordingly.

participants to alleviate transportation burdens. Job and Career

Advancement services consist of teaching job skills to high school and

college audiences; providing workplace skills/career advancement

education to those who are unemployed, underemployed and employed

(different cohorts for different populations); and referring participants to the

extensive services provided by the Department of Workforce Services.

Class facilitators will promote these supportive services, and case managers

will offer specific services when issues surface in personal communication

with participants.

Potential Barriers to Participation and How Addressed

As was explained, two of the most likely barriers to participation

include childcare and transportation, and they will be addressed as

described above. Other potential barriers include irregular work schedules,

the rural nature our service area, and cultural and/or language barriers.

Irregular Work Schedules—Individuals working in the

manufacturing/processing and hospitality/service sectors (such as tribal

casinos) usually work schedules other than 9-to-5. They may work

graveyards, or have four days on/two days off, with the schedule changing

each week. Thus, participants could find that events/ activities conflict with

their work schedules. To address this, CRE will offer flexible formats

including day, evening, and weekend sessions.

Rural Service Area—CRE's nine-county service area is 6,400 square

miles. Despite the presence of a few population centers, large swaths of this

> This short paragraph is one way to deal with the repetitiveness of many RFAs.

> Since this is not the need section, citations aren't necessarily needed to prove these assertions. These were mostly developed from common sense and experience serving a rural population.

area are extremely rural. Small, winding roads of varying quality, lack of reliable vehicles and high fuel costs can all combine to isolate area residents. In addition to providing fuel cards and transit passes to participants with financial need, we will host events and activities in a variety of locations strategically positioned throughout the service area. When possible, CRE has selected facilities on transit routes, but we usually bring services close to the residents in small-town community centers or churches.

Cultural Appropriateness-Language and cultural differences may form an additional barrier. Therefore, we made sure to include Hispanic and Native American leaders in project planning, seeking their counsel, connections and recommendations. A contract Hispanic Outreach Coordinator and a Native American Outreach Coordinator, who must come from the community they serve, will leverage their experience and relationships in their respective communities to generate interest in project Activities. We will also recruit Hispanic and Native class facilitators to deliver services. All marketing and recruitment materials will use culturally appropriate photos and content, and all print and web text will be provided in English and Spanish. Events and activities will be offered in locations central to communities with high Hispanic and Native populations. When possible, curricula proven to be effective in strengthening marriages and relationships among these people groups will be used.

Healthy Marriage Curricula and Other Strategies to Be Used and Rationale

> Don't spend time talking about possible barriers to program participation if you don't have multiple strategies for addressing those barriers.

CRE will depend upon a combination of commercially-available, evidence-based curricula as well as curricula our qualified staff have developed, tested and refined over the years. See attached resumes and the "Organizational Capacity and Experience" of this proposal for evidence of staff qualifications to write and deliver curricula.

Services/ Events	Curriculum	Rationale	Evidence-based
High School Education	Relationshipology (CRE designed)	Targets teens with skills for relationships with friends, parents, siblings, teachers, coaches, employers; addresses common teen-adult conflicts	Scores increased in emotional self-awareness, self-acceptance, anger management, empathy and listening
LifeSkills Classes	Varies based on topic – No formal curriculum needed	Topical courses taught by qualified facilitators or guest speakers (such as Credit Counseling of Arkansas)	Not applicable in most cases; strong outcome figures support Credit Counseling's content
Marriage and Relationship Education	Within Our Reach or Within My Reach – Commercial product	Professionally adapted from well-known, evidence-based PREP curriculum to target low-income couples and singles	The only marriage/ relationship content in the "National Registry of Evidence-Based Programs and Practices"; multiple citations 1996-2011 report strong positive outcomes
Jobs/Career Advancement	Winning the Workplace Challenge	Professionally adapted from PREP to target workplace relationship skills	
Valentine's Day Event	n/a –guest speaker instead	Speaker chosen based on qualifications/ publications	Speaker's references or qualifications reviewed
Pre-Marital Seminars	I Choose Us (CRE Developed)	Professionally designed based on staff experience	Successfully used with 1,250 participants

With so many different curricula to describe and to provide a rationale for, it was much easier to summarize the content succinctly in a table than to attempt to describe each narratively.

If a chosen curriculum was not necessarily evidence-based, the table emphasized its relationship to an evidence-based curriculum.

Pre-Marital Small Groups	Foundations for a Healthy Marriage (CRE Developed)	Based on established relational assessment "The Couple Checkup" and validated Prepare/Enrich content	Journal articles[5] and longitudinal study[6] strongly validate effectiveness
Marriage Mentoring	Growing a Healthy Marriage (CRE)		

> Taking time to do your research to find citations for evidence-based program activities is worth it and can make your application stand above others.

Reasonable Rationale or Research Basis for Program Models

The program model of offering a variety of non-threatening entry points into Marriage/ Relationship education services is based on our 14 years of experience with what works in our community. Ninety-minute LifeSkills classes can serve as a springboard for participation in subsequent, more intensive education, just as a dating workshop can bring participants back for pre-marital small groups. Another essential element of this program model is that project services have been designed and curricula selected to address each target population's unique characteristics and needs (such as high school students versus low income parents). Research indicates that relationship outcomes are stronger when participants are engaged over a period of time (such as 8-weeks or several months), and it is our desire to see as many people served by such educational services. However, the reality is that many couples and individuals will not make that kind of commitment. That is why other options range from 2-hour to day-long events.

> This paragraph does a good job of demonstrating that project activities have been designed thoughtfully. It is especially important in a project like this one, which has numerous activities and services which could seem unconnected if the narrative doesn't link them together for the reviewers.

---

[5] *Marriage & Family: A Christian Journal,* 2003, Vol.6, No. 4, 529-546.
[6] "Integrating PREPARE/ENRICH & Couple Communication Programs: A Longitudinal Follow-Up Study," 2007

Program Logic Model

Logic Model –CRE Healthy Marriages Initiative				
Assumptions	**Inputs**	**Activities**	**Outputs**	**Outcomes**
Beliefs about how program works	*To deliver Activities, requires:*	*Services/ Activities to be delivered:*	*Products & deliverables of Activities:*	*Results & long-term changes*
- Anyone can improve relationship skills - Low-income persons face barriers to participation - Low-income persons need services and teachers who understand their needs - Ethnic communities have higher trust with leaders from their own communities - Strong relationship skills improve employment success - Leveraging existing resources is efficient and effective	- Qualified staff - Evidence-based curricula - Variety of targeted services to meet different needs - Strategies to reduce barriers - Access to persons to be served - Trained pool of class facilitators - Community Needs Assessment - Funding - A whole-person, strengths-based approach - Strong partnership relationships with other agencies	- Conduct needs assessment/ gap analysis - Promote Activities - Select and train class facilitators - Deliver high quality marriage and relationship education - Provide wrap-around support services and case management - Teach LifeSkills content - Provide career skills education - Deliver services thru partners - Make/ receive referrals to/ from partners	- Assessment done; sets baseline for use of services - Numbers Served: • 225 high school students • 660 LifeSkills participants • 216 Within Our Reach • 105 Within My Reach • 400 individuals at Valentine's Day ea. year • 150 Workplace Challenge • 100 premarital seminars • 36 small groups • 20 mentorees - At least 2,500 case management contacts made - Est. 300 ref'd to employment services - Ads/ billboards placed - Festivals/ events exhibited at	- Increased awareness & use of marriage / relationship education - 65% of program completers a. demonstrate increased competencies in: • commu-nication • listening • conflict-management b. increased understanding of • applying skills to employment • unhealthy relationship patterns • realistic expectations of marriage - Decreased divorce rates - Strengthened relationships

This logic model is the first place where the application documents the numbers to be served by major project activities.

For this application, the author chose to fit the logic model onto a regular portrait-oriented page. The author of this proposal prefers to keep as much proposal content as possible in portrait orientation so that reviewers don't have to keep rotating pages back and forth. But this is just a personal style decision. Sometimes a table's layout is driven by how much space the table takes up, where page breaks occur, or how many columns are required.

Work Plan and Timeline

This project is based upon a detailed action plan, which includes quarterly projections of the accomplishments to be achieved—the number of services offered and the number of people served. The Timeline below indicates Year 1 activities by quarter. Following that table is a summary of Year 2 and 3 activities, contingent upon the availability of funds.

Quarterly Timeline for Year One (2011-2012)				
Task/Service	Oct.-Dec.	Jan.-Mar.	Apr.-June	July-Sept.
Conduct Needs Assessment				
Attend ACF Entrance Conference				
Finalize MOUs				
Dom. Violence/Child Training				
Recruit and Train Contractors				
Evaluate & Develop Curricula				
Design Assessment Instruments				
Bilingual Website Development				
Relationshipology (H.S. Education)				
Recruitment Advertising				
Premarital Workshops & Sm. Groups				
LifeSkills Classes				
Valentine's Day Event				
Within Our Reach (couples)				
Exhibit at Events/Festivals				
Recruit and Train Marriage Mentors				
Submit Reports to ACF				

Summary of Year 2 & 3 Activities. Contingent upon funds, educational services and advertising/ recruitment activities begun in Year 1 will continue in Years 2 and 3 at the same frequency and intervals. Services first undertaken in Year 2 include Q1: Within My Reach instructor training (curriculum similar to Within Our Reach, but specifically targets single adults), Q2-4 Within My Reach workshops, and Q1: first cohort in Marriage Mentorship groups begin.

> Without coming right out and saying it, this timeline contains some project management tasks that aren't direct services to participants, but are important to a successful project.

Collaborations, Partnerships and MOUs

The community-centered approach of this project relies on collaborative relationships to leverage resources, build community support, and increase access to our target populations. The organizations listed below have agreed to display materials promoting Project services and to accept referrals from CRE. However, most are providing more than a referral-only relationship. The table below summarizes CRE's collaborative relationships and indicates whether a signed MOU or third-party agreement has been received (will finalize MOUs by Dec. 1, 2011).

Partner Role/Contribution	Agency/Organization	Agreement Status
Training, protocol review, program advising, guest speakers	Children's Advocacy Center	Signed MOU attached**
	Children's Safety Center	Verbal confirmation
	NWA Women's Shelter	Written confirmation of willingness to sign MOU
Permission to deliver services to students on campus	Siloam Springs H.S. & Alt. School	Signed MOU on file
	Bentonville High School	Written confirmation
	Mountainburg High School	Verbal confirmation
Targeted classes on-site, facilities to offer services, childcare	Jones Center for Families	Signed MOUs on file
	Samaritan Center	
	Life Source	
Program advising; Hispanic community connections	Hispanic Women's Organization of Arkansas	Verbal confirmation
Program advising; Native American community	Cherokee Human Services	To be secured upon funding
	Creek Nation Human Svcs (Okla.)	To be secured upon funding
Delivery of Challenge course	Arvest Bank & J.B. Hunt	Verbal confirmation
	DaySpring Cards (Hallmark)	Written confirmation
Guest speakers, referrals	Child Support Enforce. Services	Written confirmation
	Credit Counseling of Arkansas	Signed MOU on file
	SARPA (Sexual Assault Recovery & Prevention Agency)	Verbal confirmation
Access to clients to deliver services; promotion of services; referrals//	Single Parent Scholarship Fund	To be secured upon funding
	Workforce Services (Ark & Okla)	Verbal confirmation
	Samaritan House	Signed MOU on file
	TANF Office	To be secured upon funding

Being able to put something in each box for partners was an important goal. The author nagged the applicant to secure the strongest commitments possible, even if only a verbal promise. The narrative is honest, but weaker commitments are mostly buried in the middle.

L. Job/Career Advancement Services

Feasible Strategy to Provide Job/Career Advancement Services. The strategies for providing job/career advancement services are clear and feasible. We are most qualified to provide services related to developing strong relationship and communication skills that can improve one's chances of being hired or advancing in a career. High school and college student classes include content on relating to co-workers and supervisors. Winning the Workplace Challenge will be delivered to already-employed individuals on-site at their place of employment (agreements secured for Year 1 locations) and to unemployed persons at a local community center. For career and skills assessments, literacy, basic education, GED preparation and other such services, we refer participants to the nearest Workforce Development office.

How Job/Career Components are Suited to the Population and Integrated into Program. The job skills and career advancement components of this project are adapted to specifically apply to members of our target populations, such as high school students wishing to become employed, currently-employed individuals wishing to sharpen their skills, and unemployed persons who can use the relationships and communication skills training our services provide as a key supplement to other job services from Workforce Development. These services are fully integrated into our program and interact seamlessly with other project services and events.

> Job services were required by the FOA, but didn't seem like a fit with the program's other priorities. Again, the narrative is honest about the applicant's strengths and promises to refer clients needing these services to more qualified providers.

Job/Career Services as Only Part of Larger Marriage/Relationship Education Program. As the budget and project work plan make clear, job/career services comprise only part of an overall comprehensive program involving marriage education and marriage and relationship skills. Marriage/Relationship enrichment remain this program's primary purpose.

Domestic Violence and Child Maltreatment

Strategy for Preventing & Addressing Domestic Violence & Child Maltreatment. CRE has developed a feasible, well-thought out strategy for addressing domestic violence and child maltreatment. At the time of intake, clients receive written and verbal notice they are providing informed consent that we will intervene if we suspect any danger in their relationships. An immediate intervention can prevent further violence. For cases of child maltreatment, CRE will follow our established Child Protection protocol for identifying signs and symptoms and following the referral process. All CRE staff will review domestic violence/child maltreatment protocols and resources from the National Resource Center on Domestic Violence. All personnel will receive ongoing domestic violence/child maltreatment training (see p. 24).

Consultation with Experts. As early as June 2006, CRE consulted with two domestic violence agencies in Northwest Arkansas—the Northwest Arkansas Women's Shelter and the Peace at Home Family Shelter regarding our domestic violence protocol. In 2011, the Northwest Arkansas Women's Shelter reviewed and updated the protocol. We consulted with the

Since faith-based programs, in particular, are often perceived as overlooking domestic violence issues in order to preserve a marriage at all costs, the author decided to state very strongly that this was not the culture at the applicant organization.

Although the table that appeared earlier in this proposal (beginning with "Partner Role/ Contribution") lists several partner relationships, the section here addresses partners specifically in the context of domestic violence and child safety.

Children's Safety Center for issues regarding children's safety and tailored our protocol accordingly.

Collaborative Partnerships. CRE will collaborate with experts from the Northwest Arkansas Women's Shelter and Children's Safety Center for safety planning, making service referrals, making connections to appropriate assistance, and increasing protections for individuals/families impacted by domestic violence. All project staff will be trained by these organizations, and both organizations have committed to providing guest speakers in classes upon invitation. For more detail on the training to be provided, see p. 24.

Comprehensive Response Plan. All personnel will be trained in the procedures for responding to disclosures of domestic violence or child maltreatment. If a participant discloses domestic violence/child maltreatment to any project personnel, that person will be immediately referred to a domestic violence agency with a physical location in our community (such as Northwest Arkansas Women's Shelter, Peace at Home Shelter, Children's Safety Center). Staff will follow procedures recommended by NWAWS for safe disclosure and referral to services, give participants resources for contacting help, and minimize barriers to reaching a shelter.

Effective Case Management

We have developed a robust, well-planned and feasible strategy for providing effective case management to program participants. Except for high school and low-income college students (in Student Support Services program), whose case management is handled by school personnel, we will provide case management to participants in all Marriage and Relationship education. Case management will be delivered by the class facilitators who will be trained in effective follow-up and on the array of service resources available for referral. During multi-session programs (several classes/ meetings over weeks or months), facilitators will call participants an average of every two weeks to review progress on the skills being learned and ask if participants anticipate any obstacles to continued attendance. On the basis of this, facilitators may refer participants to a social service or workforce agency, offer to secure childcare, send a gas card or bus pass, or make other referrals as seem appropriate. Participants who miss sessions will be contacted with an enthusiastic invitation to return next time, and the case manager will attempt to elicit information about what prevented the participant from attending the time that was missed.

Such hands-on case management is expensive, since it is personnel-heavy. Fortunately, it is expected by the funder since it is the FOA that asks us to explain how we will do effective case management.

Strategy for Providing Support Services is Feasible, Robust and Well-Planned

Our strategy for providing support services has been thoroughly described on the preceding pages. We have chosen a careful balance of what we are qualified and capable of providing (such as childcare, transportation assistance and career skills development) and leveraging a robust system of community resources and agencies from which participants can receive additional services (food bank, medical care, extensive job preparation services). Because of this careful planning and allocation of budget funds for support services, the plan is feasible to implement.

II. ORGANIZATIONAL CAPACITY AND EXPERIENCE

Organizational Capacity to Oversee Federal Grants, Fiscal Controls and Governance

John Brown University is well-positioned to manage Federal grant funds, successfully managing $0 million or more in Federal grants annually, including a five-year Healthy Marriages grant of $000,000 per year. The annual operating budget exceeds $00 million, and the university adheres to GAAP standards that ensure that funds are expended and accounted for properly. The Business Office manages university finances through its qualified finance personnel-- Comptroller, Vice President for Finance and Administration and multiple Business Office staff. Grant funds are placed into restricted accounts and spent on pre-approved grant purposes only. All purchases require a purchase order or invoice submitted by an authorized Budget Officer, and all requests for reimbursements require receipts to be submitted. The Business Office reconciles Accounts Payable, Accounts Receivable, and Payroll against approved budgets. An A-133 audit is performed annually by outside auditors, as required by Federal regulations. JBU is governed by an independent Board of Trustees with an active Finance committee. The Board carefully reviews financial statements at all of its meetings.

Financial Management Experience and Records System Allow Effective Control of Funds

JBU has been in operation since 1919, successfully managing growing

This section contains relatively standard text about organizational capacity. Once you develop such text, you can often use it in multiple applications, with minor modifications to fit the requirements of the RFA to which you are responding.

budgets during its 92-year history. Financial practices are described in the

paragraph above. Those are supported by a campus-wide data system for

accounting that produces standard financial reports, from institution-wide,

down to each department or grant project. Each Budget Officer receives a

monthly report from the Business Office to reconcile against his or her own

financial records, and the University produces annual financial statements

for distribution to the Board of Trustees and the general public through its

Annual Report. In addition, the Project Director has more than 25 years'

experience as a Budget Officer and four years of experience managing

Federal grants.

Current Capability to Organize and Operate Proposed Project Effectively and Efficiently

JBU has decades of experience managing and operating Federally-

funded and other large projects with budgets exceeding $1 million. The

institution takes pride in delivering excellence while stewarding resources

carefully. The CRE is in its 14th year of organizing, operating, and assessing

programs that develop healthy relationships. During the past five years, the

team has delivered the successful Northwest Arkansas Healthy Marriages

grant, fulfilling all grant requirements on time and within budget.

Significant planning has gone into designing project activities and ensuring

that the project is adequately staffed to reach proposed objectives.

Project Organizational Chart

The organizational chart below clearly illustrates the relationships

among project personnel, including sub-contractors (marked as "Sub:").

This section and the next are similar to the organizational capacity section from the previous section. The first time you write them, you may be tracking down information and need careful review by other staff for accuracy. But then, you can continue to use versions of the text with only minor tweaking in future applications.

The Project Director reports to the institutional president. Professional staff report to the Project Director, and support staff assist professional staff and the Director. Qualified, trained facilitators will be contracted to lead/teach classes. Members of the Hispanic and Native American Communities shall be recruited and contracted on a part-time basis to build relationships and serve as project liaison to their respective ethnic communities. Finally, a JBU faculty member shall be contracted to re-design intake assessments, design psychometrically-sound post-tests, and perform data analysis services.

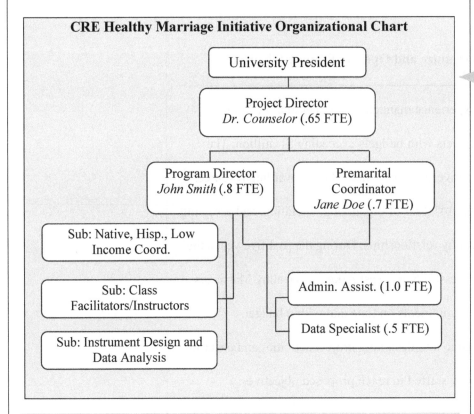

CRE Healthy Marriage Initiative Organizational Chart

University President

Project Director
Dr. Counselor (.65 FTE)

Program Director
John Smith (.8 FTE)

Premarital Coordinator
Jane Doe (.7 FTE)

Sub: Native, Hisp., Low Income Coord.

Sub: Class Facilitators/Instructors

Sub: Instrument Design and Data Analysis

Admin. Assist. (1.0 FTE)

Data Specialist (.5 FTE)

This organizational chart is an example in which the author included the names of key personnel. Notice that each person's time commitment on the grant is also indicated in the chart.

Experience in Relationship, Marriage and Other Services

CRE staff have offered workshops on relationships and premarital/ marital skills across the country in rural communities, high schools, colleges, community agencies, churches and corporations. Combined,

project staff have 65 years of experience in private counseling and marriage

enrichment and more than 35 years of teaching university courses on

relationships and marriage/family counseling. In 2005, CRE developed

Growing Healthy Relationships (GHR) for university students seriously

dating, engaged or married. The 8-hour program is <u>now offered in more

than 20 universities across the country</u>. Several thousand students have

developed their relationship skills, with focus on communication and

conflict-management. Assessments indicate growth in communication,

conflict management and relationship satisfaction among participants.

Since a good portion of the curriculum the applicant proposes to use will not be purchased commercially, but was developed in-house, the author worked here to establish the qualifications of the developers.

During the prior Healthy Marriages project, CRE provided premarital

education to more than 2,500 individuals, marriage enrichment to more than

3,500 couples, and small-group leadership training to more than 600 people.

All programs were offered free or charged only nominal fees; 42% of

project participants fell below the Federal poverty level (incomes of

$30,000 or less). Aggregate data reveal that participants increased their

communication and conflict resolution skills. Married couples experienced

increased couple satisfaction, while single individuals demonstrated gains in

identifying healthy relationships. Similarly, 92% of high school students

served reported they learned information they could instantly apply to

healthier relationships.

Experience Related to Domestic Violence and Child Maltreatment. We

consulted with two women's shelters in 2006 to develop protocols. Every program and service addresses domestic violence and child maltreatment, contact and hotline information for shelters. Curricula in all multi-hour /-day sessions include sessions on recognizing healthy/unhealthy relationships, safe ways to leave, and how to get help. All project staff have received training in domestic violence.

Experience Related to Effective Job and Career Advancement Programs. CRE staff have more than 20 years' experience teaching communication, conflict management and emotional and relational intelligence on the corporate level—skills that have direct impact career success. We have delivered these services for organizations including U.S. West, Tyson Foods, J.B. Hunt Transport and Wal-Mart. Also, JBU operates Career Services office with personnel who teach workshops on resumes, interviewing, and job search skills and who are trained to administer career assessments. These staff are available to serve as guest speakers in Project classes.

Experience and Accomplishments of Project Partners

While the CRE Healthy Marriages Initiative depends on its partners for use of facilities, access to populations or guest speakers, no CRE partners are responsible for key project services. Project staff and trained sub-contractors will deliver all marriage and relationship education services. The few exceptions to this are childcare and certain job/career services. When classes are held in community facilities like the Jones Center for Families (Washington County, Ark.), we will contract with the in-house

It would be a common mistake to make the first statement in this section and stop. Make the statement that essentially says the section is not relevant to your project, but do your best to answer the spirit of the question anyway. If you can't point a reader to a cross-reference, never leave a section under-developed.

childcare service. In the case of the Jones Center, KidsPlus offers term child care while parents use the Center. When no such services are available in a chosen delivery site, CRE will contract with local churches in good standing with the Safe Sanctuary childcare policies (which requires, among other things, background checks for all childcare workers, annual training, the presence of two adults with children, and so on). Regarding job services, CRE will refer unemployed or underemployed participants needing job skills development to the local Workforce Development Office, community college or community-based organizations with experience delivering career and aptitude assessments, GED preparation, English classes, literacy training, or math tutoring.

Plan to Train Program Staff to Address Domestic Violence and Child Maltreatment

As has been described above on p. 18, CRE has consulted with experts in domestic violence prevention and intervention for the past five years and will continue to do so. A Domestic Violence Protocol and Child Protection Protocol guides staff in the appropriate action to take. Northwest Arkansas Women's Shelter will provide half-day domestic violence training for project staff that covers topics such as what constitutes domestic violence, Arkansas law, recognizing domestic violence issues in relationships, appropriate responses to disclosures, and safety planning. NWAWS's agency-developed, research-based curriculum has been delivered to law enforcement, education, community-based organizations, and other agencies for ten years.

All project staff will attend training by Children's Safety Center and complete the Stewards of Children training, a nationally recognized evidence-based model developed by *Darkness to Light* educating adults on the steps they can take to prevent, recognize and react responsibly to the reality of child abuse. CRE staff will then train class facilitators and marriage mentors.

Community-Centered Approach

CRE depends upon its long history (and that of the University as a whole) and deep roots in the community to be successful in its program offerings. After 14 years of delivering marriage and relationship enrichment programming, project staff have developed extensive relationships with area churches, faith-based organizations, community-based organizations, and schools. We draw from the pool of university alumni (of whom there are thousands in our community) for contacts with business, churches and non-profits to identify and recruit participants, deliver activities at their locations, and to provide in-kind and other support to project activities.

In addition, the project is community-based in that project activities are selected and designed in response to a community needs assessment to be performed in Year 1. The survey firm will identify existing services, gaps in services, potential barriers, community awareness, and the topics of most interest to community members. The results of this assessment will enable us to better allocate our service delivery among the varied communities in the 9-county region.

> Work with your program people and partners to come up with details as specific as the name of the training program whenever possible. Specifics and details always strengthen your program descriptions.

III. PROJECT MANAGEMENT AND STAFFING

Description of Leadership Structure, Accountability Lines and Project Director

CRE has established a system of fiscal responsibility, which includes staff with expertise in fiscal monitoring. This system ensures compliance with internal policies and agency regulations. CRE will utilize existing procedures and controls, which have been refined and proven effective over our 14-year history, while following all applicable regulations of the US Department of Health & Human Services to ensure full compliance with funding requirements.

Leadership Structure. "Dr. Counselor" is Executive Director of CRE and a senior administrator at JBU. Upon funding, Dr. Counselor will assume the position of Project Director (65% FTE) reporting directly to the University President. Mr. John Smith will be appointed Program Manager (80% FTE), and Ms. Jane Doe the Premarital Coordinator (70% FTE). These Key Staff will report to the Project Director. An Administrative Assistant and Data Specialist will report to and support both the Program Manager and Premarital Coordinator. Mr. Smith will supervise contractors, to include three Outreach Coordinators targeting communities of potential participants (Hispanic, Native, and Low Income), workshop facilitators and group leaders, and an assessment expert to design assessment instruments and analyze report data.

Documented Experience of Proposed Senior Staff

CRE's senior staff have more than 65 years of combined experience in

Yes, this section does seem to repeat content from the text introducing the organizational chart and the chart itself. Since the author wanted to follow the outline suggested by the evaluation criteria, even when that required repetition, she chose to word the response to this prompt a bit differently in the hopes that one version or the other would garner the points from all reviewers.

private counseling and marriage enrichment and more than 35 years of combined experience teaching in university marriage and family counseling programs. In addition to expertise in the field, the senior staff also have a documented track record of managing successful federally funded projects including—during the past five years—*Northwest Arkansas Healthy Marriages*, which fulfilled all grant requirements on time and within budget. Brief summaries of staff experience are provided here; additional information is provided in the Resumes uploaded as attachments.

Project Director. Dr. Counselor has more than 30 years' experience in premarital, marital and family counseling, including several years as a senior psychologist with a group of family practice physicians and more than 12 years as clinical director of a large non-profit counseling center. Dr. Counselor has founded and directed several counseling centers and has gained extensive experience effectively managing staff, projects and large budgets. For the past 25 years, he has traveled nationwide to speak and teach on issues concerning healthy marriages and relationships.

Program Manager. John Smith is a doctoral candidate in Marriage and Family Therapy, emphasis in marriage counseling. Mr. Smith founded a community clinic in Texas where, for two years, he oversaw all aspects of clinic administration for six full-time therapists and three interns. He has taught marriage and relationship seminars and workshops nationwide.

Premarital Coordinator. Jane Doe holds an M.S., emphases in Marriage and Family Therapy and Community Counseling. She is an Associate

Absent any guidance from the RFA, the applicant defined for itself who comprised "senior staff." Since all other personnel on the grant were either sub-contractors or administrative support, this was an easy distinction to make.

Annotated Application 2—Faith-Based Applicant Delivering Community Services   213

Counselor and Associate Marriage and Family Therapist licensed by

Arkansas. Jane was a CRE graduate fellow, then served in a counseling

practice and as a school-based mental health therapist before joining the

CRE staff.

Identification of Key Staff, Responsibilities and Job Descriptions

Key Project Staff are the Project Director, the Program Manager and the

Pre-Marital Coordinator. No Key Staff positions are vacant. The Table

below summarizes the responsibilities of Key Staff and lists the

qualifications required should any staff positions come open in future.

KEY STAFF	PROJECT RESPONSIBILITIES	POSITION QUALIFICATIONS
PROJECT DIRECTOR (.65 FTE)	*Management/Oversight* • Provide comprehensive oversight of grant project • Supervise fiscal management, reporting, and assessment of grant objectives • Supervise and evaluate other Key Staff • Authorize all expenditures, maintain budget control, request and track funding draw downs • Ensure that grant reports are generated accurately and on time *Implementation/Direct Services* • Design and evaluate program curricula • Recruit and hire staff and contractors • Develop Marriage Mentor program; recruit and train Mentor couples • Develop & maintain community partnerships • Provide direct services to participants through workshops, seminars, and training	• Master's in marriage/ family therapy or related field required, doctorate preferred • Five years administrative experience, including project and budget management; grants management preferred • Five years of experience supervising personnel • Three years' teaching and/ or speaking experience • Strong interpersonal & communication skills • Demonstrated team leadership ability
PROGRAM MANAGER (.80 FTE)	• Provide day-to-day management and implementation of program activities and events • Oversee Community Needs Assessment • Manage advertising and recruitment	• Master's degree in marriage/family therapy or related field required • Three years' experience

It may sound obvious, but make sure current staff you propose to release to serve on the project meet the qualifications you list in your job descriptions. Some funding agencies require you to hire only staff who meet the requirements as written in the proposal.

	campaign; staff exhibit booth at conferences and festivals • Develop and maintain community partnerships • Coordinate with assessment contractor to design and test assessment instruments • Supervise, train, and evaluate project staff and contractors (see org. chart) • Provide direct services to participants through workshops, seminars, and training	supervising others, managing funds • Three years' teaching and/ or speaking experience • Strong interpersonal & communication skills • Demonstrated team leadership ability
PRE-MARITAL COORD (.70 FTE)	• Design and deliver pre-marital project services to the general community and college students • Produce and edit project web content, videos, and other electronic recruiting and teaching content • Coordinate production of bi-lingual print and electronic media with translation service • Staff exhibit booth at conferences and festivals • Provide direct services to participants through workshops, seminars, and training	• Master's degree in counseling or related field required • Two years' delivering pre-marital education • Strong interpersonal & communication skills • Demonstrated ability to work collaboratively

Staffing Plan Links Expertise Required with Qualifications of Proposed Staff

The Staffing Plan is closely related to the expertise and qualifications expected of Key Staff and the education and experience of staff members proposed to fill these positions. As has been described, the existing staff are highly qualified, all holding graduate degrees in counseling or marriage and family therapy, and all having several years of experience delivering services of the sort proposed by this project. See the table above for required qualifications and education and see p. 26-27 for a discussion of the education, qualifications and expertise of proposed staff. Resumes of Key staff that correspond to the Organizational Chart are uploaded as an attachment as required.

Activities Not Allowable Under This Grant

JBU understands allowable and unallowable activities and affirms that

NO unallowable activities shall be undertaken, including abstinence

education, non-programmatic capacity building or train-the-trainer

activities. JBU commits to not include fee-for-service for activities.

IV. PERFORMANCE MEASUREMENT AND ASSESSMENT

Willingness to Document and Report Performance Using OFA's Measures

John Brown University, through the Center for Relationship

Enrichment, affirms its willingness to document and report performance

using OFA's uniform measures.

Processes to Support Performance Documentation, Tracking, and Reporting

CRE has a five-year track record of successfully tracking and reporting

data under a prior Federal grant. There are well-established procedures for

collecting data for every event—registration forms, sign-in sheets, Outreach

Coordinator contact logs—and so forth. Forms and sign-in sheets are

submitted to the project's Data Specialist within one week of an event

(contact logs submitted monthly) for entry into CRE's database. This

database is able to track participants by name and also includes relevant

demographic data including ethnicity, marital status, and income levels. The

database allows the Data Specialist to produce reports to document project

Outputs (such as number of events held, ads run, partnership meetings,

These two assurances (activities not allowable and willingness to document and report) were required statements. However, the RFA gave no guidance regarding where they should appear. The author put them here, where she thought reviewers would not miss them but they don't interrupt the flow of the project description. It is not unusual to have to make strategic decisions about how to respond to some RFA requirements that lack specific guidance.

participants in services, etc.) and Outcomes (results of assessment tools). In addition, the university's robust accounting software system allows CRE to produce accurate and timely financial reports.

Willingness to Participate in Federally-Sponsored Evaluation

JBU and the CRE affirm their willingness to participate in all aspects of any Federally-sponsored evaluation as a condition of accepting funding.

V. BUDGET

Budget Justification for Operating Expenses is Consistent with Objectives/Activities

Project budget funds are reasonable and necessary to carry out Activities and reach Objectives. The budget is discussed by Federal expense category, beginning with Personnel and Fringe.

Personnel and Fringe. Salaries for project personnel are based on JBU's standard salary scale. Fringe benefits are calculated at 28.14% of salaries.

Position	Effort on Project	Project Wages
Project Director	65%	
Program Manager	80%	
Premarital Coordinator	70%	
Administrative Assistant	100%	
Data Specialist	50%	
Subtotal - Personnel		**$238,071**
Fringe (28.14% on full time staff)		$66,993
Total Sal & Fringe		**$305,064**

Travel. Travel consists of attendance at the required ACF entrance (3 staff) and annual awardees conferences (2 staff), 3 staff to a national marriage enrichment conference, partial cost (airfare only) for 3 staff to attend Georgia marriage conference, 10 staff and contractors to become certified

> Since the budget requested a lot of travel, the author chose to explain who was traveling and why. While it's not required to name the professional development conferences staff will attend, if you do know the names, be as specific as you can be. We often say "a conference such as" to keep ourselves from being tied to an exact event.

as Within Our Reach instructors and 6 to train as Winning the Workplace

Challenge instructors (required to use curricula). All travel rates are based

on actual airfare from Northwest Arkansas Regional airport and Federal per

diem tables for lodging, meals and incidentals.

Purpose and Calculation	Who Attends	Cost
ACF Conf: (air $650, meals $60/day x 5 days, lodging $180/ea x 4 nights, mileage 48 mi x $.55, parking $7/day x 5) ALL times 3 plus on-site ground transport total $100	3 required staff	$5,296
Within Our Reach Instructor Certification: (air $650, meals $60/ day x 5 days, lodging $180/ea x 4 nights, mileage 48 mi x $.55, parking $7/day x 5) ALL X 10 plus rental van $150/day x 4	10 staff and contract facilitators	$17,920
N.A.R.M.E. Conf: (air $650, meals $60 x 4 days, rooms $180 x 3 nights, mileage 48 mi x $.55, parking $7 x 4 days) ALL times 3 plus rental car $60 x 4 days	3 Key Staff	$4,695
Win. the Wkplace Chall. Certification: (meals $60 x 2 days, rooms $130-1 night) ALL times 6 plus JBU Van 450 mi x.64 =$288)	6 staff and facilitators	$1,790
Second ACF Workshop (air $650, meals $60 x 4 days, rooms $180 x 3 nights, mileage 48 x $.555, parking $7 x 4 days) ALL times 3 plus ground transport = $100	2 staff	$3,070
Airfare attend Georgia Marriage Conference $680/ea	3 Key Staff	$2,040
Total Travel		**$34,811**

Supplies. Supplies contains any item with a per-unit purchase price of less

than $5,000. Supplies are categorized into Printing, Educational Services,

Recruitment/Awareness, and Other/General. Year 1 only start-up costs

include technology for presenting classes and exhibiting at events, one

laptop, four tablet computers, and domestic violence/child maltreatment

training materials.

> You will notice abbreviations and imperfect punctuation used in the budget tables. These were used because of extremely tight space restrictions that may not be as evident in this format.

> This competition required that applicants include the year-one budget only. Here and in the table, the budget points out start-up costs that would not be repeated in subsequent years of the budget.

Printing			Cost
Posters $3.5 x 200; flyers $.18 x 2500; brochures $1.25 x 4000; postcards $.31 x 12,000; kiosk posters 3 x $1,200; banners $3,000; business cards $450; letterhead $1,700			*$18,620*
Workshops - Classes - Services	**# Served**	**# Events**	**Cost**
Education Supplies (all services): screen $300; wireless mics $500; 4 remotes $240; projector $2500; display $1,900; table drapes $300; 5 curricula packages $1,750			*$7,490*
Relationshipology - @ $37 per participant = manuals $9, food $8, incentives $20	*30*	*3*	*$3,330*
Dating Workshop - @ $32/per participant = manuals $11, food $5, packet/copies $6, incentives $10/ea	*30*	*1*	*$960*
Pre-Marital Workshops (8 hrs) - $50/per = manuals $4, breaks/lunch $20, incentives $20, packet/copies $6	*50*	*3*	*$7,500*
Community Classes (1 hour) - $9/per = $6 manuals,$3 snacks	*15*	*12*	*$1,620*
Premarital Small Groups (8-wks) - @ 36/ per = manuals and test $20, completion incentives $10, packet/copies $6	*12*	*3*	*$1,296*
Within Our Reach (8-wks) - @ $144/per = manuals/skills tools $24, packet/copies $6, meals $8 x 8 wks ($64), incentives $50	*12*	*5*	*$8,640*
Winning Workplace Challenge Wkshop - @ $47/per = manual & skills reminder tools $25, packet/copies $6, lunch $16	*15*	*2*	*$1,410*
Valentine's Day Event (6.5 hrs education and social time) – [details redacted]	*400*	*1*	*$30,756*
Mentors - curriculum 6 x $300, recruitment 30 people @ $40/per (materials, food); mentor training 20 people @ $83/per			*$4,660*
Gas cards or transit passes value $10 (need-based at discretion of case manager - 50% of individuals served)	*976*	*50%*	*$4,880*
Recruitment/Awareness Events			**Cost**
One-Time Start-Up Exhibitor Supplies–10' x 10' conference booth $3,200, 3 "close-up" projectors $1,200/ea, 2 lit. racks $450, table-top display $575, lights $450			*$8,275*
Consumable exhibitor supplies per event: give-aways, door			*$8,400*

We don't always do this, but there were so many supplies in this budget that the author grouped them in categories. The categories also served to tie the budget items back to project activities that had been discussed in the project narrative.

prizes $1,200/event x 7	
Other Supplies	**Cost**
1 Laptop - Dell Latitude E6320 13" w/ docking station, monitor, peripherals, case	*$2,580*
4 tablets for staff/contractors with peripherals, case, and data plan - $1,250/ea	*$5,000*
Resources: books, subscriptions, journal articles	*$3,000*
General office supplies: toner, paper, pens, highlighters, notebooks, Scantron forms (session evaluations and assessment instruments)	*$2,600*
Domes. Violence & Child Mal Treatment Training - 8 x $195 x 2 workshops	*$3,120*
Total Supplies	**$105,517**

Contractual. To make efficient use of project resources, CRE will contract

with firms and personnel on a limited basis to perform tasks such as the

<u>Year 1 only</u> Community Assessment, the annual ad campaign, website

development and translation. Prices are based on actual bid or our

experience. Three Outreach Coordinators will be contracted on a part-time

basis to perform targeted outreach to low-income, Hispanic and Native

populations. Class facilitators paid on a per class basis are needed since

some classes require multiple facilitators or may be running simultaneously.

Native and Hispanic class facilitators are needed to teach in those

communities.

Item and Purpose	**Cost**
Community Needs Assessment (Adair Creative) – survey, gaps analysis, report	*$35,000*
Project website - design, development, events database	*$18,000*
Bilingual website - culturally appropriate imagery	*$18,200*
3 - Outreach Coordinators (40 hr/mo x 12 mo x $20/hr)	*$28,800*
Awareness/Recruitment - *6 billboard production $900/ea; 6 billboard sites $1200/ ea x 6 mo; radio ads (7 stations x 50 spots x $53.26/spot); newspaper ads (costs vary total $6,000); website ad $300/mo; transit ($1,000/mo x two systems x 6 months)*	*$96,040*

> Since the budget for "Awareness/ Recruitment" was such a large line item, this table provides more details on what was included in that line item.

Translation Services (print materials, ads, flyers, etc.)			$8,000
Workshop Facilitator Stipends	**# Events**	**Stipend**	**Cost**
Relationshipology	3	*$1,000*	*$3,000*
Premarital Workshops	3	*$300*	*$900*
Winning Workplace Challenge	2	*$400*	*$800*
LifeSkills Classes	12	*$150*	*$1,800*
Within Our Reach	5	*$1,500*	*$7,500*
Special Event Stipends	**# Events**	**Stipend**	**Cost**
Valentine's Day (National level speaker, incl. travel)	1	*$5,500*	*$5,500*
Creek & Cherokee Festivals Special Guest at Booth	2	*$1,200*	*$2,400*
Childcare	**# Events**	**Charge**	**Cost**
LifeSkills Classes	12	*$60*	*$720*
Within Our Reach (2 hrs/wk x 8 wks = 16 hrs)	5	*$500*	*$2,500*
Total Contractual			**$229,160**

Other. Items are placed here according to RFA guidance, including local travel costs like mileage and meals, conference registration fees, rent and general office costs.

Item	**Cost**
Training Fees/Conf. Registrations: Within Our Reach 10 x $700/ea.; NARME Conf. 3 x $350; Workplace Challenge 6 x $300	*$7,000*
Exhibitor Fees- 2 Bridal Fairs, 2 Tribal Festivals, Cinco de Mayo, Health Fair, ALE Conf. - $1,000/ea x 7 events	*$7,000*
Venue Rentals - (V-Day, Within Our Reach, Pre-Marital Workshop)	*$11,199*
Local Travel within 6,400 sq. mile service area – 14,204 miles @ $.55/mi	*$7,757*
Lodging in Service Area – 10 nights at $99/night	*$990*
Staff local meals - Partnership meetings, during trade shows, seminars, day-long events as applicable (meals avg. $20/ea)	*$2,880*
Jones Center Rental $150/mo x 12 – work and supplies space for Hispanic Coordinator and facilitators delivering education at Center	*$1,800*
Postage - postcard campaign qty. 12,000 * .44 = $5,280; general postage/ shipping $1,500	*$6,780*
Staff cell service pro-rated - ProjDir/ProgDir/Pre-MarCoord 3 x $90 cell plans x 12 = $3240 / 2 = $1620	*$1,620*
Total Other	**$49,876**

Notice that the budget items are very specific regarding what was being purchased. You are not bound to purchase the exact items mentioned or attend the exact events listed, but the additional detail proves you have carefully planned your project. You would be expected to expend your grant funds on items very similar to those you describe in your budget.

Reasonable, Feasible and Proportional Nature of Budget to Project Scale

JBU is applying for a grant in Range B - $300,000-$799,999. The proposed annual budget of $724,428 is reasonable and feasible, given that CRE is completing a five-year Federal Healthy Marriages grant reaching only the four Arkansas counties for $540,000 annually. Expanding into Oklahoma with new education and wrap-around supportive services, and focused outreach to the Hispanic and Native communities adds reasonable costs to the project budget.

Allocation of Funds Among Proposed Program Components

The line-item detail p.1-4 clearly states how funds are allocated among project components.

Cost of Project are Reasonable, Allocable, and Program-Related

Project costs are reasonable given the large 9-county service area to be reached in person and by the promotional campaign. The cost per participant in educational services and events are reasonable and directly program-related. All expenditures can and will be clearly allocated to approved Project Activities.

Budget Includes Funds for All Required Items

The budget includes funds for required travel to the ACF entrance conference and annual meeting in Washington, DC.

Commitment to Comply with Non-Supplanting Provisions of the FOA

No project funds will supplant currently available resources or current budgets for Project Activities. JBU commits to comply with the FOA's non-

This section and the section titled "Costs of Project are Reasonable," were required by the RFA. Even though they may seem redundant, the author included them both and answered them slightly differently.

This section header has a typo that wasn't discovered until after the grant was funded. While we do our best to produce perfect proposals, mistakes sometimes slip through. Fortunately, they are rarely fatal!

supplantation provisions.

VI. BONUS POINTS

Providing Comprehensive Services Including Job & Career Advancement Services

As the Project Narrative clearly explains and illustrates, the CRE Healthy

Marriages Initiative will provide comprehensive marriage and relationship

skills education and training, targeted to a range of ages, ethnicities and

marital status. Job and Career Advancement Services are included.

Detailed, Reasonable and Feasible Plan to Partner with Local Child Support Agency

The local office of the Arkansas child support agency has communicated

via email their enthusiastic support of the proposed project. They will send

agency staff to serve as guest speakers at appropriate events. They were

unable to obtain a signed MOU/third-party agreement from the state office,

but attributed that to a normal bureaucratic delay and assured us that the

MOU will be available within 120 days of funding.

> Since there were no instructions about where in the application to address bonus points, and there was not an attachment for bonus points, the author elected to place them prominently at the end of the narrative. Whenever possible, it's best to assert your bonus points and explain why you should receive them. Never assume that a reader will award them automatically.

Annotated Application 3—Working with Tight Space Restrictions

Environmental Protection Agency (EPA)

Funding Opportunity Name and Number

Regional Indoor Air Environments: Reducing Public Exposure; Funding Opportunity Number—EPA-OAR-ORIA-12-04

Background of Application

The application for the Regional Indoor Air Environments Grant Program was submitted in April 2012. The applicant and its partners had submitted federal grants in the past and had informally collaborated. This was the applicant's first application to this funding agency.

The application was included in the workbook to demonstrate effective ways in which to communicate a significant amount of information within tight space constraints. The narrative is very tight, with little luxury for white space. Judicious use of tables and extensive subheadings help point the reviewer to all required content.

Finally, understanding that the funder was not the typical health and human services funder, the grant proposal focused on both visually showing and narratively discussing what changes would occur within the community as a result of the grant and, more importantly, how. The author made sure to state that the application aligns with EPA goals. She also provided strong comparison data to demonstrate need in the community.

Information from the RFA

In the interest of space, we can't include the entire RFA. (See the CharityChannel website for this book to review the RFA.) We can, however, bring to your attention two elements of interest.

In the *Writing to Win Federal Grants* book, we told you that sometimes agencies will indicate that grants will be spread across the United States. Below, we provide an excerpt from the RFA that is a perfect example of a federal agency defining how it intends to make awards across the country. Note that the actual amount of each grant varies by region in addition to the number of awards to be made by region.

Such information may inspire you to collaborate with other eligible organizations to increase your chances of receiving funding if your region is receiving only a small number of awards (as was our situation). Two eligible organizations collaborating on a grant application may have a better chance of receiving some of the funding for their region than if they decided to compete against one another.

EXCERPT...

Eligible Funding Ranges and Anticipated Number of Awards

EPA Region	Available Funding	Anticipated Number of Awards
Region 1	Proposals for projects taking place in a defined geographic area in Region 1 (e.g., neighborhood, city, county or state) cannot exceed $50,000 for the two year project period and projects with a Region wide focus cannot exceed $70,000 for the two year project period.	Three to six assistance agreements.
Region 2	Proposals must be between $50,000 and $150,000 for the two year project period.	One to four assistance agreements.
Region 3	Proposals must be between $50,000 and $120,000 for the two year project period.	One to three assistance agreements.
Region 4	Proposals must be between $50,000 and $120,000 for the two year project period.	One to two assistance agreements.
Region 5	Proposals must be between $50,000 and $120,000 for the two year project period.	Two to four assistance agreements.
Region 6	Proposals must be between $25,000 and $50,000 for the two year project period.	One to four assistance agreements.
Region 7	Proposals must not exceed $60,000 for the two year project period.	One to four assistance agreements.
Region 8	Proposals must be between $40,000 and $160,000 for the two year project period.	Two to three assistance agreements.
Region 9	Proposals must be between $20,000 and $70,000 for the two year project period.	Two to four assistance agreements.
Region 10	Proposals must be between $30,000 and $90,000 for the two year project period.	One to three assistance agreements.

The next excerpt contains the evaluation criteria to which the proposal was written. They are very brief. Unfortunately, as is common with federal funding announcements, other instructions (both general and specific) were provided elsewhere in the RFA. The author used both the evaluation criteria that are reproduced below and the added instructions to guide her writing. This is why reading the RFA from cover to cover is important. When the evaluation criteria are brief, it is even more important to look for other instructions.

EXCERPT...

V. APPLICATION REVIEW INFORMATION

All applications will first be reviewed against the threshold eligibility factors in Section III.C of the RFA by regional staff. Applications that pass the threshold review will then be evaluated based on the criteria below by regional review panels—each region will review the eligible applications for projects to be performed within their region. In addition, EPA Region 9 is the lead region for the Navajo Nation and any proposed project for work in the Navajo Nation, regardless of state boundaries, will be reviewed by Region 9. Applicants should explicitly address the following criteria as part of their application package submittal. Each application will be rated under a points system, with a total of 100 points possible.

A. Evaluation Criteria

Criteria	Points
1. <u>Regional Priorities:</u> Under this criterion, the Agency will evaluate the quality and extent to which the narrative proposal includes a well-conceived and high quality strategy for addressing at least one of the regional priorities that apply to the region where the project will be performed as described in Section I. B. **(25 points)**	25
2. <u>Environmental Results – Outputs and Outcomes:</u> Under this criterion, the Agency will evaluate: **(i) (10 pts)** whether the proposed project goals, objectives and activities are realistic and demonstrate the ability to achieve substantial and measurable outputs and outcomes, **(ii) (10 pts)** whether the proposed project describes practical and feasible activities, methods, and materials to achieve each goal and objective, and identifies baseline information to measure the efficacy of each activity, and **(iii) (5 pts)** the effectiveness of the applicant's plan for tracking, measuring, and reporting on progress toward achieving expected project outputs and outcomes. Applicants should include a milestone chart demonstrating a reasonable time schedule for the execution of tasks associated with their proposed project.	25
3. <u>Disproportionately Impacted Communities:</u> Under this criterion, the Agency will evaluate the extent to which the proposed project is likely to benefit segments of the population that are or have been traditionally disproportionately and/or adversely impacted by environmental hazards or risks, such as minorities, children or low-income individuals, as described in Section I.B. Scope of Work.	10
4. <u>Community Effect:</u> Under this criterion the Agency will evaluate the extent to which the proposed project activities address environmental and/or public health concerns affecting the community or region where the project is to be performed.	5

Criteria	Points
5. Partnerships: Under this criterion, the Agency will evaluate the extent to which the proposed project activities describe plans to utilize formal or informal partnerships or collaborate with others to perform the project and how these partnerships will make the project more effective. Proposals for projects that have listed partners should include commitment letters from every listed project partner; if not, it may affect the applicants score for this criterion. Applicants who propose to use partners must note the provisions in Section IV.G and H including how proposals with identified partners will be evaluated.	5
6. Programmatic Capability and Past Performance: Under this criterion, applicants will be evaluated based on their ability to successfully complete and manage the proposed project taking into account their: **(i) (5 pts)** past performance in successfully completing and managing the assistance agreements described in Section IV,C,2.b.iii. of the announcement, **(ii)(5 pts)** history of meeting the reporting requirements under the assistance agreements described in Section IV.C,b,2.iii, of the announcement, including: whether the applicant submitted acceptable final technical reports under those agreements and the extent to which the applicant adequately and in a timely manner reported on their progress towards achieving the expected outputs and outcomes under those agreements; and if such progress was not being made whether the applicant adequately reported why not. Note: In evaluating applicants under the above criterion, the Agency will consider the information provided by the applicant and also may consider relevant information from other sources including agency files and/or prior/current grantors (e.g., to verify and/or supplement the information supplied by the applicant). If you do not have any relevant or available past performance or past reporting information, please indicate this in the proposal and you will receive a neutral score for these subfactors (a neutral score is half of the total points available in a subset of possible points). **If you do not provide any response for these items, you may receive a score of 0 for these factors**	10
7. Staff Expertise/Qualifications: Under this criterion, the Agency will evaluate the following factors: **(i) (5 pts)** the applicant's staff expertise/ qualifications, staff knowledge, and resources or the ability to obtain them, to successfully achieve the goals of the proposed project, and **(ii) (5 pts)** the description of the applicant's organization and experience relating to the proposed project.	10
8. Budget/Resources: Under this criterion, the Agency will evaluate whether the proposed project budget is appropriate, reasonable, and cost effective to accomplish the proposed goals, objectives, and measurable environmental outcomes in addressing regional priorities, and provides an approximation of the percentage of the budget designated for each major activity.	10

A. SUMMARY INFORMATION

Organization name: (DOH)	Any County Department of Health
Address:	111 South Main Street
	Anytown, State 11111
Contact person:	Jim Smith
Phone number:	(555) 212-9999
Fax number:	(555) 212-8888
Email address:	insertnamehere@someagency.com
Type of Eligible Organization:	Local government
Funding Requested:	$60,000 for project period (2 years)
Project Period:	October 1, 2012 - September 30, 2014
EPA Region:	Anytown, EPA Region Somewhere

In this situation, the Summary Information page requirements were spelled out in the RFA. We substituted generic information about the applicant for inclusion in the workbook, though the text of the proposal is what was submitted.

Description of Project Activities: This project will focus on residents in Any County. The specific target is the All-American School District (AASD). According to school district nurses approximately 880 out of 4,500 students are known to have asthma. DOH will provide education materials to caregivers and persons with asthma on the management of indoor environmental asthma triggers including trigger identification, control and/or avoidance in homes. The project will include in-home assessments as an element of the educational process. In addition, the Anytown Asthma Consortium will provide classroom training to healthcare professionals at the North County Health Center in the management of indoor environmental asthma triggers, including trigger identification, control and/or avoidance of triggers. The program approach will encourage the use of the EPR3 asthma guidelines. The addition of in-home assessments and asthma health literacy education will help build a more robust asthma care system. Our staff will also raise awareness of asthma, asthma triggers and their abatement among school district staff including school nurses.

In the project summary and approach the author introduced each of the key elements: 1) what the applicant would do, 2) how activities complied with the EPA region goals, 3) what activities would occur, and 4) who the project's partners were.

B. WORK PLAN

i.   Detailed Project Summary and Approach

DOH's project is fully consistent with the EPA Region's goals and will focus on two objectives: First, the education of caregivers and persons with asthma on the management of indoor environmental asthma triggers including trigger, identification, control and/or avoidance in homes, schools, and elsewhere in the community. DOH will also offer **in-home environmental assessments** as an element of the education process. Second, the program will raise awareness of asthma among health professionals including school nurses and healthcare professionals at the North County Health Center in the form of classroom training on the management of indoor environmental asthma triggers, including trigger identification and/or avoidance.

DOH's approach is to integrate current best practices of the EPR3 guidelines into the patient's overall care and treatment building on the services already offered by our partners: Kids Health Van, the All-American School District, and the medical care offered at the North County Health Center.

Local situation: Asthma remains a common, chronic health issue in our region. The asthma and bronchiolitis hospital admission rate among youth is 402 per 10,000 population and is greater than the state rate of 385. Mid and North County rates (919 and 869 respectively) are well above state and county rates. Emergency department (ED) visits for children in our county are one and a half times higher than the State. A similar pattern is seen with youth ED visit rates for asthma. Mid and North County rates (1,092 and 2,080, respectively) are markedly higher rates than County-wide rates.

Project Staff include: a health education coordinator and a licensed lead risk assessor. These individuals will be responsible for the education intervention for the recruited families. In-kind services will be provided by Jon Jones, MD, MPH who will educate and train professional healthcare providers as outlined below.

Program Activities by DOH include In-Home Consultation Service to a) perform an in-home environmental assessment to identify family-actionable items to reduce asthma triggers, and b) improve family asthma self-management skills. DOH staff activities will also include the distribution of information about asthma and trigger reduction in the community. All families will be encouraged to find and use a health care provider. The DOH operates the North Central Health Center that serves the All American School District area.

The graphic below provides an overview of the project activities and changes expected:

When discussing the local situation, the author found great data from the state and county health departments. Using comparison data demonstrated the severity of the problem.

The diagram that appears on the next page is a good example of using an illustration to effectively demonstrate what the project will do. We recommend using a show and tell approach. Use diagrams to show how, and use narrative to tell how.

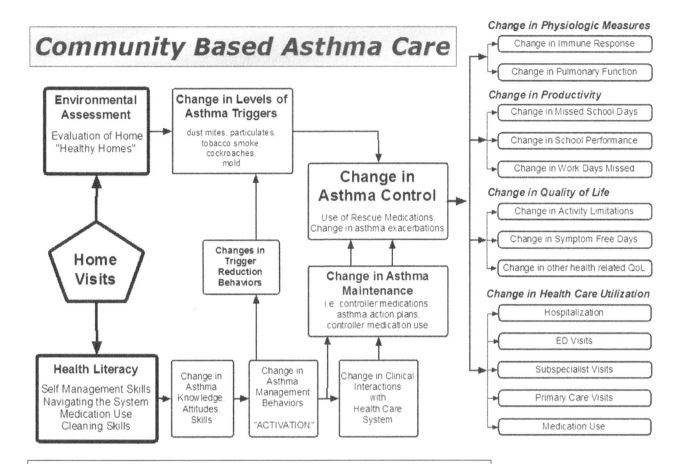

In addition to the In-Home Environmental Assessment Consultation, the program will also reach out to health professionals at the schools and the North Central Health Center with presentations on the implementation of the EPR3 guidelines and environmental triggers of asthma.

The program components are detailed below:

Identification, Referral, Contact and Enrollment:
School nurses have identified 880 students with asthma. All families of a child with asthma will receive a package of information describing environmental triggers of asthma and other information about asthma and asthma treatment. This package will be mailed by the School district to homes.

To enter the home environmental consultation program families will be recruited through referral from our partners. Our partners include the All-American School District, Kids' Health Vans, and Community Housing's 24:1 Initiative. Once patients are referred, they will be contacted by project staff and offered the opportunity to have a series of 2 or 3 in-home environmental consultations. These in-home visits will include a home environmental assessment for triggers and health information about the diagnosis and management of asthma including medication use. A second

> Tight page limitations forced the author to be very brief when describing the project. But brevity is no excuse for vague thinking. Include as much specific detail about your project as possible, even in shorter narratives.

in-home visit will be done at 3 months and a third visit (or a phone call follow-up) will be done at 6 months. These follow-up contacts will be used to reinforce messages and assess changes in behavior.

In-Home Consultation Services to Improve Health Literacy
DOH Staff will visit 45-50 families per contract year to deliver evidence-based individual family in-home consultations. Materials delivered will include an informational packet that discusses asthma and its symptoms, environmental triggers that may affect the return of symptoms, a home environmental checklist and a list of exposure reduction/elimination activities that can be performed at the home of the client.
Time frame: 1.50 hours each
Materials: Asthma Education Participant Information (Pre test evaluation form), Home Environment Assessment Workbook, Asthma Action Plan, Creating a Healthy Environment for Children with Asthma booklet and Acting on Behalf of My Child to Control Asthma DVD.
Activity: Follow-up consultation (Post test), by phone or face-to-face, will be completed for families that agree to being contacted for follow-up questions and ascertaining improvement in the child's asthma symptoms following initial consultation. Follow-up consultation shall occur 90 and 120 days following initial consultation.
Time frame: .50 hours each
Materials: Asthma Education follow-up form

Environmental Home Assessment
Activity: An in-home assessment will consist of the administration of an asthma home assessment workbook to assess indoor environmental triggers in the home and a walk-through assessment of the client's home to observe obvious sources of indoor air pollution and environmental asthma triggers, including environmental tobacco smoke (ETS).
Time frame: 1.30 hours each
Activity: An on-site indoor air quality assessment utilizing the air quality monitors provided by the staff that measure carbon monoxide (CO), carbon dioxide (CO2), humidity, and temperature will also be conducted.
Time frame: included above
Materials: Help Yourself to a Healthy Home booklet, Indoor Environmental Asthma Triggers Checklist and indoor air quality instruments.
Activity: Families will be provided results of assessment within one week. Staff shall identify strategies and develop recommendations with key stakeholders in the community to connect resources available within the community and/or at a state level to address perceived needs. Results will include; an evaluation letter, healthy homes suggestions, and a resource reference guide.
Activity: Families needing a health care home or primary care provider (PCP) will be referred to DOH's North Central Community Health Center (NCCHC). This center is located within the project community.

> Sub-headings call out program specifics, making it clear the plan is detailed and complete, even if the description of the plan is brief and there is not the luxury of adding white space to set off each section.

Distribution of Education Materials
Phone consultation will be offered and the asthma assessment workbook will be offered for families to complete on their own. Outreach and awareness building educational activities will include distribution of posters, flyers, presentations to parents/teachers and health fairs. Families unable to participate in in-home consultations or in-home asthma assessments will be mailed additional educational materials.

School Administration and Health Profession Staff Education
Jon Jones, MD, MPH of the Asthma Consortium (AC) will meet with the school nurses at scheduled staff meetings several times throughout the year. He will also meet with principals and teachers as needed to make the school staff aware of the availability of asthma trigger reduction services and their importance in the overall management of asthma. At least two school staff trainings will be conducted during the contract period. Dr. Smith will also meet at least four times with the physicians, nurses, social worker and lay outreach staff of the NCCHC to talk about the impact of environmental triggers on asthma outcomes and the EPR3 guidelines. He will also attend community meetings of the 24:1 Health and Wellness Initiative to assist in recruitment of families and caregivers for the in-home environmental consultation.

Work Products: No new work products will be developed. Materials used in the education process and in-home evaluations are evidence based, including some materials available from the EPA such as EPA 402-F-04-017,EPA 402-F-03-030, EPA 402-F-04-021, EPA 402-K-02-003, EPA 402-F-09-004.

> The author chose to demonstrate familiarity with EPA materials. Speaking your funder's language is important. Also, many funders prefer that you leverage existing resources. This approach can keep costs down.

Public Benefit: This program builds on existing partnerships in the community by adding and emphasizing an essential element of EPR3 guidelines: environmental trigger reduction. It also enhances the knowledge of families and the medical community, and reinforces the synergy among families, school nurses and practitioners. This helps build a more robust care system for asthmatics. It also helps build community involvement and empowers families to act by providing them with the knowledge and skill to improve the health of their children.

Project Alignment with EPA Strategic Plan and IAQ Priority Area Goals:
Our project is aligned with EPA's Strategic goal of *Improving Air Quality*, specifically indoor air quality. It is consistent with one of the five cross-cutting fundamental strategies, namely *Working for Environmental Justice and Children's Health*. It supports the goal of reducing exposures and risks 5s, specifically reducing exposures to indoor asthma triggers.

> The author does more than simply say the project aligns with the EPA strategic plan and priorities. This gets specific in naming the precise goal and strategies with which the project aligns.

Effective/Proven Approaches: Our evidence-based approach will be similar in scope to the Seattle-King County Healthy Homes Project:

Implementation of a Comprehensive Approach to Improving Indoor Environmental Quality for Low-Income Children with Asthma.

Audience Served: The site of our project is North County, USA, specifically the All-American School District (AASD). Our partners have ongoing activities aimed at the AASD students. In its 2011 Community Health Needs Assessment the County is divided into 4 regions. North, South, Mid and West regions. Our project will recruit the families of the 880 asthmatic children enrolled in the All-American School District located in northern most tip of the Mid County region. Mid and North county area have high unemployment and high percentages of adults without high school diplomas. Mid and North county have substantially lower mean annual income compared to more affluent West County.

About the NSD: Twenty-four (24) separate municipalities are either completely within, or overlap, the All American SD. The total school district enrollment is 4,500 in grades K-12 and is approximately 80%

A map of the service area was included in this space.

African-American. Sixty-three percent (63%) of the housing units are detached. The district operates five (5) elementary schools, one (1) middle school, one (1) high school, one (1) early childhood center, and one (1) alternative learning center. Zip code 99999 most closely overlaps the AASD; according to the Information for Community Assessment (ICA) web site, 96% of the ER visits for children under 15 are African American. (The map above shows its position in the County. School locations are shown.)

Partnerships and Collaborations: DOH partners in the project area include Community Housing, Healthy Kids Van, and All-American School District. These partners already have ongoing cooperative activities related to identifying, treating, and referring children with asthma to primary medical homes. School nurses are full time at each of the elementary, middle and high schools. None of these partners offers in-home environmental assessments. DOH will build its education activity on these existing resources and recruit caregivers and children with asthma from its service base. The St. Asthma Consortium will help with health profession education services.

You can obtain or create maps from a variety of sources. The one used in this proposal came from a free online map. Sometimes we draw circles or arrows to indicate a service area or important feature.

Underlining specific language helps emphasize important points you want reviewers to notice. In this case, the author emphasized how the proposed in-home assessments are not being provided by other organizations.

The first source of referrals will be Healthy Kids Van (HKV). HKV is operated by the Anytown Children's Hospital. On a rotating basis using a large van HKV visits partnering local school districts, Head Start programs, local day care centers, and other community sites to offer services. HKV's mobile office provides screenings for hearing, vision, anemia, lead, dental, asthma, scoliosis, height/weight measurements, and immunizations. The program was developed to bring health care to children aged 1-18 years in our community. HKV visits each of the schools in the All-American School District and works with the school nurses to offer asthma assessments, spacers, and Asthma Action Plans.

The second source of referrals will be from school nurses. The AASD has 7 school health nurses in the district. The school nurses hold the rescue inhalers for students. These nurses are involved in day-to-day asthma care for children at school and are likely to have an opportunity to interface with parents and caregivers.

A third source of referrals and family recruitment will come from the Community Housing's Wellness Initiative. Community Housing has served as a catalyst to bring the 24 municipalities and the school board to work more closely together on a variety of community issues. In 2009, ten Mayors joined forces with Community Housing and each other to address the impact of the foreclosure crisis on their municipalities that were all within or overlapped the All-All-American School District. That partnership has now grown into a community building initiative that includes each of the 24 communities served by the school district, and is appropriately named the 24:1, (i.e. twenty-four municipalities, one vision) Initiative. Community Housing has secured its position as the lead agency and has a five-year funding commitment to provide staffing that will facilitate the development of a community-driven plan in the vital areas of: community engagement, education, community health and wellness, commercial and residential real-estate development, research and resource development.

DOH staff will attend community meetings of the Wellness Initiative and other 24:1 activities, make presentations as appropriate to engage families, and publicize the availability of in-home evaluations and trigger reduction education.

A fourth source of referrals will be from calls from County residents made to the Healthy Homes/Lead Poisoning Prevention Program for evaluation of indoor mold levels. The County receives 800 to 1,000 indoor environmental calls per year.

Practicality, Feasibility and Replicability: Our project offers families an opportunity to learn about asthma triggers in their own home. Other regions in the country (some with Medicaid funding which is lacking in our State) have provided these in-home services with lowered medical costs and improved patient outcomes. The Community Guide recommends home-based multi-trigger, multi-component environmental interventions for children and adolescents with asthma. In addition to environmental intervention, these programs include general asthma education and/or training and education to improve self-management skills.

ii.   **Environmental Results – Outcomes, Outputs and Performance Measures**

1] In-Home Caregiver Activities *DOH Staff*	Environmentally Related Outputs	Short/Intermediate Term Action Outcomes	Long-term Health Outcomes (see graphic page 2)
Deliver asthma education/outreach and **in-home environmental consultations** targeted toward **asthma patients & caregivers** that will help families reduce exposure to indoor environmental asthma triggers in homes.	600 to 800 families will get education materials via mail 45-50 patients and caregivers will receive in-home environmental consultation and asthma education. 20-30 outreach activities per year, increasing the number of children and low income adults.	60% of families will demonstrate increased knowledge of indoor environmental asthma triggers and mitigation solutions. (pre-test/post-test) 30% of families with asthma will reduce their exposure to their environmental asthma triggers in their homes.	↓ # of ER visits and hospitalizations for asthma ↓ in other indicators of asthma morbidity, i.e. # of inpatient hospital admissions, sick visits to PCPs, school days missed, ↑ in symptom-free days, rescue medication use and Quality of Life indicators

2] Health Profession Related Activities *J. Jones, MD, MPH*	Environmentally Related Outputs	Short/Intermediate Term Action Outcomes	Long-term Health Outcomes (see graphic page 2)
Deliver education to **health professionals,** i.e. school nurses, doctors, social	6 provider trainings and services delivered.	↑ # of health care professionals understanding the value of and performing environmental	↓ # of ER visits and hospitalizations for asthma ↓ in other

This diagram is actually a logic model, using the format that the funder required. We have reduced it in size to fit within this workbook. The headers are different from a traditional logic model, but the content is similar.

workers, and public health nurses at NCCHC to use environmental evaluation for asthma patients	40-50 health care professionals and/or school personnel educated about indoor environmental asthma triggers and mitigation solutions.	trigger history (pre and post test) ↑ # of health care providers who understand and implement the EPR3 guidelines of asthma care	indicators of asthma morbidity, i.e. # of inpatient hospital admissions, sick visits to PCPs, school days missed, ↑ in symptom-free days, rescue medication use and Quality of Life indicators

Performance Measures

Internal monthly Process Indicators will be used to analyze, assess and report on the progress of the program. Activities include number of consultations, environmental assessments, follow-up, education and outreach in the community, program logs, and interviews with caregivers. For the two year reporting period, a semi-annual and annual progress report will be provided each year. To comply with HIPPA, reports will be limited to statistics only.

> Here the author tells reviewers what data will be collected and reported.

Process Indicators

Process objective	Status/ Indicators
Recruitment plan developed and implemented	• Comprehensive recruitment plan and supporting materials targeting schools and community developed/implemented within 30 days of the start of 1st year contract. • Assess effectiveness and adjust if needed.
Work with families on an ongoing basis to increase knowledge, improve asthma care, improve the home environment	• Enroll 40-50 clients each year of two year project. • Provide in-home consultation and environmental assessment. • Follow-up with each client 90 and 120 days after initial consultation.
Provide educational materials	Throughout contract period
Education and outreach	Throughout contract period
Provider trainings and services	2-3 trainings per contract year.
Contract Reporting	Semi-Annually and Annually or as contract dictates

> Notice how the author differentiated between process and outcome indicators by placing them in two separate tables. (The table for outcome indicators appears on the next page.)

Outcome Indicators

Indicator	Baseline interview	Exit interview
Number of families		
Number of symptom-free days (past two weeks)		
Percent with a hospital stay, past 12 months		
Percent with an ED visit, past 12 months		
Percent with an unscheduled office visit, past 3 months		
Percent of persistent patients with a written action plan		
Percent of persistent patients on controller medication		

Home Environment Outcome Indicators

Indictor	Baseline Interview	Exit Interview
Percent of families vacuuming at least once/week		
Percent of homes with visible moisture problems		
Percent using mattress and pillow covers		
Percent with a working kitchen fan ventilated to exterior		
Percent with a working bathroom fan		
Percent with pets that come inside		
Percent of homes with visible mold		
Percent of homes with evidence of pests		
Percent with someone who smokes inside the house		

> The Home Environment Indicators specifically show changes in knowledge and skills, which are lasting measures of change.

iii. Programmatic Capability and Past Performance

1. The Any County Department of Health (DOH) is accredited by the Institute for Community Health. DOH has a long history of receiving and managing federal and state grants. In 2010 DOH were awarded over $8 million in grants and contracts including the U.S. Department of Health and Human Services and the Centers for Disease Control and Prevention (CDC).

2. Federal Program: Healthy Homes Lead Poisoning Prevention Program
Size of Award: $100,000
Success: Current contract, ongoing project
History: All reports were submitted in a timely manner. Targets and outcomes were successfully achieved without modification.
Technical Reports: Final technical reports were submitted in June 2010 as required by the contract.

3. DOH successfully completed the Early Childhood Asthma Initiative (a $50,000 grant). DOH provided services to over 600 day cares and 170 pediatric healthcare providers as family and caregiver consultations, group training and education for parents/caregivers, follow-up consultations, on-site indoor air quality assessments, asthma education materials for childcare providers, caregivers and families and children with asthma. Activity reports were conducted electronically and were submitted by the (15th) business day of the month following the previous month's services. Documentation requested included participant form for consultations, child care environmental assessment form for initial assessment and follow-up. Child care environmental log, child-care asthma quality improvement invoice worksheet, a department vendor request for payment form, log(s) for each child care facility for which IAQ assessment and/or asthma consultation services were provided, a training sign-in sheet for each group training/education session conducted and a summary of families of children with asthma perceived needs, and strategy to link families and child care centers to local and state resources. The final deliverable of the contract included a strategic development plan. DOH completed this project two months ahead of schedule.

iv.   **Organization and Staff Experience and Qualification**

The vision of the Any County Health Department is that the DOH will be a progressive public health department providing a full array of services that includes assessment, policy development and assurances of health information, disease and injury prevention, and environmental health.

The mission of the Healthy Homes Program (HHP) is to improve the environmental health of residents and visitors of the County through promoting healthy housing and eliminating the incidence and prevalence of lead poisoning for all who live in or visit the community.

The HHP addresses multiple childhood diseases and injuries in the home. HHP takes a holistic and comprehensive approach to these activities by focusing on housing-related hazards in a coordinated manner, rather than addressing one separate hazard at a time. Environmental concerns include mold, lead, allergens, asthma, carbon monoxide, home safety, pesticides, and radon. Some of the County Department of Health's highest priorities include lead poisoning prevention and reducing asthma triggers in the home environment. The Healthy Homes Program was awarded approximately $150,000 which included the Healthy Homes/Lead Poisoning Prevention Program and the Early Childhood Asthma Initiative Program grant.

In a section like this, you want to persuade the funder that your organization is qualified on two levels: 1) to deliver the proposed activities, and 2) to properly administer a federal grant.

This paragraph establishes the applicant's experience delivering similar programming and also its experience with prior federal grants.

Full time staff include Jane Doe, MSW and Jennifer Smith, MPH (resumes are included). Both staff are Licensed Lead Risk Assessors, have successfully completed the National Healthy Homes training, Essentials for Healthy Housing Practitioners Course, have completed six (6) hours of asthma training through the Department Child Care Health Consultation Program in the last three years, and have successfully completed 2.6 hours of Asthma Management and Education sponsored by the Asthma and Allergy Foundation of America.

Ms. Doe has been employed by the County Department of Health for over 21 years. Ms. Smith has been employed by the County Department of Health for 4 ½ years. In 2011 DOH provided over 77 environmental assessments to families throughout the community.

The Asthma Consortium (AC) is a 501(c)(3) not-for-profit organized in 2000. AC was one of seven sites for the Centers for Disease Control and Prevention's Controlling Asthma in American Cities Project (CAACP). AC also received funding from CDC for Asthma Management for At-Risk Children (AMARC) Grant (2009-11). AMARC funded asthma environmental capacity building by providing Healthy Home training for over 80 individuals from its partnering agencies. The AC's board chairman is Jon Smith, MD, MPH.

Mentioning previous funding and/or one's selection to participate in previous projects also establishes expertise and credibility.

Annotated Application 4—Writing for Online Applications

Federal Emergency Management Agency (FEMA), Department of Homeland Security

Funding Opportunity Name

Assistance to Firefighters Grants (AFG)

Background of Application

This application was from a volunteer fire department in a small semirural community in Texas. Assistance to Firefighters Grants (AFG) are submitted online via FEMA's proprietary application submission system (not Grants.gov). The project narrative was limited to five pages only.

In this system, the project narrative has to be written in a word processor and then pasted into a text box on the application web screen. This means that all formatting, such as bold or italics or underlining, is lost and that automatic bullets often don't survive being pasted into the website. We often create our own bullets by inserting an en dash followed by a space just to set text off with what looks like bullets.

The space allocated for the narrative is limited, which is why this narrative may sometimes come across as choppy or too brief in sections. It is important to know that the AFG application consists of several additional pages of information about the applicant department, its service area, its budget, the number of calls, its inventory of equipment, and status of training that are all entered into boxes or selected from drop-down menus. We have made a PDF version of the entire application from the Sabine Volunteer Fire Department available at the *Writing to Win Federal Grants* website so you can see how the narrative fits into the larger whole.

Sabine Volunteer Department FEMA Equipment Request 2009

Introduction to Sabine Volunteer Fire Department and Service Area Characteristics

The Sabine Volunteer Fire Department is located in Gregg County, Texas. The Department serves 8,000 people throughout its 97-square mile primary response area. Sabine VFD also provides automatic and mutual aid to Gregg County (273 square miles) and the eastern portion of Smith County, which contains another 316 square miles. Adjacent to the department's primary response area are the cities of Longview, Texas (pop. 76,816) and Kilgore, Texas (pop. 12,024), the community of Gladewater, Texas (pop. 6,829) and numerous smaller communities.

The Sabine Volunteer Fire Department is in the center of the East Texas Oil Field, "the largest and most prolific oil reservoir in the contiguous United States" (*Handbook of Texas Online*). The large oil and gas extraction, storage and transport industry means that Sabine VFD's primary response area is comprised of 40% industry – almost all of it related to the oil and gas industry.

Interstate 20, a primary cross-country highway, bisects the fire district, carrying 33,000 vehicles per day (*TXDOT, 2007*). Add into this mix hundreds of miles of underground pipelines, above-ground storage tanks, oil and chemical transport trucks, the nation's most important East-West pipeline and the Eastman chemical factory (Texas' largest inland chemical complex), and **Gregg County's risk as a potential terrorism target is significant.** If the critical infrastructure supporting these industries is attacked or experiences a hazardous event, **a catastrophic loss of life or catastrophic economic loss could occur.** Eastman chemical is located on the outskirts of Longview (pop. 76,816). The oil and gas field industries adjoin, cross and parallel Interstate 20 as well as two major Texas highways (259 and 135) and a major US highway (80, part of old Route 66), all of which carry critical transport and have numerous bridges and overpasses.

The remaining 60% of the service area is rural, either comprised of grass, forest and agricultural lands (30%) or residential (30%). Homes are rarely located near hydrants. Many are isolated, surrounded by woods or fields. Mutual aid regularly takes 10-12 minutes to arrive; therefore, the Sabine Volunteer Fire Department's presence and ability to respond rapidly makes an incredible difference in the safety of lives and property.

Project Description

Identified Problem

The Sabine Volunteer Fire Department is forced to rely on Personal Protective Equipment (PPE) and Self-Contained Breathing Apparatus (SCBA) that do not meet NFPA standards. Every single item of equipment

Since the department is small and in a rural area, local statistics were included to explain how the department may be called upon to respond to larger incidences than might be expected of a small department.

Even with the tight space limitations, item names were written out the first time they were used. You can never assume that those reading your proposals are experts in your project area.

is second-hand—donated by other departments who discarded it because it was not compliant. All of the PPE and SCBA owned by the Sabine VFD is 10 years old or older. Of the Department's SCBA, none meets 1997 standards and none has a PASS safety device.

The increasingly worn-out Personal Protective Equipment (PPE) and Breathing Apparatus used in the Sabine VFD is compromising the Department's mission, placing the safety of its volunteers in jeopardy, and risks potential fines if equipment is not brought up to standard. Because of the condition of the equipment, the Department often cannot conduct aggressive interior attacks on structural fires, meaning that more property loss occurs.

The safety of volunteer firefighters who answer the call to protect those in danger is compromised by outdated SCBA that may fail at any time. Similarly, firefighters are placed in danger by the outdated, non-compliant PPE, which exposes them to dangerous heat. Nor is there the ability to decontaminate equipment after incidents. This can accelerate its decay, further compromise its effectiveness, and places the health and safety of the firefighters at risk.

Though the Department's volunteers are extremely loyal and serve at enormous personal sacrifice, the Department has great difficulty recruiting new volunteers and expanding its service when it cannot assure firefighters of the most basic protection against the many risks of serving.

Solution

As was mentioned above, the Department's current PPE and SCBA have been handed down from other Departments that were upgrading to meet NFPA standards. While the Sabine VFD is grateful for this generosity, continuing to use sub-standard PPE and SCBA that places fire-fighters at risk and hampers their ability to respond to emergencies is a hazard that must be eliminated. Sabine firefighters need adequate protection, and citizens of Gregg County need adequately equipped firefighters for the protection of their lives and property.

Therefore, the project calls for equipping 100% of the volunteers with NFPA-compliant PPE, purchasing NFPA-compliant SCBAs with integrated PASS, and adding a washer/extractor and dryer to properly care for the PPE. This project proposes to purchase the following items:

Personal Protective Equipment

Nineteen (19) full sets of turnout gear/PPE for volunteer firefighters, to consist of:

- Helmets
- Visors

Annotation notes (margin):

Instead of just saying the equipment is old, the author made word choices to paint a picture in reviewers' minds—e.g. worn out, compromising, risk, safety, jeopardy, property loss.

The last two sentences in this paragraph cram into a small space important details about the importance of cleaning firefighter's gear. Since a very expensive washer and dryer were in the budget, it was important to establish the need for those items here.

This paragraph makes an explicit link between the community's need for fire protection and the department's need for safe equipment in order to protect the community.

On another portion of the online application, the Department documented how many personnel were on its active duty roster to support this request for 19 of each item.

- Hoods
- Coats
- Gloves
- Pants
- Boots

We also propose to purchase a washer/extractor and a dryer for decontaminating PPE. This will significantly extend the life of the PPE and preserve its integrity. The washer/extractor and dryer will protect the health and safety of firefighters as well as the general public by ensuring that all Personal Protective Equipment items are properly decontaminated between each incident.

Self-Contained Breathing Apparatus with Integrated PASS Devices
Ten (10) 45-minute SCBAs, with extra tank, and with integrated PASS Devices. The number of SCBA devices does not exceed the number of seated positions in our fleet.

> Always try to anticipate things about your proposal that may seem confusing. In this case, the proposal explained elsewhere why the department only needed to purchase 10 breathing apparatus even though there were 19 firefighters. Leaving that sort of possible question unanswered can sink a proposal.

What Standards Will Be Met
- All PPE items will meet NFPA 1971, 2007 edition
- The washer/extractor and dryer will meet NFPA 1851
- SCBAs will be compliant with NFPA 1981, 2007 edition
- PASS devices will be integrated, auto-on devices that meet NFPA 1982, 2007 edition

Plan to Provide Training Since no Training Funds are Requested
Texas fire departments are very fortunate in that the State Forestry Department provides generous grants to cover training costs for volunteer departments. These grants, which we regularly apply for and receive, meet 100% of our department's training needs. The Department currently has volunteers enrolled in training classes to reach Firefighter I. When that training is complete, we will begin Firefighter II courses.

> The funding agency requires applicants to document why they are not requesting training funds if these are not included in the grant budget.

Project Costs
The total proposed project cost will be $117,000. This is broken down as $51,186 for PPE:
   $5,700 for Helmets, $646 for Hoods, $20,140 for Coats, $15,675 Pants, $7,790 Boots, and
   $1,235 for Gloves.
Another $18,200 is budgeted for the washer/extractor and dryer and $63,000 for SCBA.

> This is probably one of the simplest budget breakdowns the author has ever provided for a $117,000 grant request. There were more details provided on a budget form, including likely model numbers, brands, and sizes.

<u>Financial Need</u>
Why Federal Funds Are Needed
The project cannot be funded solely through local resources for several reasons. First, the department is a small, rural department with an annual budget of less than $40,000. The department is currently paying off a note

for a 1984 pumper and a 2001 brush truck. **Clearly, the budget cannot support a significant equipment purchase.** Of the Department's annual revenue, 35% comes from county taxes, 50% from donations, and 15% from fund drives and bingo. Unfortunately, revenue from our annual mailing to the community was down $7,000 in 2008, and we anticipate similar results in 2009. Income from Bingo has even dropped $1,000 per month. With the bulk of the Department's budget being spent for fuel, the department cannot afford a major expenditure for PPE and SCBA.

During the recession years when this application was written, donations were down, as they were for most non-profits. However, a department of this size could clearly never afford such a major investment from its own budget.

Other Attempts to Fund Needs

Sabine Volunteer Fire Department operates efficiently on a limited budget. Gregg County supplies funds that are approximately equivalent to the Department's annual fuel costs, and an external grant covers insurance premiums and training costs. Community donations and small fundraising events organized by our volunteers can help meet general operating costs and are sometimes enough to help purchase minimal equipment. However, these sources of income are not adequate to replace the second-hand, unsafe equipment that our firefighters currently use.

Annually, the Department sends out a mail appeal to the community and runs monthly bingo games. However, income from these efforts goes to the Department's general operating expenses and is not adequate to purchase equipment. We have submitted grant proposals for PPE to FM Global and to Hamburger Helper's Community Assistance fund. Both have been denied.

Many federal applications require a response to a question similar to this one—"what else are you doing to raise funds?" Our goal with this answer was to demonstrate that the Department was not just sitting around waiting for the federal money fairy. They have done their best with limited resources.

Financial and Community Trends/Changes

The national financial and economic crisis has also hit rural areas of East Texas hard. Unemployment jumped two percentage points from Spring 2008 to Spring 2009 (*Bureau of Labor Statistics*). While local industries ramped up when oil prices were extremely high, these industries are now cutting back as wholesale oil prices again decline. We know from past experience that our call volume increases during times of economic crisis, especially arson fires, which can be particularly dangerous to fight. In addition, even before the economic downturn, the Department was experiencing annual call volume increases, with the number of structural fires we responded to doubling from 2006 to 2008.

Providing local, on-the-ground details can make your application stand out and seem more genuine. As grant writers, we may not know details such as arson fires increasing during economic downturns. In this case, the assistant chief had the history and institutional knowledge to share with the author.

Costs and Benefits

Frequency of Use vs. Cost

The Sabine Volunteer Fire Department responds to almost 200 calls each year, including mutual aid. The PPE will be used for every single call, and SCBAs will be used for all fire calls as well as some Haz-Mat calls. Over the years this equipment will be used, the cost is reasonable.

Increased Efficiency

Having current PPE and SCBA that meet required standards is primarily a safety issue. However, the Department will also realize efficiency gains from meeting required standards, which will allow the volunteer fire department to continue functioning as a fire department. Knowing that all of the equipment to be used will perform properly, immediately, will save time.

Benefit to the Department
The Sabine Volunteer Fire Department will benefit in several ways from the purchase of updated PPE equipment, the washer and dryer, and SCBAs with PASS. First and foremost is improved safety (see next page). Second, the increased confidence in equipment will lead to more effective fire fighting. If firefighters know that they can trust their PPE and SCBA, they can focus their energy on the emergency at hand instead of worrying that a critical piece of equipment might fail and place their lives in danger. Third, the increased morale and provision of adequate safety equipment may also enable the Department to recruit more firefighters.

Benefit to the Community
Gregg County and surrounding areas will benefit from the updated equipment, as it will improve fire suppression and safety for residents as well as reduce losses by business and industry. Having proper equipment will allow the department to engage in aggressive interior fire attack operations, which it does not dare conduct now. This will result in reduced damage to property during structural fires. The community depends upon the Sabine VFD for its protection. Updated PPE and SCBA equipment will ensure the safety of our firefighters, the efficiency of response to fires and emergencies, and the security of residents and businesses.

Most Economical Solution
Purchasing NFPA-compliant PPE and SCBA is the most economical solution for our volunteer fire department, which has depended on hand-me-downs. Using second-hand equipment that does not meet standards is a false economy and daily places the lives of our firefighters at risk. Bringing 100% of our force into NFPA compliance allows the Department to get a discount, making the per item cost less than if it just purchased items one at a time as funds became available. Purchasing the washing and drying systems is good stewardship, as they will extend the life of the PPE and protect health and safety.

Consequences of Not Receiving Award
The consequences of not funding this project could be disastrous for both our firefighters and the community. Of course, the major concern is the possibility of injury or a fatality. Even a minor injury can shake our firefighters' confidence and open the Department to costly lawsuits. One such lawsuit could close our doors forever and place 8,000 residents at risk. The Department serves a 97-square mile district, and without this all-

It is important to find something to say in response to each application prompt, even if, the question is really not applicable to your project or you don't meet that criterion. The three sentences of this paragraph are clearly a stretch, but it is better than leaving a question unanswered.

Reducing property damage and increasing community safety are priorities of this funding agency. That is why this application repeatedly emphasizes the positive impact on community safety and fire suppression.

Being able to draw conclusions about what may happen if the project is not funded is a valuable skill. Sometimes the applicant is a good source of this knowledge. Other times, you have to ask the right questions.

volunteer force, area residents, businesses, and industries would have no local fire protection (other than distant municipal departments that may not have the capacity to respond in a timely manner). Furthermore, we are unable to fight structural fires as aggressively as necessary, thus leading to increased property loss. The lack of adequate, NFPA-compliant equipment hinders our ability to effectively serve the community, as the potential consequences of a substantial failure could be much more devastating.

Impact of Project on Daily Operations and Community Safety

Effect Upon Daily Operation of the Department

Providing NFPA compliant PPE and SCBA to the Sabine VFD will remove significant safety hazards for our firefighters. Firefighters responding to a call can immediately pull on their PPE and head out the door or put on their SCBA to enter a building, confident that the equipment will protect them, that they will be able to handle dangerous situations in a controlled manner, and that the community will be better protected. **This will be a dramatic improvement over the current situation which is fraught with uncertainty and safety concerns**.

Effect Upon Department's Ability to Protect Lives and Property

Having PPE and SCBA equipment that is compliant with NFPA standards will improve our Department's ability to protect lives and property by keeping our firefighters safer. They can respond to emergencies with confidence. In addition, we can more effectively fight structural fires with proper, reliable equipment, increasing our ability to reduce property losses.

Improving Firefighter Safety

The new equipment will have a large impact on improving firefighter safety. The current PPE and SCBA is so old and so worn out that there is great potential for injury. Standards are set by NFPA in order to protect firefighters, and that is why obtaining compliant equipment is our priority. The PPE will equip 100% of our force with up-to-standards protective gear. The new SCBA units will come with integrated PASS devices, important safety tools with motion and heat sensors to warn firefighters of danger and an alert strobe light that helps injured firefighters to be quickly located and rescued if necessary.

Frequency of Use

The new PPE equipment will be used every time the Department responds to a call, and SCBAs will be used for every interior fire incident. These items are the first defense firefighters have against the emergencies they respond to.

How Results Will be Measured

It will be easy to measure the results of this project – the Sabine Volunteer Fire Department will own 19 sets of PPE, 10 SCBAs and an appropriate

It is common for federal applications to ask for the same information over and over again. It's usually best to respond to each prompt as many times as you are asked, rather than referring a reader back to an earlier section of your proposal. It may feel frustrating to repeat yourself, but work to state things a little differently each time if possible.

washer/extractor and dryer. The Department will continue to collect statistics on all calls responded to, any injuries, and any loss of property.

Conclusion

The Sabine Volunteer Fire Department proposes to purchase enough PPE to bring 100% of our force into NFPA compliance, **which earns this proposal a "high competitive" rating**. The Department plays a critical role in protecting key potential targets of interest spread throughout East Texas, including 85 miles of Interstate highway, oil and gas wells, storage tanks, trans-continental pipelines, a refinery and large chemical complex. Having adequate safety equipment is crucial to protecting the lives and property of residents of Gregg County, Texas.

Any time your proposal is eligible to receive priority points, be sure to work that in somewhere. Don't depend on agency staff or reviewers to make that connection for you.

Index

A

activities, 21, 47, 50–51, 53–60, 63–64, 69, 73, 80, 106, 121, 128, 159–60, 197, 225–27
annotated proposals, 137–76, 177–222, 223–38, 239–46
  contents of, 134–35
AOR (authorized organizational representative), 26, 29, 38, 40
application package, 9, 25–26, 32, 38, 41, 48, 99, 108, 178
authorized organizational representative. *See* AOR

B

budget, 67–83, 119, 191
  annual organization, 9, 44
  federal categories, 32, 34, 67–68, 70, 73, 77, 79–80, 216
  form (SF-424A), 32–37
  multi-year, 32
  program, 20, 32, 34, 69, 121
  negotiator, 118
  restrictions, 121
  sample, 216–21, 242
budget checklist, 70–72
budget narrative, 67, 73, 79
  sample, 216–21, 242
budget templates, 73–79

C

capacity, organizational, 5–7, 8, 12, 121, 169, 204–5
Catalog of Federal Domestic Assistance. *See* CFDA
CFDA (Catalog of Federal Domestic Assistance), 13–18
checklist of internal documents, 8–9
contracts, 4, 38, 68, 89, 96, 115, 117, 118–19
contractual (budget category), 68, 71, 72, 75, 78, 79, 219–20
cover sheet. *See SF-424*

D

diagrams (using in proposals), 150, 228–29, 234
Disclosure of Lobbying Activities form, 43

E

evaluation, 121, 154, 161–62, 164, 166–67, 172
  capacity, 20–21, 169–71
  partner responsibilities, 90, 92–94, 96–97
  report, 8, 161, 164, 166–67, 169, 198, 213, 215
  sample plan, 134, 170–71
  services, 169
evaluation criteria, 135, 178, 181, 182, 211, 225–26

evaluator, 20, 51, 72, 75, 139–40, 146, 154, 159, 161–62, 164, 166–67, 169–71, 172–73
executive director, 6, 9, 11–12, 21, 38, 42, 88, 94–95, 118–19
Executive Order 12372, 26, 29, 122

F

federal budget categories, 34, 67–68, 70, 73, 77, 79–80, 216
footnotes (using in proposals), 134, 142
forms, 12, 25–48, 73, 178
  grant summary, 21–22, 23
  sample, 27–31, 33–37, 39–40, 42, 43, 45, 47
  time and effort report, 128–30
  travel report, 123–27
FTE (full-time equivalency), 74, 79, 81, 102–3, 106
full-time equivalency. *See* FTE
funding opportunity feasibility analysis, 20

G

grant opportunities, 7, 13, 14, 19, 21, 23, 121
  executive summary, 21–22
grant proposal, 8–10, 26, 104, 115
Grants.gov, 4, 10, 11, 13, 24–29, 38, 40, 48, 239
  application package, 25, 47
  forms repository, 48
  lobbying form, 12, 41–42
  user ID, 11, 117

I

in-kind contributions, 20, 67, 69, 73, 80–82, 96, 103, 106, 121, 128, 172

L

letters of commitment, 81, 101, 112, 115, 120, 226
  sample, 113, 114
letters of support, 82, 101, 108, 112, 115, 120, 134

  sample, 109–11
logic model, 49–65, 134, 135, 179
  sample, 54–59, 64, 197, 234
  templates, 50–51, 61–64

M

matching funds, 17, 20, 22, 33, 35, 69, 74, 77–78, 80–82, 119, 121–22
MOUs, 22, 81, 85–99, 115, 119, 179, 199, 222

N

National Grants Management Association (NGMA), 131

O

objectives, 5, 8, 51, 54–55
  sample, 138–40, 159–67, 180, 187, 235–36
organization, faith-based, 44, 177–78
organizational charts, 9, 101–6, 115, 134–35
  sample, 102–3, 105, 107, 205–6
organizational self-assessment, 5–6
outcomes, 8, 50–65, 119, 121, 135, 159, 187, 197, 225–26, 234–36
outputs, 50–51, 54–59, 63–64, 187, 197, 225–26, 234

P

page budget, 178–79
partners, 20–222, 52, 85–96, 99, 101, 103, 106–7, 108, 112, 115, 118–19, 120, 131, 135, 162, 175, 199, 223, 226–27
partner roster, 86–87, 199
postaward meeting, 120–21
postaward procedures, 117–20
postsubmittal record, 118
program design, 6, 60, 67
program summary form, 21–22
Project Performance Site Location(s) form, 47
project period, 22, 118, 121–22

R

research, 13–14, 18, 23–24
reviewers, 4–5, 49, 50, 73, 88, 99, 102, 104, 106, 108, 112, 115, 133, 139, 141, 144, 146, 148, 152, 154, 159, 162, 174, 175, 177–78, 181, 182, 184, 186, 196, 197, 211, 215, 223, 232, 235, 241, 246
RFA review checklist, 20

S

SF-424, 26–28, 32, 179
SF-424A, 25, 32–37, 48, 68, 73, 79, 179
SF-424B/SF-424D, 9, 12, 38–40, 122, 179
SF-LLL, 12, 41–42, 179
Standard Grant Information Form, 10–11

staffing plans, 101, 106, 134
sample, 172–74, 213–15
summary of grants under management, 121–22
Survey of Equal Opportunity for Applicants, 44–46

T

timeline, 101–2, 134–35, 137
sample, 198
travel expenses, 123–27

W

work plan, 101–2, 134
sample, 159–67, 181–83, 198

If you enjoyed this workbook, you'll want to pick up the companion book, *Writing to Win Federal Grants: A Must-Have for Your Fundraising Toolbox,* published by the CharityChannel Press **In the Trenches™** series.

IN THE

Trenches™

Writing to Win Federal Grants

A Must-Have for Your Fundraising Toolbox

Cheryl L. Kester, CFRE
Karen L. Cassidy, GPC

Master federal grants by learning how to:

- Create compelling need statements and budgets
- Design detailed projects for more competitive proposals
- Assemble proposal development teams and effective partnerships
- Step up your game by developing evaluation plans suited to federal grants

Multiple examples from successful proposals demonstrate these concepts in action.

CharityChannel.com/bookstore

*Charity*Channel
PRESS™

If you enjoyed this book, you'll want to pick up the other books in the CharityChannel Press **In the Trenches™** series.

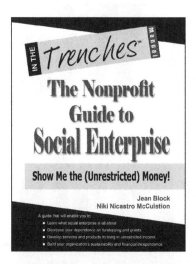
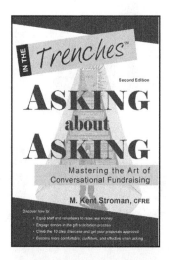
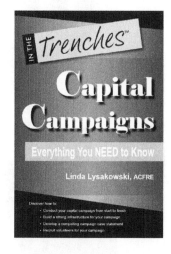

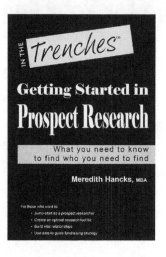

CharityChannel.com/bookstore

IN THE Trenches™

YOU AND YOUR Nonprofit

Practical Advice and Tips from the
CharityChannel Professional Community

This is surely the book I wish I had decades ago.
—Bob Carter, Chair-elect, Association of
Fundraising Professionals (AFP)

Edited by:
Norman Olshansky
Linda Lysakowski, ACFRE

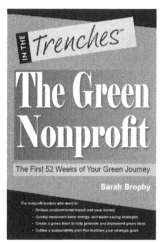

IN THE Trenches™

The Green Nonprofit

The First 52 Weeks of Your Green Journey

Sarah Brophy

For nonprofit leaders who want to:
- Reduce environmental impact and save money
- Quickly implement basic energy- and water-saving strategies
- Create a green team to help generate and implement green ideas
- Outline a sustainability plan that matches your strategic goals

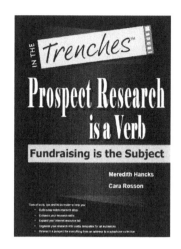

IN THE Trenches™

Prospect Research is a Verb

Fundraising is the Subject

Meredith Hancks
Cara Rosson

Tons of facts, tips and tricks inside to help you:
- Build a tip-notch research shop
- Enhance your research skills
- Expand your Internet resource list
- Organize your research into useful templates for all audiences
- Research is prospect for everything from an address to a telephone collection

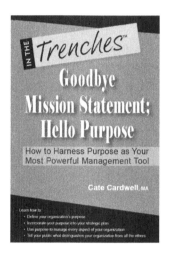

IN THE Trenches™

Goodbye Mission Statement; Hello Purpose

How to Harness Purpose as Your
Most Powerful Management Tool

Gate Cardwell, MA

Learn how to:
- Define your organization's purpose
- Incorporate your purpose into your strategic plan
- Use purpose to manage every aspect of your organization
- Tell your public what distinguishes your organization from all the others

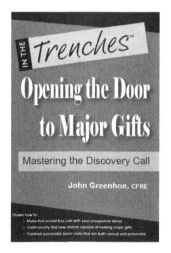

IN THE Trenches™

Opening the Door to Major Gifts

Mastering the Discovery Call

John Greenhoe, CFRE

Shows how to:
- Make that crucial first visit with your prospective donor
- Continuously find new donors capable of making major gifts
- Conduct successful donor visits that are both casual and purposeful

IN THE Trenches™

Succeed in Your Nonprofit Funding Partnerships

Analyzing Their Costs and Benefits

Joanne Oppelt, MHA, OPC

A guide for:
- Preparing profitable budgets
- Choosing lucrative fundraising activities
- Ensuring your organization stays in business
- Talking about your agency with corporate and institutional funders

IN THE Trenches™

Fundraising Research Made Easy

A Practical Guide for Fundraisers

Meredith Hancks, EdD
Cara Rosson

Are you a fundraiser? Learn to:
- Research your top donors and prospects
- Build a set of research skills
- Expand your Internet resource list
- Set goals to fit research into your fundraising plan

IN THE Trenches™

7 Nonprofit Income Streams

Open the Floodgates to Sustainability!

Karen Eber Davis

Need sustainable income?
- Understand the 7 nonprofit income streams
- Develop a dependable income strategy and plan
- Learn the practical steps to take to implement your plan

IN THE Trenches™

Raise More Money from your Business community —the Workbook

Jump Start Your Corporate Fundraising Today!

Linda Lysakowski, ACFRE

This workbook will help you:
- Develop an economic impact statement
- Create a list of prospective business donors
- Build an annual corporate appeal involving volunteers
- Learn how to identify the decision makers and how to reach them

CharityChannel.com/bookstore

Charity Channel
PRESS ™

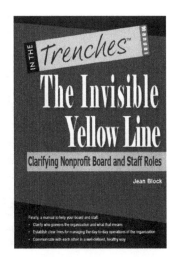

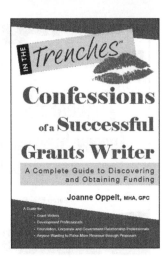

CharityChannel.com/bookstore

*Charity*Channel
PRESS™

And now introducing **For the GENIUS® Press,** an imprint that produces books on just about any topic that people want to learn. You don't have to be a genius to read a **GENIUS** book, but you'll sure be smarter once you do!

ForTheGENIUS.com/bookstore

Just Published!

Casino
Video Poker
for the GENIUS

Take the mystery out of
video poker and boost
your casino fun!

Linda G. Nowell

FOR THE GENIUS IN ALL OF US

ForTheGENIUS.com/bookstore

Just Published!

ForTheGENIUS.com/bookstore

Lightning Source UK Ltd.
Milton Keynes UK
UKOW07f2154260116

267124UK00005B/155/P